D1423632

European Culture and Society
General Editor: Jeremy Black

Published

Lesley Hall   *Sex, Gender & Social Change in Britian since 1880*
Neil MacMaster   *Racism in Europe, 1870–2000*
W. M. Spellman   *European Political Thought 1600–1700*

European Culture and Society Series
Series Standing Order
ISBN 0–333–74440–3
(*outside North America only*)

You can receive future titles in this series as they are published by placing a standing order. Please contact your bookseller or, in case of difficulty, write to us at the address below with your name and address, the title of the series and the ISBN quoted above.

Customer Services Department, Macmillan Distribution Ltd
Houndmills, Basingstoke, Hampshire RG21 6XS, England

RACISM IN EUROPE 1870–2000

Neil MacMaster

palgrave

First published 2001 by
PALGRAVE
Houndmills, Basingstoke, Hampshire RG21 6XS and
175 Fifth Avenue, New York, N.Y. 10010
Companies and representatives throughout the world

PALGRAVE is the new global academic imprint of
St. Martin's Press LLC Scholarly and Reference Division and
Palgrave Publishers Ltd (formerly Macmillan Press Ltd).

ISBN 0–333–71119–x hardback
ISBN 0–333–71120–3 paperback

This book is printed on paper suitable for recycling and
made from fully managed and sustained forest sources.

A catalogue record for this book is available
from the British Library.

Library of Congress Cataloging-in-Publication Data

MacMaster, Neil, 1945–
    Racism in Europe, 1870–2000/Neil MacMaster.
        p. cm.
    Includes bibliographical references and index.
    ISBN 0–333–71119–X—ISBN 0–333–71120–3 (pbk.)
        1. Racism—Europe—History—19th century. 2. Racism—Europe—
History—20th century. 3. Europe—Race relations. 4. Europe—Ethnic
relations. 5. Social Darwinism—History—19th century. I. Title.

D372 .M33 2001
305.8'0094—dc21   2001019446

10 9 8 7 6 5 4 3 2 1
10 09 08 07 06 05 04 03 02 01

Printed in China

CONTENTS

Acknowledgement

I wish to thank Dr Jim House of Leeds University for his very helpful and constructive criticism of an earlier version of the manuscript. His detailed comment has enabled me to make various improvements, although any outstanding weaknesses are all my own.

INTRODUCTION: THE ROOTS OF MODERN RACISM

Some General Considerations

This book is not centred on the theory of 'race', but explores, within a historical framework, the development of racism within the changing context of European society between 1870 and the end of the twentieth century. However, certain theoretical perspectives underlie the overall structure and interpretation, and we begin with these in order to make explicit the argument that is being presented.

Since 1945 mainstream sociology has argued that 'race' is a social construct. Racial categories cannot be explained through a scientific system of classification based on biological/genetic methods, but are ideological constructs, forms of boundary definition between groups that have evolved within specific historical and social contexts. While categories of 'race' have no ontological status, no concrete reality that can be measured, modern European society has tended to believe in the division of the world's population into distinct biological groups, of 'black', 'white', 'Asian' or other peoples, that are permanently divided and arranged into a hierarchy of superior to inferior types. A recognition that there is no essence to 'race', no scientific validity to the subdivision of humankind into fixed subgroups, is of importance to the central concern of this book, which is the historical construction and meanings of racism. 'Races' may not exist, but there has been, and continues to be, a widespread belief in such categorization and this belief, in turn, has had enormous implications for the way in which 'white' Europeans have historically set out to dominate, exploit and kill 'inferior' peoples. So while 'races' may not exist, racism, or the belief in such biological differences, has had enormous impact on behaviour and practice, from the highest levels of government policy to everyday social relations in the pub and on the football terrace.

1

The central issue under investigation is *racialization*, those processes through which one group (usually the 'white' majority) has set about the task of targeting other groups (frequently non-European minorities) as inferior, a process involving ideological constructions (those with black skins are 'less intelligent') as well as an apparatus of legal, political and social discrimination and oppression. Racism is always a dynamic process, a set of beliefs and practices that is embedded in a particular historical context, a particular social formation, and is thus continuously undergoing change, a plastic or chameleon-like phenomenon which constantly finds new forms of political, social, cultural or linguistic expression. This rooted-ness of racism, deeply lodged within the changing structures of European society, explains in part why it has proved so difficult for sociologists or dictionary compilers to arrive at a satisfactory and reasonably simple universal definition of 'racism', since it is constantly undergoing change through time.

To complicate matters even further, it will be argued that the his-toric development of racism in relation to particular object groups has often been so specific, and formulated through unique stereo-types and entrenched patterns of discrimination, that it makes more sense to speak in terms of *racisms* in the plural, rather than in the terms of a universalizing *racism*. During the nineteenth and twentieth centuries European racism, it will be argued throughout this book, assumed two paradigmatic forms, that of anti-black racism with its his-toric roots in slavery and colonial conquest, and racial anti-Semitism grounded in a totally different tradition of Christian oppression, segregation and pogroms dating back to the Middle Ages. Most academic work on European racism has tended to operate either in terms of a binary opposition between white and black (particularly true for Britain), or between Jewish and non-Jewish people. As the sociologist Robert Miles has pointed out, it is no longer possible to theorize European racism on a truly Continental scale in terms of only its colonial or of its anti-Semitic modalities. The failure to develop a comparative approach is rooted both in a traditional division of labour in which scholars of colonialism and anti-Semitism have remained entrenched within their segregated fields of study, or from an assumption that the two forms are so radically different as to belie any comparison. However, both modalities are universally denoted by historians as forms of racism, and, this being so, any attempt to analyse the development of modern racism should be able to provide an explanatory framework that can include both types.

By concentrating on these two modalities I do not wish to imply that there was not a myriad of other racisms in Europe, but a work of this length has necessarily to be selective. As will be discussed later (Chapter 2), the category of 'black' is itself ambiguous and rife with problems of definition. In Britain the term 'black' has often been used in the post-war period as a political category that includes all non-European minorities, whether of Caribbean, Asian or Arab origin, on the grounds that they have shared a common class position in European society as an exploited and racialized stratum. In this study the term 'black' is explored mainly by reference to those peoples of African origin, particularly from sub-Saharan Africa or the ex-slave societies of the Americas. The reason for this is that the black, in the past designated as a 'Negro' type, played a fundamental role in the elaboration of a science and discourse of race, of a particular form of stereotyping and representation that was central to European culture. The connotations of blackness have been so powerful in Europe that the term 'black', as a standard template of the biologically or culturally inferior, has been universally mobilized in European society in a cross-referential way to racialize almost all other minorities, designated as 'black', from Jews and Gypsies, to the Irish and Chechens. While, for the purposes of analysis, a wider categorization like 'colonial racism' might sometimes be more useful, what is lost by this is the way in which racial stereotypes were historically constructed, through slavery and the colonial domination of Africa, and with reference to quite specific cultural markers and representations.

The decision largely to restrict the investigation of colonial racism to the stereotype of the black African or Afro-Caribbean does create some problems, in particular since it largely excludes the particular forms of racism that developed in relation to other non-African minorities and which assumed quite different and distinctive formulation. In France during the twentieth century, for example, racism has been most virulent towards immigrants from the Maghreb, particularly Algeria, and has been structured in terms of Orientalism, a tradition rooted in the long conflict between Christian Europe and the Muslim and Arab world of the Middle East and North Africa. In this study Orientalism, as well as the development of distinctive currents of racism targeted at Asians (Chinese, Indians, Vietnamese) and other minorities (Turks, Kurds, Somalis . . .) have been largely ignored, apart from some passing reference. Inevitably, a short work of this kind attempting to cover a truly enormous subject, both in its complexity, geographic diversity and long time scale, will leave out as much as it contains, but the intention is not to be all-inclusive or encyclopaedic, but rather to provide an interpretative outline that focuses on a more restricted range of core issues. It is hoped that what is lost in this process is more than compensated for by exploring more thoroughly what we consider to be the dominant modalities of racism throughout the modern age; anti-Semitism, anti-black and self-referential white racism. By following through the contrasting threads of these racisms between 1870 and 2000, it is intended to provide a general historical and interpretative framework that will throw light on the key issues or processes in the development of modern racism. In other words, the aim is to provide an analysis that enables us to understand the past in terms of how specific racisms emerged or were constructed, without necessarily trying to give equal weight to all groups that may have been defined in the past as a 'race'.

The period covered in this book is that of a 'long' twentieth century, from 1870 to 2000. It is a major premise of the study that the period from about 1870 formed an important watershed that witnessed the elaboration and diffusion of a more radical and modern form of racism across the entire landmass of Europe. This new development manifested itself in a simultaneous deepening of hostility towards both blacks and Jews. An official in the British Colonial Office, looking back in 1908 with regret at the dashed hopes of an earlier phase of liberalism and black emancipation, noted that, 'contrary to what might have been hoped and expected, and undoubtedly was hoped and expected half a century ago, the growth of democracy and science and education has not diminished but increased antipathies of race and colour.'[1] Contrary to expectation, more virulent and universal forms of racism were the companion of modernity and an age of 'progress'. Likewise, the great German anthropologist Virchow, writing in the 1890s, was perplexed by the reversion to an irrational and outmoded anti-Semitism. How could this happen, he mused, in 'our time, so sure of itself and of victory by reason of its scientific consciousness? . . . . Even now it is standing baffled before the enigma of anti-Semitism, whose appearance in this time of the equality of right is inexplicable to everybody.'[2] This shift in emphasis was symptomatic of a new form of political anti-Semitism that began to spread throughout Germany, Austria and other parts of Central and Eastern Europe, undermining and attacking the gains of an earlier phase of Jewish emancipation. Across European society the Enlightenment tradition, founded on a belief in rationality, in scientific progress and a social and political order based on equality and universal human rights, appeared to be under attack and increasingly on the defensive.

Was it a mere coincidence that colonial racism and anti-Semitism within Europe began to assume more negative formulations at the same time? George Mosse, one of the few historians to speculate on the nature of the two racisms, tended to see them occupying quite discrete and largely unconnected geographic spaces. Anti-black racism was centred in the West European imperial and maritime powers with a long history of slavery and colonialism, societies in which 'contact with blacks was intimate and constant', while the core of anti-Semitism was located in Central and Eastern Europe, the demographic and cultural heartland of world Jewry, where 'the highly visible Jews took the place of the blacks as the "foil" of race'.[3] Mosse's division of Europe into two racial zones presents a false dichotomy and fails to address the comparative issue. The common-sense assumption that the intensity of racism increases according to the degree of contact with a numerically large minority presence, a kind of 'threshold of tolerance' theory, has no empirical validity. High levels of racism can exist in relation to minorities that are virtually, if not totally, absent from a given society or nation. Britain and France, both great colonial powers, became centres of strong anti-Semitic movements in the late nineteenth century, in spite of the fact that Jews constituted, respectively, 0.5 and 0.2 per cent of the total population. Likewise, as will be demonstrated, the culture of Central and East European societies with a weak or non-existent colonial tradition was suffused with racialized, anti-black stereotypes.

The simultaneous deepening of racisms across Europe after the 1860s, both in their anti-black and anti-Semitic forms, suggests a general pattern of causation. I would agree with those who interpret racist ideology as a specific component of modernity, and in particular of a scientific project which, in the words of Avtar Brah, 'confidently stalked the world identifying, categorising and classifying fauna, flora and peoples; asserting its "neutrality" whilst marking hierarchies of "race", class, and gender'.[4] But this racial discourse, which was developed during the eighteenth century, began to assume a particularly important function during the last third of the nineteenth century, as it became a key ideological expression for new forms of virulent nationalism and for social groups in crisis, undergoing an unprecedented pace of industrialization, urbanization and economic change.

While the ideological formulations of nineteenth-century nationalism frequently found expression through racism, it is important not to conflate the two terms so that any differentiation becomes meaningless. The modern nation-state emerged not only as a process of political, legal and institutional control over the population contained within a delimited territorial space, but also as an imagined community, a *Volk* or people, whose identity was formulated by those boundaries that separated off those who belonged, the 'we-group', from all those foreigners and outsiders who remained aliens or potential enemies. Group identity, it has been argued, can never be defined in a void, but only over and against those Others who are essentially different from 'us'. The modern state, impelled by the need to generate a powerful sense of cohesion and shared identity among its citizens (for purposes of warfare, economic unity etc.), frequently underpinned nationalism through appeals to *ethnicity*, to essentially cultural manifestations of belonging that included shared religion, language, traditions and history. Such forms of nationalism readily lent themselves to the more radical forms of group closure and exclusion constituted by racism. Where racism differs from ethnicity is in the elaboration of a *naturalized* identity, a fixed and unchanging quality that is imprinted in the 'blood' or the biological essence of a group of shared descent. The nation is the family writ large, an issue of 'kith and kin'. As Etienne Balibar notes: 'The symbolic kernel of the idea of race is the schema of genealogy, the idea that filiation of individuals transmits from generation to generation, a substance both biological and spiritual.'[5] For nationalists bent on more radical forms of group boundary maintenance, ethnicity, and in particular language, did not create a sufficiently impermeable screening mechanism against Others (language could be learned), while racism introduced a more absolute principle of closure: the Other could never, even with the greatest will, cross over the symbolic boundary line since difference was indelibly stamped into the body. In the period after 1860, during which a scientific racial discourse achieved increasing power and legitimacy or hegemony in European society, what can be witnessed is a racialization of nationalism, a process that reflected both internal crisis as well as deepening international tension, militarism and insecurity.

What was distinctive about the racial watershed of the late nineteenth century was not that it was based on a revolution in ideas – the scientific classification of 'race' had already appeared in the eighteenth century – so much as the extent to which 'race' became an almost universal or standardized key for the interpretation of human history, as well as for the understanding of contemporary society and its future evolution. The motor of history lay in the realm of Social Darwinism, the war for survival between stronger or weaker races, and in theories relating to degeneration, racial purity, eugenics, military conflict and imperial conquest. This racial *Weltanschauung* remained dominant throughout the period from 1870 to the Second World War, and this is why particular emphasis is placed in this study on the key transition that took place from *c*.1870 since the new paradigm that appeared at this watershed was to remain hegemonic throughout the first half of the twentieth century.

There is a danger in interpreting racism as a history of ideas, as a process of knitting together the texts of major thinkers, of the philosophers of race, from Robert Knox and Gobineau to Darwin, Nietzsche and Houston Stewart Chamberlain. Such an emphasis can lead to an overly idealistic interpretation of history, the view that racial theories influenced practice in an unproblematic way: the educated élites, we are led to believe, from professors to government ministers, read such sources and translated their messages into actions, from legislative and political programmes, to research institutions and educational practice. However, as will be seen below in the discussion of Social Darwinism, the ideas of the theorist (Darwin) were not uniformly adopted, but rather more frequently moulded or selectively adapted to fit in with or to legitimate the pre-existing political goals or ideological agendas of social or political movements. The development of racial ideology did not stem from the impact of science and ideas, but rather the reverse: race science was invariably structured as an expression of underlying preoccupations, whether stemming from class position, nationalism, colonialism, economic crisis or other considerations. Fundamentally, all racism/s are a cultural manifestation, a reflection or expression of tensions or problems within a society, rather than a phenomenon derived from an autonomous and somehow 'objective' sphere of scientific investigation and theory.

Even more complex is the relationship between the racial formulations of the educated élites, of political decision makers and demagogues, which tended (even when 'irrational') to be elaborated as a body of more or less systematic ideas, and the more 'common-sense' racism of the masses (a language of the 'jungle', of 'cannibalism' or simply the 'wog' or the 'nigger'). The racism of the street, of the factory, the public house or football terrace, was rarely formulated as a scientific logic, such as 'Blacks are inferior to whites because they have a smaller brain capacity or represent a lower evolutionary type,' but far more as a set of stereotypes, 'jokes', insults and platitudes that were embedded in popular culture. The spread or deepening of such a 'racism of the masses' could have far more serious implications for target minorities than a sophisticated treatise elaborated in the study of the race scientist.

Tzvetan Todorov has expressed this distinction by reserving the term 'racialism' for doctrines or ideology and 'racism' for behaviour. He comments: 'The ordinary racist is not a theoretician; he is incapable of justifying his behavior with "scientific" arguments. Conversely, the ideologue of race is not necessarily a "racist", in the usual sense: his theoretical views may have no influence whatsoever on his acts.'[6] To understand the history of twentieth-century racism we need to look at the interrelationship between theory and praxis. One of the central, and still largely unresolved, problems in the history and sociology of racism is the extent to which ideologies filtered down to influence public behaviour or, vice versa, whether ideologues (whether theoreticians or political leaders) responded to popular racist behaviour, such as violence, rioting and grass-roots campaigns, by modifying their ideas and policies. The position that I have taken throughout this study supports the idea that the genesis of modern racist practices has been most crucially a top-down process through which élites have played the greatest role in initiating action or forming a wider public opinion. As Teun A. van Dijk has argued, it is the educated élites within national and local authorities, the judiciary, police forces, education, academic research and the media who hold the power both to construct dominant discourses, as well as to formulate and implement policies.[7] Racist ideologues and propagandists knew perfectly well how to translate the central ideas of scientific racism, Social Darwinism and biological superiority into popular forms and slogans. As Anne McClintock remarks, scientific racism down to the 1850s remained 'relatively class-bound and inaccessible to most Victorians', but then through mass marketing or 'commodity racism', imperialism was able to 'package, market and distribute evolutionary racism on a hitherto unimagined scale'.[8]

In suggesting that historically modern racism has been generated through a 'top-down' process, it is not being argued that popular racism played an insignificant role or was lacking in its own dynamic. However, time and again during the period from 1870 to 2000 the origins of organized or political racist currents, the processes of initiating or mobilizing a populist momentum, can be traced to the crucial role of the European middle classes and of the state. Any particular 'outbreak' of political racism, in the form of organized movements, from parties to leagues, associations and pogroms or riots, followed a regular pattern in its development through time. An ideal typical model, or interpretive schema, can be proposed as follows. Racial prejudices and stereotypes have, to a lesser or greater extent, always been widely diffused within modern civil society, transmitted from generation to generation within the family or by wider social networks, or via a myriad of cultural routes, from images in advertisements to school textbooks and church sermons. In a first stage such racial stereotypes can be viewed as existing in a primarily 'benign' form; sedimented within the culture of the general public they can remain latent over long periods of time, without ever translating into overt forms of verbal or physical violence or of organized racism.

However, such a latent cultural racism can, particularly within a context of economic, social or political crisis, offer a resource for political élites as a means to whip up or mobilize the populace. In a crucial early transition to organized forms of racism, the state and the bourgeoisie played a crucial role in opting whether to dampen down racism, to control or block its manifestations, or whether to encourage its popular expression. Through the mobilization of prejudice, either from the level of the central or local state apparatus, élites can create and then harness racism as a political resource and source of power.

While the intervention of élites was often crucial in initiating or kick-starting racist movements or currents of opinion, frequently, popular racism would take on its own volition and autonomy once it had been set in motion. In the dialectic between state racism and popular racism, the crucial drive for 'upping the stakes' has derived from the bourgeoisie or from the educated fractions of the working class holding positions of power as minor civil servants, police officers, trade union leaders and politicians. Government leaders and politicians, in undertaking racist actions, have frequently justified this as a necessary response to popular pressure, whereas they themselves have all too frequently taken the ini-tiative, through discourse and policy initiatives, in precipitating the very racism to which they claim they are having to react and give way. For example, during the year 2000 governments across Europe generated a highly negative perception of asylum seekers as 'bogus' refugees, a threat to national identity and culture, a drain on the welfare state, and a source of disease and criminality. This, in turn, legitimated and accelerated widespread popular racism at the local level, especially in reaction to state policies of geographic dispersal, a wave of racism that politicians then claimed, in principle, to oppose (see Chapter 7).

A final theoretical point concerns the almost universal linkage between race and gender. The rise of the contemporary feminist move-ment from the 1960s onwards provided a powerful and radically new impulse to the theorizing of difference. Feminist writers have had a major impact on the way in which categorizations of inferiority have been created through signifying systems based on notions of an essential nature and biological specificity. In the nineteenth and twentieth centuries women (like races) were generally considered to be internally programmed by 'Nature' to fulfil certain functions within a patriarchal order: characteristics of softness suited to the nurturing and care of both children and adult males, of 'natural' obedience to the superior intellectual and physical abilities of men, and so on. The sciences of anthropology, medicine and psychiatry that were obsessively fixated on the black body, on the location and measurement of 'markings' and signs of inner difference, carried out a similar project on the female body. Through this interlocking field of enquiry, as Nancy Stepan has argued, 'gender was found to be remarkably analogous to race, such that the scientist could use racial difference to explain gender difference, and vice versa'.[9] Through this equation, European women, who were challenging male domination, were claimed to have small brain weights and deficient brain functions, analogous to the lower races, which likewise were thought to depend on the superior intellectual direction and care of the white colonial master. European women were described as having slightly protruding jaws, analogous to the ape-like jaws of lower races, while in an inverse direction, inferior races were frequently 'feminized', described in terms of 'unmanly', soft, physically weak or low intellectual characteristics.

In this study space does not allow an adequate treatment of this enormously fertile area of investigation, but a number of key facets can be kept in mind:

- White self-referential racism (see Chapter 1) was constructed through a discourse that presented European women as lower than men on the evolutionary scale and analogous to biologically inferior peoples.
- Lower races were in turn reduced by 'science' to the status of women, or frequently made effeminate, sexually ambivalent or homosexual. Winwood Reade, in *Savage Africa*, noted in the mid-nineteenth century: 'But if the women of Africa are brutal, the men of Africa are feminine. Their faces are smooth, their breasts are frequently as full as those of European women; their voices are never gruff or deep. Their fingers are long; and they can be very proud of their rosy nails ... the men have gracefully moulded limbs, and always are after a feminine type.'[10]
- Just as most males in the late nineteenth and early twentieth centuries assumed that the maintenance of the European social and political

order depended crucially on masculine hegemony (including a kind of 'ownership' of women), so within the colonial sphere white domination was almost universally regarded as dependent on the black male not reversing the power relationship by having sexual relations with white women. Hence the obsessive fear of miscegenation, racial pollution and degeneration.

- The colonial/racial order was, however, quite concomitant with white males entertaining sexual relations with black or Asian women, who were thus frequently represented in terms of erotic imagery, of naked black bodies or Orientalist unveiling and harems. White male sexual fantasies of conquest and control of inferior, but supposedly lubricious, black females was integral to the social psychology and culture of imperial domination. Assertion of sexual rights over women, like the medieval *droit de seigneur*, was a statement of power.

- The self-confident 'sexual economy' of white hegemony was, however, frequently disrupted or challenged by profound anxieties and ambiguities that manifested themselves in racisms and stereotypes that were quite different in structure. The black male, for example, could be viewed as a powerful, physical challenge, the sexually potent stud who presented a danger to white male sexual dominance through rape or through repressed homo-erotic powers of attraction. Conversely, blacks could be feminized, although such stereotypes were more frequently applied to the Jewish male as a physically weak, degenerate specimen than to Africans.

- Increasingly, during the twentieth century, the potency of black women was viewed in terms of a 'breeding capacity', a biological power of demographic reproduction which, in contrast with the low and declining fertility of unhealthy or degenerate white women, posed the growing threat of global 'race wars' in which the civilized order would eventually be 'inundated' by swarms of inferior peoples.

- Lastly, it can be noted that in the history of racism between c.1870 and the present, feminist writers have shown that far more attention needs to be given to the social, economic and political position of women from the minority groups. For example, until the 1970s most accounts of migration into Europe related almost solely to males. However, although black and Asian men did predominate in the earliest migrations (as seamen or labourers), women had always played a significant part in such movements. After 1945 a growing percentage of all immigrants were women, and as such they became the target of quite specific forms of racism. This should be kept in mind throughout the following account, in which space has not always allowed as detailed a treatment of this field as the subject merits.

The Origins of a Science of 'Race'

The remainder of this introductory chapter sets out to explore in more detail the conditions under which a typically modern form of racism began to spread within European society from the 1860–70s onwards. To understand the nature of the new racial paradigm requires some examination of the earlier forms of racism that were about to undergo a major shift or reformulation. A true science of 'race', an attempt to classify the human species into a range of differing biological subgroups, did not emerge clearly until the eighteenth century with the work of thinkers like Linnaeus, Buffon and Blumenbach. The Age of the Enlightenment was one in which self-confident reason set out to impose order on the natural world by elaborating systems of classification that would enable the underlying structures and patterns of the material universe, regulated by the laws of nature, to be identified and analysed. The scientific work of the Swede Linnaeus involved a vast scheme, an epistemological project, to systematize knowledge of the teeming chaos of animal and plant forms through a coherent system of classification that would establish the underlying biological similarities of species and types. The great breakthrough of Linnaeus in the *Systema Naturae* (1735) was to classify man in the same Order of quadrupeds as the ape and sloth, a revolutionary step that broke with Genesis and a Scriptural interpretation of the place of man within a divine order, and located him zoologically as part of the animal world. In the second edition of 1740 he went on to subdivide man into four races, according to skin colour: the white European, the dark Asian, the black African and the red American.[11] However, a more representative figure of the science of race was Johann Friedrich Blumenbach (1752–1840), professor of anatomy at Göttingen, regarded as the father of modern anthropology. In the third edition of his *On the Natural Variety of Mankind* (1795), Blumenbach divided mankind into five races, including the famous white 'Caucasian', but most crucially he upheld the theory of monogenesis, as had Linnaeus and Buffon.

Monogenesis – the defining mark of European racial ideology between *c*.1750 and 1850 – upheld the descent of all races from a single original group, and in doing so was in conformity with both Biblical tradition and with the Enlightenment concept of the essential unity or brotherhood of man. Blumenbach thought that the different races had evolved from a common ancestral group (which was characteristically white) through a process of 'degeneration' and the accumulative impact of differing climate, diet, disease and mode of life. His contention that, regardless of race, men 'are all related, or only differ from each other in degree',[12] was an essential component of the 'humanitarian racism' that remained dominant down to the mid-nineteenth century.

The period from the late eighteenth century down to $c.1860$–70 was one in which most European thinkers emphasized the shared characteristics and fundamental equality of all mankind. The Enlightenment, as well as the American and French Revolutions, promoted the values of a universal humanism, through which all men, regardless of class, religion, colour or nationality, shared the same essential being and fundamental rights. This was also the age of emancipation, which saw the gradual extension of the abolition of the slave trade and slavery between 1794 and 1865, as well as the civil and political emancipation of the Jews (France 1789, Belgium 1830, Prussia 1850, Austria-Hungary 1867, Germany 1871). A few thinkers during this period did come up with radical forms of racial difference, but the main drive of the age was towards a view of human progress in which eventually even the most primitive peoples would receive the benefits of civilization and Christianity. Blumenbach was a represenative figure of the age of Enlightenment and progress, and expounded a tolerant racial science. 'Negroes', for example, usually viewed as at the bottom of the racial hierarchy, he found to have a 'good disposition' and 'they can scarcely be considered inferior to any other race of mankind taken together'. They would show the same natural 'tenderness of heart' as other peoples, as long as this sentiment 'has never been benumbed or extirpated on board the transport vessels or on the West India sugar plantations by the brutality of their white executioners'.[13] This was a classic abolitionist position: if blacks seemed inferior and morally vicious this had nothing to do with innate racial characteristics, but with the damaging effects of slavery. Remove this evil, and Africans would be as perfectable as Europeans.

From $c.1850$ onwards European society began to show evidence of a shift towards a more intolerant racism that constructed more radical biological differences between groups. A distinguishing feature of the ideological formulation of the emergent, modern racism was that it set out to create radically impermeable boundaries between races. The British anatomist Robert Knox can be taken as an early precursor of this shift. In *The Races of Men* (1850) he placed an absolute biological division between races such that it was impossible for any interbreeding to result in lasting hybrid or mixed types. History could show that each race had remained absolutely unchanged over thousands of years, regardless of nationality, climate, migrations or other conditions. Knox's theory was founded on a racial determinism: the laws of nature dictated that the Negro was irrevocably inferior to the Saxon race (the highest type) and was lacking in the major 'qualities which distinguish man from the animal', among them the power of 'pure reason' and the ability 'to observe new phenomena and new relations'.[14] In several passages he suggested that the fair Saxon race – 'a tall, powerful, athletic race of men; the strongest, as a race, on earth' – was inevitably bound to exterminate the weaker, dark races. This had already taken place with the Tasmanians, and although this was perhaps regrettable, as 'a cruel, cold blooded, heartless deed', Knox did not regard extermination as an ethical or religious issue: this was simply the playing out of the inexorable laws of nature.

Knox's theories were characteristic of the modern race science that became dominant between 1870 and 1914. A number of features distinguish the transition to the distinctive modern form of racism. Firstly, so all-determining was the theory of race that it provided the universal key to an understanding of the whole of human history as well as of the contemporary social and political order: 'Race,' claimed Knox, ' is everything: literature, science, art, in a word, civilization, depends on it' and 'in human history race is everything';[15] words echoed in Disraeli's famous bon mot 'Race is all!'. From the mid-nineteenth century onwards 'race science' became the dominant epistemology, a tool for the unlocking of every conceivable social, cultural and political phenomenon, and the discourse of race infiltrated gender, class and nation.

Knox's work was prophetic of a deepening crisis in late nineteenth-century liberalism, an atmosphere of growing European intolerance and inherent superiority towards minority peoples. For example, in his off-hand dismissal of the 'hideous', 'lazy' and baboon-like Hottentot and Bosjeman races, Knox asked if they were doomed: 'I suppose so: they will soon form merely natural curiosities; already there is the skin of one stuffed in England; and another in Paris.'[16] Although Knox did not use the term 'polygenesis', the idea of the totally separate and fixed characteristics of races was implicit throughout his work, a theoretical position that broke away from both the Christian tradition of descent from Adam, with its connotations of a shared humanity, as well as the scientific monogenesis of the Enlightenment and the concept of the universality of man. As Nancy Stepan has shown, such an emphasis on the fundamental

heterogeneity of mankind remained the dominant racial discourse throughout the period 1850–1945, in spite of the implications of Darwin's theories
which demonstrated the evolutionary interconnectedness of the human
species. The idea of the fixed and immutable quality of race lent itself
more readily to a racist praxis that emphasized a hierarchy of superior
and inferior types, and the radical segregation, exclusion or domination
of lower forms.

Knox also pointed towards the future trend in racial science in his
emphasis on the existence of distinct races internal to Europe. The
humanistic racism of the Enlightenment tradition that was dominant
from 1750 to 1850 deployed a simple demarcation of global population
into a few categories, most commonly European (white), African (black),
American (red) and Asian (yellow). In this system the people of Europe
were presented as a homogeneous block, *homo europaeus albus*. Knox,
however, argued that Europe was divided internally into a range of
races (Saxon, Celt, Slavonian, Sarmatian etc.) that were just as distinctive
as Red Indians, Hottentots and other 'savages'. Moreover, the dynamics
of contemporary history could be interpreted as a struggle between
these European groups, a 'war of race against race'.[17] This shift in physical anthropology after 1850, which can be linked to a growing form of
aggressive nationalism and inter-state tension that divided Europe, is of
importance to the emergence of two quite different forms of racism; one
that was directed towards Others who were seen as essentially outside
the borders of European society (anti-black colonial racism), and another,
more paranoid form, that targeted alien groups that were located inside
Europe, embedded within the heart of the host society.

The classic instance of the 'enemy within' was the Jew. Here again,
Knox was innovative in his categorization of Jews as a distinct biological
race. During the age of emancipation (1782–1871) the Jews were seen as
primarily a religious and cultural group, and it was a basic premise of
emancipation that they could indeed become fully integrated and even
assimilated into the national majority group. However, from the late
1860s onwards the Jews were increasingly defined not only as an alien
presence within the nation, 'a state within the state', but as a quite distinctive racial group that would remain eternally separate from the
people of Europe. Christian tradition had defined the Jew as a deicide,
as the living rejection of Revelation, but, at the same time, the Church
maintained the possibility of conversion and even associated the final
conversion of the Jewish people with Christian eschatology, the Millennium and the return of Christ. Now, scientific forms of racism meant

that the Jews would always remain Jews, locked into the hereditary destiny of their race. Johannes Nordmann, in *The Jew and the German State* (1861), provided an early example of this new form of thinking that, from 1879, was to be denoted by the neologism 'anti-Semitism'. According to Nordmann, the closed character of the Jewish community and marrriage endogamy had allowed a distinct racial minority to survive unassimilated in Europe: 'Seclusion and inbreeding over many thousand years strengthened the thorough domination of the race type and made the way of thought a part of it. Jewish blood and Jewish sentiment became inseparable and we have to conceive of Judaism not only as religion and congregation but also as the expression of racial peculiarity.'[18] Wilhelm Marr, the leading anti-Semitic theorist, emphasized that in the new approach, befitting a secular age of scientific progress and inquiry: 'There must be no question here of parading religious prejudices when it is a question of race and when the difference lies in the "blood".'[19]

The period from the 1870s onwards witnessed a European-wide reaction among the bourgeoisie against liberal humanism and against the political movements that had seen the final emancipation of black slaves and of the Jews. In both instances the radical difference between Europeans and the Other was naturalized; a difference built into the biological essence of each group. The absolute boundary between each race was constructed as a scientific theory and hence, in a secular age when purely religious interpretations of the world were being sapped by materialism, such racial forms of thinking would have appealed to growing numbers of the educated classes and provided a powerful form of legitimation for such concepts. The modern form of racism was spreading simultaneously both across the maritime colonial states of Western Europe (in an anti-black form) as well as across swathes of Central and Eastern Europe (primarily in the form of anti-Semitism).

So far we have tended to examine the emergence of modern racism from earlier forms in terms of ideas (of Blumenbach, Knox and others). However, as has been argued, it would be a great mistake to try and interpret the synchronicity of modern racism, its simultaneous appearance across the face of Europe, as a consequence of the spread and impact of new ideas. It was rarely the case that thinkers, even the most sophisticated scientists like Darwin, discovered biological truths about race that then simply spread into society, but rather there was an inverse relationship in which scientific racism tended to reflect the general beliefs and values of the wider society and the changes it was undergoing. Ideas of race were not a cause, but more frequently an expression of racism. The construction of 'race' was achieved through a system of marking and stigmatization, of generating taxonomies, that depended crucially on the 'naturalization' of group difference. The process through which genetically superficial differences, usually the most visible and external qualities of skin tone, hair texture, height and facial features, became symbolic markers or signifiers for not only racial categorization, but also for essential forms of moral, mental and cultural inferiority, was central to modern racism.

The founding race theorists, like Linnaeus and Blumenbach, as we have seen, elaborated complex systems of classification that divided human beings into distinct groups using primarily the methods of comparative physical anthropology. Most race theorists, from Linnaeus to Gobineau, were 'armchair' anthropologists who formed their ideas not from the direct observation of 'native' peoples, but from the accounts of travellers (missionaries, sailors, soldiers, explorers), from their drawings, and the close measurement of skeletons and, in particular, of human skulls. Blumenbach was quite typical: he never travelled further than Switzerland, Holland, England and France, and his main scientific technique was the classification of what he called his 'Golgotha', his private collection of 245 skulls imported from around the world. The physical anthropologists, whose approach remained dominant between the mid-eighteenth century and the early years of the twentieth century, classified each race type using a scientific language that listed the main component features of skin, eye colour, hair type, skull shape and other somatic features. Blumenbach described the African or 'Ethiopian' race as follows: 'Colour black; hair black and curly; head narrow, compressed at the sides; forehead knotty, uneven; molar bones protruding outwards; eyes very prominent; nose thick, mixed up as it were with the wide jaws; alveolar edge narrow, elongated in front; the upper primaries obliquely prominent; the lips (especially the upper) very puffy; chin retreating.'[20] While such a seemingly objective and rational language would appear to constitute the very core of racist scientific methodology, this impression is illusory. The crucial message of the scientist lay not in the typology, but in the aesthetic, moral, and cultural characteristics which were 'slipped in' and attached to each somatic type. Linnaeus, for example, tabulated and classified the African as follows:

Black, phlegmatic, relaxed.
Hair black, frizzled. Skin silky. Nose flat. Lips tumid.
Women without shame. Mammae lactate profusely, crafty, indolent, negligent.

Anoints himself with grease.
Governed by caprice.[21]

The key racial element here lies not in the physical 'markers' (these can be quite neutral), but in the qualities to which they are attached: Africans are shameless, crafty, indolent, negligent, capricious. The scientists did not discover such qualities by direct observation of Africans, but through the numerous, and often lurid or highly subjective, accounts of travellers that lay to hand in the libraries of Europe. The race ideologues thus picked up the pre-existing prejudices and stereotypical attitudes of European and white colonial societies, repackaged them as scientific theory, and then mirrored them back to a literate public. A century and a half after Linnaeus, physical anthropologists were still operating in an identical way. A. H. Keane, professor at University College, London, and a leading expert on race at the turn of the century, in his popular *Man, Past and Present* (1899) provided a taxonomy which included a description of racial 'temperament'. The Sudanese Negroes were 'sensuous, indolent, improvident, fitful, passionate and cruel, though often affectionate and faithful; little sense of dignity, and slight self-consciousness, hence easy acceptance of yoke of slavery; musical', while the Southern Mongols were 'somewhat sluggish, with little initiative, but great endurance, cunning rather than intelligent; generally thrifty and industrious, but most indolent in Siam and Burma; moral standards low, with slight sense of right and wrong'.[22]

Throughout the nineteenth and twentieth centuries racist stereotypes of the black operated with an unchanging and restricted repertoire of characteristics, a list that was repeated *ad nauseam* in newspapers, novels, travel writings, bar-room jokes, children's adventure books, encyclopaedias, advertisements and vaudeville. The black was generally described as lewd and oversexed, lazy, diseased, dirty, of low intelligence, child-like (requiring supervision), violent, immoral, lying and thieving. Race scientists did not then use some advanced methodology to locate the essential inferiority of the black, but rather they reflected and reiterated the predominant values of the society and age in which they were embedded. Both Linnaeus and Keane described the African as 'indolent'.

An examination of just this one attribute, the 'myth of the lazy native', illustrates how the process of racialization was embedded in concrete historical processes of domination. When technologically advanced European adventurers and colonizers moved into Africa, they brought with them a capitalist work ethic, a set of cultural attitudes towards clock time and systematic labour, that was totally alien to the pastoral and agrarian economies of Africa. Europeans failed to recognize the hard labour involved in, for example, traditional patterns of extensive herding or hunting. Africans were thought to laze about in the tropical heat, occasionally lifting an indolent hand to pluck a banana from an ever-fertile forest: a fundamental reason why, since necessity is the mother of invention, it was argued that Africans had never built cities or achieved any degree of civilization. Whenever colonizers tried to harness African labour to their own ends, in plantations, gold mines and railway construction, they invariably met a high degree of resistance, not only to the violence deployed, but also to the very processes of unremitting, measured toil. Europeans, who regarded it as their natural right to dominate and exploit such 'primitive' and backward peoples, viewed such opposition as perverse, and an expression of the inherent laziness of all blacks. It is typical of the contradictory or irrational nature of racial stereotyping that such a fixed idea could be sustained despite the fact that the incalculable wealth produced by the labour of black plantation slaves was a foundation-stone of West European capitalism. However, the idea that black peoples were biologically and ineradicably lazy, in turn, served an important ideological function and was used to legitimate the need for European masters to supervise and control the labour potential of primitive peoples who, without such direction, would never lift themselves from savage torpor towards a civilized order.

The myth of the lazy native, a key component of modern racism, like most racist stereotyping, tells us much more about the Eurocentric preoccupations of the dominant society, about the projections of white Europeans, than about the social reality of African society. Studies of racism which remain restricted to ideas about race will tend to exaggerate the autonomy of science and largely fail to locate the social, economic and political processes that can explain such a phenomenon. The shift in the paradigm of racism in about c.1860–70 to a new form, the assertion of radical biological difference, was not then a consequence of scientific innovation, but rather the reflection of a profound transformation in European society. However, this is not to argue that race science was simply an epiphenomenon and had no impacts since, as Michel Foucault has shown, particular types of knowledge or discourse can also constitute a form of power. In a rapidly secularizing age, of immense industrial and technical advance, science carried enormous prestige and powers of legitimation. This is one key reason why the 'arts of race', in order to carry conviction, needed to be reformulated in scientific rather than in traditional religious terms

Racism, Modernity and the 1870 Turning-Point

The simultaneous appearance of a modern, exclusionary racism in its anti-black and anti-Semitic forms right across Europe after 1870 cannot, therefore, be adequately understood as a breakthrough in racist ideas alone, an innovative moment in science, but needs to be investigated within the broader context of social, political, economic and cultural change. In particular, note can be taken of five major factors that provided a particularly powerful impetus towards a modern form of racism:

- An anti-liberal shift in politics, a deep cultural pessimism, that was a conservative reaction to the upheavals and dislocation produced by rapid economic and social change.
- The appearance of militarism and xenophobic nationalism linked to an age of growing international insecurity and competitiveness.
- The rapid expansion of the 'New Imperialism' and aggressive forms of colonialism, particularly in Africa.
- The extension of the popular franchise and the growth of new 'mass-party' organizations in which, for the first time, matters of 'race' (both of Empire and of anti-Semitism) became mobilizing issues.
- Growing literacy and a revolution in mass-communication technologies that enabled both racial texts and representations, from film to advertising, to be diffused with unparalleled force.

We next provide a brief summary of these key factors, which will then be expanded upon in later chapters. Before doing so, however, it is important to note that the spread of capitalism and the making of 'bourgeois Europe' was an uneven process, with some regions undergoing an early stage of industrialization (notably in Britain, and parts of France), while other areas (Southern and Eastern Europe) remained predominantly underdeveloped peasant societies. This made a difference in the extent to which secular and modern forms of racism took root, but the impact of modernization was by 1870–1900 being felt even in the most backward zones. For example, the wave of anti-Semitic pogroms that spread across the Ukraine and Black Sea coast areas at the turn of the century, although still finding expression in more traditional Christian forms

(Jews as deicides), was undoubtedly linked to the rapid economic growth of cities like Odessa.

By 1870, and the close of what Hobsbawm has dubbed the 'Age of Capital' (1848–75), Europe was accelerating through an unprecedented series of changes that were driven by rapid industrialization, the spread of steam power across the Continent, the growth of factory and mining towns, and the migration of land workers into urban centres. The pace of change can be illustrated by the extremely rapid growth in cities: between 1850 and 1900 the population of London increased from 2.3 to 6.4 million; Paris from 1.3 to 3.3 million, Berlin from 446 000 to 2.4 million, Hamburg from 193 000 to 895 000. Although this could be seen as the age in which the bourgeoisie was triumphant, possessing an unprecedented degree of wealth and power, it was also – as Marx showed in detail – a period of immense social stress and insecurity. The bourgeoisie felt threatened from below by the growth of a vast and oppressed proletariat which was beginning to convert to socialism or anarchism, and to organize in trade unions and mass political parties. Bourgeois confidence in the onward march of capital was severely dented by the stock exchange crash of 1873, a crisis that inspired a strong anti-Semitic reaction, and by the Great Depression that lasted through to the 1890s. Rapid economic transformation meant that numerous social groups, from traditional landowner/aristocracies to peasants and handcraft workers, were faced with inevitable decline and the disintegration of an old rural or small-town society that was seen through a haze of nostalgia and regret. The disruptive impacts of capitalism created the conditions under which many groups and organizations, profoundly disturbed by modernism, responded by seeking stability and solace in a conservative or reactive agenda. It was these groups who were to prove susceptible to the appeal of racism, and in particular to anti-Semitism which targeted the Jews as the 'enemy within', seen as responsible for both the growth of speculative and commercial capitalism that was 'parasitic' on the honest labour of European peoples, and for the subversion of the existing order via the secretive organization of socialist and revolutionary movements.

A powerful conservative and anti-liberal politics began to spread across the face of Europe after 1870, from Berlin to Moscow, in opposition to the laissez-faire 'Manchester' ideology of free trade, held as responsible for the depredations of unregulated capitalism. Among conservative élites the disintegration of the old order and its hierarchical certainties was characterized by nostalgia for a mythical rural or volkish past in which grateful peasants were bound by mutual ties to protective lords, a society rooted in tradition, the ways of ancestors, and hallowed by strong religious faith. Thus, although today we are often struck by the triumphalism and splendour of late Victorian Europe, the apparent self-confidence of its grand architectural statements, for many élites this was not the age of progress and certainty, but of profound pessimism and of what Fritz Stern has aptly named 'cultural despair'.[23] The disquiet with modernism was widely translated into a *fin-de-siècle* pessimism that regarded European civilization as threatened from within by a process of physiological and racial degeneration. The work of Count Gobineau, *Essai sur l'inégalité des races humaines* (1853), was a key precursor of this late nineteenth-century trend, founded as it was on a profound remorse for a declining aristocratic order, a nostalgia that was translated into racial terms. In particular, the crisis of civilization and degeneration was expressed as a profound fear of interbreeding with lower race-class types, a sexual phantasm of pollution and intermingling that could only be contained through projects of segregation, exclusion or elimination. As Benedict Anderson states, white racism 'dreams of eternal contam-inations, transmitted from the origins of time through an endless sequence of loathsome copulations'.[24] It was this anxiety that inspired the evolution towards racial eugenics and what Foucault has termed bio-power, state strategies to maximize the demographic potential and 'efficiency' of the nation.

A second fundamental aspect of modern racism was its integral associ-ation with the rise of nationalism. As we have seen, the nation-state, like racism, developed as an imagined community which was defined through the elaboration of boundaries that determined who did or did not belong to the 'people'. From the late fifteenth century onwards, monarchies throughout Europe engaged in dynamic processes of state formation that extended power over peripheral regions and minorities, and attempted to enforce a homogeneous 'space of belonging', through the elimination of minority languages, the imposition of religious ortho-doxy, uniform and centralized bureacracies, and other processes. This process of 'nationalization' began to assume a proto-racist form in Spain at a very early stage with the total exclusion of Jews and Moriscoes in 1492. The statutes on the purity of blood (*limpieza de sangre*), which were enforced by the Spanish Inquisition between 1449 and 1834, have been frequently interpreted as an unusually early form of racism in that 'New Christians', in spite of conversion, remained indelibly tainted with Jewish or Moorish blood from one generation to the next. However, the concept of indelible staining (*macula*) derived from both a Biblical tradition of the impure as well as from the aristocratic ideology of lineage (the avoidance of misalliance and marriage outside the group of 'noble blood') that should not be confused with modern forms of biological racism. It was not until the late eighteenth century that the first signs of a racialized nationalism began to appear. The revolutionary shift from dynastic states (in the possession of monarchs) to nation-states (constituted by citizen/peoples) saw an abandonment of an older concept of 'race' that was founded on the aristocratic principle of lineage, the transmission of hereditary 'good blood', and the prevention of misalliance and tainting, controlled by strict rules of class endogamy and genealogical tables. In the nineteenth century the model of group purity that operated at the level of the family, the lineage or the dynasty was extended outwards to encompass the boundaries of the nation-state. As Stella Cottrell has noted, the language of the new forms of British patriotism that appeared after 1800 was one of pedigree, lineage, ancestry and nobility, in which the historic continuity of the nation/people was expressed as 'the British Blood that flows in our veins'.[25] Hence the discourse of modern racism was, and continues to be, suffused with a much older language that defined the rules of belonging through notions of 'blood', fictive kinship (the nation as 'family') and a horror of miscegenation and tainting by inferior groups.

What the modern form of racism provided after mid-century was a powerful ideological means of expressing a much more rigidly defined nationalism. The boundaries of the national community could be policed in a far more absolute way, since those Others who were regarded as alien (Jews, Gypsies, the Irish, blacks) could never be assimilated or cross over, since they were locked into an ineradicable biological difference. A distinctive watershed appeared during the 1880s as Western states, including the USA and white dominions, moved from an earlier 'liberal' phase in relation to international migration, towards increasingly restrictive controls at national borders. Nation-building involved new passport regimes, work quotas and other bureaucratic mechanisms for the policing of territory and the exclusion of aliens seen as racially incompatible. By 1870 the romantic phase of national liberation, of heroic Polish struggle against Russia, of Greek against Turk, of Italian unification, was giving way to a phase of growing tension and insecurity between the major European powers, Britain, France, Germany and Russia. Significantly, as these antagonisms deepened, the science of race shifted from a preoccupation with the global categorization of non-European races and a simple, unified concept of European white/Caucasian identity, to an internal racism that began to elaborate an increasingly complex subdivision into distinct European types (Aryan, Celt, Nordic, Mediterranean, Alpine . . .). Nationalist ideologues began to express growing international tensions inside the boundaries of Europe in the language of race and of Social Darwinism. However, the obsessive drive towards an 'integral' nationalism, one that could assure the external strength of the state in international conflict only through an internal cohesion based on racial purity, was to find its most widespread formulation through political anti-Semitism. Right across Europe the Jews, regardless of their numerical presence, were regarded as a 'stateless other', a racial group that threatened the integrity of the host society since their hereditary values would always tie their allegiance to international forces (capitalism, socialism, freemasonry, liberalism) that were perceived to present the greatest danger to national survival. While national antagonisms were often racialized (the English dislike for the Irish, the German for the Pole, the French for the Italian), these were restricted and nation-specific: what distinguished the Jews from all other groups, apart from the Gypsies, was that they constituted a truly 'international insider'.

A third major feature of the period after 1870, integrally linked to the surge of aggressive nationalism, was the growth of the 'New Imperialism'. In particular, the 'scramble for Africa' led to a remark-ably rapid partition of the Continent between 1880 and 1912. The involvement of a considerable number of old and new imperial states in this process – Spain, Portugal, Belgium, England, France, Germany, Italy and Denmark – meant that maritime, West European societies were inevitably affected by colonial propaganda and by forms of racism that were tied to the imperial mission. The fact that colonial expansion and intra-European competition was so much centred on the 'Dark Continent' during this period meant that media attention and racist propaganda was focused on the image of the black. The same aggres-sive and defensive forms of nationalism that gave rise to militarism, patriotism and a search for national efficiency internal to Europe, also inspired the extension of this contest out beyond the boundaries of Europe in the struggle to seize colonial territories and to control their raw materials, markets and labour power. The French newspaper *Le Temps* commented, after the shock of the defeat by Prussia in 1871, 'cruelly defeated in Europe, we must look for compensation elsewhere'.[26]

Throughout the age of the 'New Imperialism', c.1875 to c.1914, as well as into the inter-war period, European powers in Africa engaged in an oppressive racial praxis, systematic and 'legalized' brutality and segregation, widespread killings, and genocidal wars (from the Belgian atrocities in the Congo and the German extermination of the Herero in South-West Africa, to the Italian campaign in Ethiopia) that inevitably had an impact on 'civilized' metropolitan societies. In this study we are concerned primarily with racism as it developed internal to Europe and space does not allow a fuller treatment of the colonial sphere, but, clearly, the direct contact with Africans overseas and the development of a complex apparatus of institutionalized racism backed up imperial ideologies of racial superiority and had a major impact on metropolitan society. Colonial societies were not only the originators of discriminatory ideologies, such as elaborate codes to prevent miscegenation, but, far more crucially, they provided the context in which racial practices were implemented through tough legal systems, oppressive policing regimes, segregation and a host of other measures. In the period after 1870 many colonial regimes, from South Africa to Indonesia and Algeria, witnessed a shift from more benign towards more oppressive forms of racist regime. This racism flowed back and impacted on metropolitan societies through numerous channels, from the impact of pro-imperialist propaganda and political leagues to the career circulation between Europe and overseas of numerous colonial state officials, army officers, missionaries, academics and businessmen who brought 'home' racist attitudes. As Ann Stoler has argued, colonial empires acted as 'laboratories of modernity', testing grounds and models for the European bourgeois order.[27]

Fourthly, the racialization of European politics after 1870 coincided with the growth of new forms of mass political organization. Between the 1860s and 1914 there was a drive towards electoral reform and the extension of the vote throughout Europe. Although universal male suffrage was introduced in a piecemeal way (Imperial Germany 1871, Britain 1867 and 1885, Belgium 1893, Finland 1906, Italy 1912), the size of electorates increased dramatically. The gradual extension of the vote to lower middle-class and working-class males was accompanied by the growth of mass political parties that began to develop new organizational structures and forms of popular agitation. In some national contexts, as in France during the Dreyfus crisis, in Germany and Austria after 1879, and in England at the turn of the century, this could have a dramatic impact on the politicization of anti-Semitism. For the first time in modern Europe race became a mobilizing issue, a concern that could begin to have a dramatic impact on the behaviour of the voting public. The period 1870–1914 also saw the proliferation of an immense number of campaigning organizations, of leagues and associations, that were dedicated to imperialist and racist propaganda, from the British Primrose League (1883), the Imperial Federation League and the Empire League, to German organizations like the Pan-German League and the Navy League. The growing comfort and rapidity of transport systems, by train, tram and automobile, accelerated mobility and encouraged the movement of propagandists, as well as the regular meeting and exchange of ideas between anti-Semites, race scientists and eugenicists in annual conferences and colloquia, both nationally and at the European level. For example, the First International Anti-Jewish Congress, held in Dresden in 1882, was attended by delegates from various parts of Germany, Austria and Hungary; while the Second International at Chemnitz the following year attracted representatives from Austria, Hungary, Russia, Romania, Serbia and France.

Finally, and linked closely to the emergence of mass politics, was the spread of education and of new technologies of communication. Primary education expanded considerably during the late nineteenth century, and adult illiteracy declined between 1870 and 1900 in the Austrian Empire from 50 per cent to 23 per cent, in France from 31 per cent to 17 per cent, in Belgium from 31 per cent to 19 per cent, although levels remained high in Italy (69 per cent to 48 per cent), in Spain (72 per cent to 56 per cent) and in Russia and Poland (81 per cent and 74 per cent in 1897). The creation of a literate, mass readership revolutionized popular culture and vastly increased the channels through which colonial and racist ideas could be diffused. Technical changes, including rotary presses, mechanized type-setting and photographic reproduction, opened the way to a cheap mass-circulation press. By 1914 modern machines could print 50 000 copies of a 12-page newspaper in an hour, and the circulation of the popular *Daily Mail*, for example, increased from 400 000 copies in 1898 to one million in 1901, while *Le Petit Parisien* went from 690 000 copies in 1890 to 1.5 million in 1914. This period also saw an enormous proliferation of visual materials, from postcards and advertisements to cigarette cards, that reproduced racist images of barbarous 'fuzzy-wuzzies', cannibals and naked savages or of evil, hooknosed Jews bent on world conquest. School textbooks, children's adventure stories, popular national histories and missionary leaflets became a vehicle for the depiction of the victorious civilizing mission of the white races that were taking modernity and enlightenment to the savage. The commercial cinema expanded with phenomenal speed after 1898, and by 1917 British audiences had reached 20 million a week in some 4000 cinemas.

Historians, it can be noted in conclusion, disagree among themselves as to the period in time when racism first began to manifest itself: some date it back over millennia, as an almost universal feature of human societies; others point to the beginnings of European global expansion and conquest from the fourteenth century and the beginnings of capitalism; while a third and fourth group centre consecutively on the growth of Enlightenment science in the eighteenth century or the rapid growth of industrialization and nationalism in the nineteenth century. Such disagreement is a significant reflection of varying definitions, a lack of clear agreement as to what precisely is under discussion. There cannot be a universal definition of racism that will hold true for all periods of history, and even for all societies at the same moment in time, simply because racist ideologies are plastic in form, continually being reworked and modified and made operative under different historical conditions. However, such a position runs the danger of total relativism, while our argument that it makes sense to talk of racisms rather than a singular racism still raises the problem that differing modalities of race, as subsets of a general category, must still share some common features to make such an identification possible. One answer to this conundrum, and adopted throughout this study, is to accept an ideal typical definition that restricts racism to those belief systems which categorized individuals in a deterministic way, whether expressed through biology or culture, such that they were incapable of moving from one social position to another. A systematization of essential group difference, one that broke away from older concepts of 'race' as lineage, appeared with Enlightenment science. What distinguished the late nineteenth century was not so much the elaboration of a new science of race, in spite of all the talk of a Darwinian Revolution, but rather the sheer speed with which a discourse of radical biological difference was diffused within European society and became an almost universally accepted way of thinking about history, contemporary politics and national identity. The following three chapters (Part 1) explore the way in which this modern form of racism established a solid foundation within Europe between 1870 and the outbreak of the First World War.

PART 1
1870–1914

The age of the 'New Imperialism' was to see the emergence of a modern racism that emphasized the ineradicable biological and cultural difference between Europeans and external colonial 'Others', as well as the simultaneous and deepening divide between Europeans and internal groups that were seen as 'alien', particularly the Jews. The forms of scientific and popular racism that took root during this period established all the essential features of the racism that assumed a wider and more threatening political form during the inter-war period. Part 1 ends on the eve of the First World War since this marked a crucial watershed, the collapse of the German, Russian and Austrian Empires, revolutionary turmoil, and conditions for the growth of fascist and right-wing nationalistic movements. Chapter 2 examines the impact of colonial and anti-black propaganda during the age of high Imperialism, and how this assumed a widespread form within the boundaries of Europe in spite of the small black presence. Chapter 3 looks at the growth of anti-Semitism, which provided beyond any question the dominant form of political racism throughout the period 1870–1945. However, before examining these two predominant forms of racism, Chapter 1 investigates the nature of white 'self-referential' racism which assumed a particularly acute expression between 1870 and 1914 through Social Darwinism, eugenics and ideas of national hygiene and efficiency. White *fin-de-siècle* Europe experienced a profound sense of anxiety about its own racial substance, and a fear of physical degeneration, that it tried to counter through state intervention and bio-power.

1

THE WHITE RACE: DEGENERATION AND EUGENICS

One of the paradoxes of European racism is that its language seems to be centred on, or engrossed with, the negative characteristics of the Other, blacks (libidinous, dirty, lazy . . .) or Jews (grasping, parasitical, cunning . . .), whereas the reverse side of the coin, the construction of European 'whiteness', is strangely absent. The overwhelming concern with the moral and physical features of the Other means that the European is occluded; within most texts white identity and its essential characteristics are implicit, taken for granted, and thus become the unspoken norm, the measuring stick, from which all other racial groups deviate. The invisibility of whiteness, its unstated nature, derives from the fact that in Western culture, through language and representation, whites have an almost universal and central role as the standard of biological and aesthetic excellence. Few Christians take conscious note, let alone realize the significance, of the fact that the predominant Western image of Jesus Christ, a Jewish Palestinian, is of a blue-eyed Aryan, with long, fair tresses. It is only in recent years that scholars have begun to explore more systematically the historical and psychological processes through which 'white' identity has been constructed. This 'self-reflection' by white Europeans is central to an understanding of how racism has historically functioned: as Richard Dyer comments: 'As long as race is something only applied to non-white peoples, as long as white people are not racially seen and named, they/we function as a human norm. Other people are raced, we are just people.'[1]

Racist ideologies are invariably relational and work through binary oppositions between 'Us', the superior group that engages in the process of racialization, and 'Them', the inferior target group. Social psychology suggests that the 'Other' is crucial to the process by which boundaries or frontiers of identity are constructed: 'You know who you are, only by knowing who you are not.'[2] A key feature of racial categorizations of the Other is that they invariably represent a projection and a negative inversion of the central moral, aesthetic and cultural values of the dominant group. As was seen in the Introduction, when Europeans described blacks as inherently lazy, what they meant implicitly was that white Europeans were naturally dynamic, busy and enterprising. And likewise, if blacks were libidinous, dirty, diseased, ugly, thieving, cowardly, stupid and superstitious, then Europeans were sexually restrained and monogamous, clean and healthy, fair and beautiful in form, honest and brave, intelligent and moral. Europeans, through racializing the Other, simultaneously racialized themselves. Such rules of binary opposition are common to many types of group boundary definition, from family, tribe and village, to nationalism and ethnicity. Where modern racism differs from these other forms is that it naturalizes difference in absolute biological or cultural terms so that barriers between collectivities are rendered impermeable. The French racist theoretician Vacher de Lapouge typically formulated this by the claim that it was impossible for immigrants ever to become French: 'The prince can no more make a Frenchman from a Greek or a Moroccan than he can bleach the skin of a Negro, make round the eyes of a Chinaman or change a woman into a man.'[3]

In this chapter we are concerned with self-referential racism, the processes by which Europeans designated themselves as a superior race, as opposed to hetero-referential racism and the negative stereotyping of inferior Others which, although part of the same process, will, for the purposes of analysis, be treated in later chapters. Self-referential racism is of particular interest during the period before the First World War since European society was haunted by the spectre of its own degeneration, while, at the same time, many felt that they had discovered the solution to physical decay in the first scientific methods for the eugenic breeding of a superior racial type. The European racial project had as much to do with technologies for the transformation of its own group biological substance, as it did with the segregation, exclusion or extermination of 'inferior breeds'.

Race and Degeneration

Degeneration was an age-old theme in European thought, but in the past the idea of social decadence had been treated in moral and religious terms: for example, eighteenth-century thinkers portrayed the decline and fall of ancient Rome, as well as the imminent fall of modern European civilization, in terms of luxury, excess, a softening of the will and a physical exhaustion that was a consequence of moral turpitude. In the second half of the nineteenth century the concept of degeneration moved to centre stage, became an all-pervasive concern, and found a new authoritative expression through scientific theories of evolution, morbidity and psycho-physical abnormality.

The language of degeneration was widely deployed in relation to 'inferior' races, and in particular to the idea that interbreeding between races, or 'miscegenation', inevitably led to an irreversible deterioration in the physical and intellectual qualities of hybrid groups. A radical opposition to 'race-mixing' had been a widespread feature of colonial and slave societies from the seventeenth century onwards: the French, for example, legislated against intermarriage in Guadeloupe in 1711 and in Louisiana in 1724, to prevent what one missionary called, 'a criminal coupling of men and women of different species, whence comes a fruit which is one of Nature's monsters'.[4] Colonial racism of this type was eventually integrated into nineteenth-century 'scientific' racist systems, like the highly influential *Essai sur l'inégalité des races humaines* (1853–5) of Count Gobineau. Gobineau, who was to have a major impact on German racism after the turn of the century, elaborated a theory of history in terms of the inexorable decline of civilizations through racial mixing and the degradation and enervation of the Aryan, the most brilliant and superior type. However, within the borders of *fin-de-siècle* Europe, as opposed to colonial society, the central preoccupation was not with the dangers presented by misalliance with inferior races, largely absent from the Continent, so much as with the generalized biological deterioration of the white race itself.

The term 'degeneration' was used to refer to a whole range of social pathologies that threatened the biological substance of the European race(s), from alcoholism, tuberculosis and venereal disease, to lack of physical training, cretinism and sexual perversion. While the late nineteenth century was superficially an age of unprecedented optimism in the power of science and progress, among its writers and artists, from Ibsen and Zola to Gerhart Hauptmann, there were all the signs of a morbid and deepening pessimism, in which the metaphors of disease, madness and decay proliferated. As Max Nordau commented in his book *Degeneration* (1892): 'We stand now in the midst of a severe mental epidemic; of a sort of black death of degeneration and hysteria.'[5] The growing anxiety that Europe was confronted with a profound inner crisis, a process of biological decay, was to receive its most sophisticated analysis and resolution in Social Darwinism and the science of eugenics and 'racial hygiene'. The drive towards the 'rescue' of the European race or of the national stock between *c*.1870 and *c*.1914 needs to be placed within the broader context of the Darwinian Revolution.

Social Darwinism

Darwin's key work, *On the Origin of Species* (1859), had an enormous and rapid impact throughout Europe, from Russia to Portugal: translations appeared in all the major languages, for example, German and Dutch editions appeared in 1860, French (1862), Russian (1864), Italian (1864–5) and Spanish (1877). Darwin's evolutionary theory was by no means the only one that determined social and political thought in the period after 1860. For example, for some decades the impact of Darwinism in France was quite weak since French scientific thought remained largely entrenched within the paradigm of neo-Lamarckian evolution, which maintained that acquired characteristics could be inherited. However, despite the many theoretical and often contradictory strands that went to make up late nineteenth-century evolutionary theory, Darwinism undoubtedly provided the paradigm of the age, the most influential and sophisticated explanation for the mutation of species. In *The Origins* Darwin studiously avoided applying his theory of natural selection to humans since, in an age when Christianity was still extremely influential, he wished to avoid controversy. However, the cat was out of the bag and, well before Darwin came to explore the implications of his theory for human evolution in *The Descent of Man* (1871), numerous scientists had eagerly seized upon his ideas and, in applying them to human societies, began to develop the general body of theory known as Social Darwinism. The basic premise of Social Darwinism was that natural selection had, over geological time, ensured that those organisms which were best adapted to the environment would survive and pass on their inherited advantages, while the weak and maladaptive would die and, in doing so, fail to reproduce. Social Darwinists believed that such processes of selection were at work within contemporary societies: it was in the long-term interests of the human species that competition and war should ensure the reproduction of the strongest and most intelligent individuals and the most biologically superior race-nations. The influential Social Darwinist Karl Pearson, for example, wrote that the scientific definition of a nation, 'is that of an organized whole, kept up to a high pitch of internal efficiency by insuring that its numbers are substantially recruited from the better stocks, and kept up to a high pitch of external efficiency by contest, chiefly by way of war with inferior races, and with equal races by the struggle for trade-routes and for the sources of raw material and of food supply.'[6]

Social Darwinism assumed the form of a 'class-racism', an expression of the mounting fear of the European bourgeoisie faced with the growth of huge and dangerous proletarian slums in the major cities, from London and Paris, to Vienna, Berlin and St Petersburg. The poor, pullulating in urban rookeries, provided a concentrated mass in which epidemics, crime, immorality and Socialism could breed, threatening to burst out and to swamp the civilized order in a wave of primitive barbarism, as it had in the Paris Commune of 1871. As George Sims said of the London poor:

It has now got into a condition in which it cannot be left. This mighty mob of famished, diseased and filthy helots is getting dangerous, physically, morally, politically dangerous. The barriers which have kept it back are rotten and giving way, and it may do the state a mischief if it be not looked to in time. Its fevers and its filth may spread to the homes of the wealthy; its lawless armies may sally forth and give us the taste of the lesson the mob has tried to teach now and again in Paris.[7]

The deep anxiety of the educated élites faced with the 'rise of the masses' and access to the vote, the spread of revolutionary political movements and trade unions, found expression in a racialization of the working class. Louis Chevalier has shown how the Parisian bourgeoisie increasingly deployed a language that described the *classes dangereuses* in racial terms, as primitive and instinctual beings who carried all the inherited stigmata of the savage – sexual potency, low intelligence, moral corruption, violence and raw animality.[8] The French historian Taine, who studied medicine and psychiatry, deployed an evolutionary and medical language to plot the course of French history: with the Revolution of 1789, he wrote: 'we see all of a sudden spring forth the barbarian, and still worse the primitive animal, the grinning, sanguinary baboon, who chuckles while he slays.'[9] The Italian criminal anthropologist Lombroso, in line with an older tradition of phrenology, developed after 1870 a photographic system to record the primitive features of the criminal type who, like some evolutionary throwback, showed all the hereditary features of the savage. The criminal, he claimed, was:

> an atavistic being who reproduces in his person the ferocious instincts of primitive humanity and the inferior animals. Thus were explained anatomically the enormous jaws, high cheek bones, prominent super-cilliary arches, solitary lines in the palms, extreme size of the orbits, handle-shaped ears found in the criminals, savages and apes, insensibility to pain, extremely acute sight, tattooing, excessive idleness, love of orgies, and the irresponsible craving of evil for its own sake, the desire not only to extinguish life in the victim, but to mutilate the corpse, tear its flesh and drink its blood.[10]

The idea that modern man might contain, buried within himself, dark instinctive forces that threatened to overwhelm the thin veneer of civilized behaviour also found expression in the psychoanalytic theory of Sigmund Freud, as well as in literature, from Stephenson's *Jekyll and Hyde* to the unspeakable horror faced by the adventurer Kurtz in Conrad's *Heart of Darkness*.

Although space does not enable the full treatment which it deserves, it can be noted that the language of race was invariably also a language of gender, and of a science that presented women as biologically and morally inferior. As Nancy Stepan has shown, women, like primitives, were thought to be of a lower order, less evolved and similar to children in their intellectual and emotional development.[11] Women were also prone to regression, particularly when in a crowd, to descend into atavistic forms of savagery, blood-lust and even cannibalism. As with class, the naturalization of difference between male and female was used as an ideological barrier to the rise of feminism. If women constituted a separate 'race', and were locked into the inferior and hereditary characteristics of their group, there was no way that educational reform, or any other measures, could enable them to undertake the functions of the superior male. So entrenched and universal were sexist differentiations in European society and culture that the perceived absolute separation of male and female could also work in the opposite direction, to feminize inferior male races.

Returning to Social Darwinism and eugenics, a central idea of these movements was that the further modern societies developed, the more they created welfare systems that interfered with the laws of natural selection. For tens of thousands of years prehistoric man, and even more recent pre-industrial man, had progressed as a racial type in intelligence and physique through the harsh but necessary impact of disease, famine and tribal warfare that remorselessly weeded out sickly individuals or entire non-adaptive groups. As Ribot commented in his *Heredity* (1875), medical science and improved resources 'makes more and more certain the future of children, by saving the lives of countless weak, deformed, or otherwise ill-constituted creatures that would surely have died in a savage race, or in our own country a century ago'.[12] Across Europe, Social Darwinists pointed to the same, underlying problem of the modern age: the immense growth of cities created the social problems associated with overcrowding in filthy, airless slums, a brutalized 'residuum' that sought to escape its miserable existence through alcoholism and sexual licence, and which sank ever deeper into physical and moral degeneration. However, this pale and wretched 'race', instead of dying out, was able to survive through the growing intervention of charitable organizations, and local and central government welfare. During the second half of the nineteenth century all European states engaged in welfare programmes that attempted to alleviate the conditions of the urban poor, from slum housing regulation, health inspection and sewerage disposal, to medical dispensaries, public hospitals and soup kitchens. The concern of the Social Darwinists was that society was artificially keeping alive those sickly individuals who would, according to the 'laws of natural selection', have died out. The economist Alfred Marshall commented in 1885: 'Charity and sanitary regulations are keeping alive, in our large towns, thousands of such [feeble] persons, who would have died even fifty years ago. . . . Public or private charity may palliate their misery, but the only remedy is to prevent such people from coming into existence.'[13]

What was particularly disturbing to the Social Darwinists was the growing demographic imbalance of society, for while the improvident poor continued to breed without restraint, producing large numbers of enfeebled children, the educated élites were beginning to have smaller and smaller numbers of offspring, owing to late marriage, the use of birth control, egotism and a lack of patriotic duty. The Social Darwinists translated the bourgeois fear of being outnumbered by the 'masses' into racial terms. An underlying assumption in the work of many thinkers was that the élites constituted a kind of hereditary 'gene-pool', in which the highest racial qualities of intelligence, moral strength and physical beauty were preserved. The degeneration of the racial stock of the nation as a whole carried major implications for the modern state. Social Darwinists were less concerned with the consequences of evolutionary theory for the individual, than with the survival of the fittest as a contest between entire racial groups or race-nations. The language of Darwinism became an expression of growing militaristic aggression and economic tension between states, a contest for power and domination both within the European continent as well as overseas in Africa and elsewhere. Those states that were the 'fittest', that were able to preserve or regenerate the racial substance of the nation, would inevitably be victorious in the competition with others, and in so doing would fulfil the destiny of the human race as a whole by ensuring that the most superior peoples would survive to reproduce the future species on a higher level.

The Social Darwinism of Ernst Haeckel

Probably the most influential Social Darwinist in Europe was Ernst Haeckel (1843–1919), Professor of Anatomy at Jena, and his ideas, translated into numerous languages, may be taken as typical of those which were sweeping the Continent before the First World War. Haeckel, unlike the cautious Darwin, was a keen propagandist who saw it as his prophetic mission to broadcast the lessons of evolutionary theory, the scientific key to universal understanding. Haeckel's most famous work, *The Riddle of the Universe* (1899) had gone through ten German editions by 1919 and was translated into 25 languages, while in 1906 he founded the Monist League to ensure that evolutionary science would become the basis of individual and state actions. Haeckel had a huge impact: not only was he a gifted populist, but his promise to unlock the secrets of the material universe, the laws of evolution and biology that controlled human destiny, was attractive to the general public, while his prestige as an outstanding scientist added legitimacy to his Social Darwinism.

As a young man he had held to a progressive, liberal politics, but during the 1860s he moved to the right, becoming an ardent supporter of Bismarck and German unification and nationalism. As a nationalist he was haunted by a deep dread of the biological deterioration of the German people. Like most of his contemporaries, he held that non-European races were radically inferior: for example, he held that Negroes were 'incapable of a true inner culture and of a higher mental development'.[14] However, in keeping with a major shift in post-1870 racism, he was more preoccupied with the elaboration of theories that centred on the internal subdivision of European peoples into distinct races: a concern that linked in directly to the deepening competition between European states. Thus he regarded the German Aryans as the highest form of human evolution, the group that had been able to 'outstrip all other branches in the career of civilisation'.[15] Haeckel was quite typical of the European-wide movement towards a racialized concept of the nation: he rejected a liberal view of the nation-state as an expression of democratic will, a constitutional and voluntaristic binding together of individuals, regulated by contract and law, for a conservative organic theory of community based on race, language and history. This *volkish* concept of the nation, rooted in the German Romantic and anti-Enlightenment tradition and the idea of an organic community, lent itself ideally to elaboration in the new language of evolutionary biology.

In Haeckel's Monist philosophy it was the duty of the most advanced race-nation to ensure not only its own survival, but to maximize its power, the species domination of territory, since this was in the long-term interest of all future human kind. This could only be achieved if the individual, instead of trying to maximize his own happiness, heroically sacrificed himself to the higher good of the organic community. Such a theory could lend itself to an extremely authoritarian form of politics. In the struggle for the survival of the fittest race, a contest in which millions were pitted against each other in a fight to the death, the survival of the individual was of little significance. The life of each person was of relative value, depending on the contribution which he or she could make to the continuity of the group as a whole. Haeckel's Social Darwinism opened the door to a disquieting vision of individual human life as expendable according to racial criteria of 'species worth'. Since Negroes were closer to apes and dogs than to Europeans, he wrote: 'we must, therefore, assign a totally different value to their lives.'[16] This view, which was held widely by those commenting on colonial expansion, led to the acceptance of the necessary extermination of lower types, like the Tasmans or the Hottentot. Applied to the eugenic purification and strengthening of the national race it opened the door to the elimination of the biologically weak. Haeckel's anti-humanist philosophy, in line with the ideas of Nietzsche (1844–1900) and some other contemporaries, attacked Christianity for its promulgation of a moral code which was fundamentally 'dysgenic' since it valued the life of the weak and feeble, and preached peace, submission and reconciliation rather than determined struggle. Since the Christian West, over two millennia, had laid an emphasis on the over-valuation of individual life, this had only served to distort natural selection and led to the evolution of a sickly humanity. In taking such a position Haeckel claimed not to be operating from any system of moral values; rather the iron laws of nature determined every-thing, no matter how harsh its dictates may have seemed.

Warfare and Colonial Conquest

The logic of an *internal* racism, centred on the biological fitness of the nation, can be seen in its connection to militarism and the degree of pre-paredness of the racial community to engage in a struggle for survival with other global competitors. The racialization of European nationalism can be illustrated by the tension between France and Germany after the Franco-Prussian War and the annexation of Alsace. The leading French anthropologist De Quatrefages claimed in 1872 that the invasion of France and the barbaric bombardment of Paris was the work of a 'Prus-sian race' that was corrupted by mixing with dark Mongoloid Finnish and Slavonic elements: in contrast, the French and Southern Germans were of a more advanced Aryan type. This triggered a major controversy with the progressive German anthropologist Virchow, who believed that the differences between peoples were more cultural than physical. Throughout Europe the growing concern over racial degeneration found expression in the statistical analysis of the physique of military recruits: in 1866–7 the French press had reported widely on the increas-ing number of stunted individuals who were unsuitable for the army. In Britain the high level of illness and deformity found among those recruited during the Boer War led to the establishment of a Parliamentary Inquiry in 1902. Among the public, this linked into a deepening gloom and anxiety that was rooted in a dim awareness that Britain, challenged by Germany, France and the USA, was in decline as a world power.

Such anxiety was a key element in the growth of the eugenics movement after 1900. In 1900 the leading Social Darwinist Karl Pearson lectured with enthusiasm on the positive and progressive functions of war: the struggle for existence meant 'suffering, intense suffering', but a redeeming feature of sacrifice was that the fitter race would survive 'the fiery crucible out of which comes the finer metal'.[17] Pearson, like so many of his con-temporaries, assumed without question that he was himself a member of the master group, of that 'organized whole' that was 'kept up to a high pitch of internal efficiency by insuring that its members are substantially recruited from the better stocks, and kept up to a high pitch of external efficiency by contest'.[18] However, some eugenics experts were concerned that warfare, by leading to higher mortality among the cream of the nation's stock, the young, courageous, fit and intelligent officer class, would damage the racial stock. The German biologist Ploetz even advocated that the physically unfit should be sent to the battlefield, while the superior type was reserved for racial reproduction. As we shall see below, during the First World War Britain and France deployed huge numbers of 'inferior' black colonial troops in the most deadly front-line assaults, thus conserving the 'national race'.

The Social Darwinist drive towards the eugenic creation of a powerful, militarized community that could triumph in any conflict with other European states also linked up to colonial expansion and Social Imperialism. During the age of 'New Imperialism' and the partition of Africa (1875–1912) European powers were concerned to procure a strong growth rate in the metropolitan white population, of a hardy and intelligent 'breed', in order to settle and govern the new colonies and to defend them against the challenge offered by other European nations, as well as against indigenous 'lower races'. Galton, the founding father of eugenics, who had travelled widely in Africa, looked to a future in which the Anglo-Saxon race would achieve demographic world domination. In no nation was a 'high breed more necessary . . . for we plant our stock over the world and lay the foundations of the dispositions and capacities of future millions of the human race'.[19] For Haeckel, who worked for imperialism through both the Monist League and the Pan-Germanic League, the establishment of new colonies, particularly a *Mittelafrika* in the Congo, would ensure the 'creation of a healthy and biologically fit German community in all parts of the world'.[20] The geographer Friedrich Ratzel coined the term *Lebensraum* to express the concept of an expansionist organic national community that would be built upon *Lebensreform*, a programme that would regenerate racial vigour through a holistic sense of nature. Each major European colonial power had ambitions to be not only the empire, but also the white race, on which the sun never set.

Race and the Eugenic Movement

Eugenic ideas were widely debated in Europe from 1860 onwards, although the term, which means 'good in birth' or 'noble in heredity', was not invented by Francis Galton until 1883. The movement has been frequently analysed in relation to *negative* eugenics, which emphasized the most controversial forms of suppression of the racially feeble, and *positive* eugenics, which promoted steps to encourage or enhance the birth rate of the biologically superior individuals or groups. Negative eugenics has received more attention from historians since its methods appear to have laid the basis for the worst excesses of National Socialism. There is undoubtedly a risk of falsifying history by reading back into European history, from the stance of the post-Holocaust age, signs of the road to Auschwitz, of a coherent exterminationist logic, where none existed. Our understanding of pre-1914 history can be distorted through the selection of evidence pointing towards a genocidal logic and the failure to recognize countervailing information. However, that having been said, the prevalence of ideas about population 'culling' in European society, and across the political spectrum, does point to the spread of authoritarian forms of thought and a disturbing trend towards the dehumanization of both the working-class 'residuum' and of minorities (the Jews, the disabled, immigrants).

Negative eugenics proposed the drastic termination of the 'breeding' capacity of individuals or groups that were perceived to carry hereditary traits that would damage the future biological fitness of the race-nation. Most of the adherents of negative policies shared the 'germ-plasm' theory of Weismann (or similar ideas) according to which the genetic characteristics of parents which were transmitted to offspring could not, in any way, be transformed by environment. This led to the logic, often pushed to the extreme, that programmes of social reform, health care, education and general welfare were radically dysgenic since not only could they not improve the genetic quality of the sick and degenerate, but they also ensured their 'unnatural' survival. The main solution to this was sought through the enforced sterilization or castration of criminals, the physically handicapped, the mentally ill and the diseased, whose condition was regarded (in a secular version of Original Sin) as the outcome of impurity, nature's 'punishment' of racial degenerates for their alcoholism, uncontrolled sexuality and atavistic savagery. An alternative strategy was to enforce the isolation of the degenerate in 'total institutions', prisons, hospitals, asylums and work camps, so that they were prevented from reproducing. Haeckel, for example, proposed that criminals should be executed since their criminality was an inherited characteristic that could not be reformed, while the insane and incurably feeble could be referred to a commission which could adjudicate on euthanasia 'by a dose of some painless and rapid poison'. Haeckel also admired the Spartans, as did Hitler, for their careful selection of new-born children and the killing of those who were 'weak, sickly, or affected with any bodily infirmity'.[21] Some German and British doctors so lost touch with their professional ethics as to tolerate venereal disease, tuber-culosis and other deadly microbes as 'the friends of the race' through elimination of the unfit.[22] As we shall see, however, such radical ideas were the exception and, before 1914, made little political impact and rarely translated into legislation.

Positive eugenics was concerned with supportive natalist programmes to ensure that the maximum number of sound babies would be born, an issue of demographic 'quantity' or, more frequently, of 'quality', meas-ures to encourage and foster the birth of children to couples selected from the superior physical and racial stock. Eugenic thinkers in Britain, France and Germany were interested in finding the means to encourage marriage only between ideal partners, or at least couples who were free from negative genetic qualities that might be inherited by their offspring. Galton and the psychologist Havelock Ellis both supported the idea of encouraging ideal partnerships by ensuring that those intending to marry were able to offer the guarantee of eugenic 'certificates'. One writer stated in 1904:

When a young man and a young woman, offering themselves for marriage, can produce certified records of their ancestry back for three or four generations, showing that their progenitors have been entirely, or largely, free from nervous prostration, sick headaches, neurasthenia, hysteria, melancholia, St Vitus' dance, epilepsy, syph-ilis, alcoholism, pauperism, criminality, prostitution and insanity... then it may truly be said that such a union may be correctly styled a EUGENIC MARRIAGE.[23]

In France there was a long eugenic campaign to introduce a premarital examination law that would screen for tuberculosis, venereal disease, alcoholism and the 'abnormal'. In Germany during the 1880s a group of young biologists, centred on Alfred Ploetz, made plans for utopian colonies that would screen the health and biological suitability of incoming members to guarantee racial purity. Ploetz himself went through an agonizing search for a wife who would be of the correct German stock. Similar 'sanitory utopias' promoted in England by Galton, Richardson and Bellamy included 'faddish' proposals for clean air, temperance, cycling, sunshine and land-work, alongside measures for racial health and selection.

One controversial aspect of the proposals for breeding colonies was differences of opinion over the criteria to be used for selecting those who constituted the ideal racial stock. As we have seen, the deep anxiety of broad sectors of the European bourgeoisie, confronted with the growth of an impoverished and potentially revolutionary working class, frequently translated into a racialization of class conflict. The lower orders were seen, quite literally, as a different and savage race. However the lower orders tended to have large families, while the bourgeoisie were already restricting their family size with success: the nightmare scenario of the educated middle classes was that they would be outnumbered and swamped by the primitive lower orders, just like the small numbers of European masters in the colonies who could be overrun at any moment by native hordes. Within European society, if the genetically unfit 'race' was the degenerate working class, then the superior breeding group came from the middle-class professionals and intelligentsia to which the eugenicists themselves belonged. The eugenicists, recruited from a bourgeois meritocracy, on the whole opposed the concept of aristocracy, since the rules of primogeniture did not guarantee status and power on the basis of biological fitness and intelligence, but from laws of inheritance that could promote the most physically and mentally feeble individuals. In general, eugenic projects to guarantee the greater breeding capacity of the superior racial stock can be interpreted as one facet of bourgeois crisis and insecurity at the turn of the century, a project to increase the demographic weight of the élites within the 'age of the masses'.

Eugenicists, however, did not project a utopian society in which only the super-élite survived, since this carried the worrying prospect of a social order devoid of workers and servants. Vacher de Lapouge held that Europe was inhabited by two key racial groups, the blond, Aryan and long-skulled *Homo Europaeus*, robust, energetic, of high intelligence and a natural conqueror, and the *Homo Alpinus*, a smaller, darker, short-skulled and more primitive type, who served as slaves to the former. The goal of eugenics was to prevent the latter outbreeding the former and becoming dominant, but, at the same time, the strong though inferior Alpine race needed to be retained as a work-force. Once again it can be seen that an anthropological science that analysed class in terms of race served as a thin disguise for the *status quo* and a legitimation of existing class relations. There was a close linkage here to the rationale of colonialism: the racism that described black slaves as of low intelligence, but physically strong and ideally suited to the work of the plantation economy, was similar in structure to the racism that denoted the working class as a biological group that was naturally suited to industrial labour. The broader ideas of Social Imperialism and national efficiency were closely tied in to the needs of industrial capitalism. State welfare and eugenic programmes were directed towards the breeding of a strong, energetic and dedicated work-force. The economic and productivist functionality of eugenics was also shown by the detailed calculations that were made as to the enormous social costs presented by the care and institutionalization of criminals, the feeble-minded and the sickly, dysfunctional beings who would be better eliminated. American studies of the delinquent and feeble-minded descendants of a notorious New York family, the Jukes, estimated that they had cost the state government two million dollars by 1916, while the cost of sterilizing the original Jukes pair would have been 150 dollars. During the inter-war period Sicard de Plauzole, in his *Principes d'Hygiène* (1927), developed a Taylorist eugenics that would procure the best 'human capital' at lowest cost: 'the art of procreating, perfecting and utilizing man as a work-producing machine'.[24]

Thus the eugenics movement in Europe can be located within a much broader development of social imperialism and of state welfare programmes to improve national 'efficiency', or as Michel Foucault has termed it, strategies of 'bio-power'. As military and economic tensions increased between European powers, so governments began to realize that it was in the national interest to promote the overall physical health and well-being of the working class. Marxists had traditionally interpreted the capitalist system as one that would inflict deepening levels of exploitation and misery upon the working class. However, conservative leaders, from Bismarck to Joseph Chamberlain, came to see that social welfare programmes (medical and unemployment insurance, pensions, health care) could serve to undermine the position of the revolutionary left, reduce class conflict, and generate a sense of corporate and national solidarity. The total energy of the race-nation would be gathered together and focused in the most powerful way on the struggle with other nations. Such diffuse forms of 'national socialism', which were influential across the political spectrum, were linked to further aspects of self-referential racism, of which two are considered here: firstly, the role of motherhood; and secondly, sporting techniques for the production of ideal white bodies.

Eugenics, Race and Motherhood

By the 1880s there was growing concern that a decline in birth rates and high infant mortality was undermining the demographic potential of the nation: more babies were required to provide future workers, soldiers and an 'imperial race' to fill the empty spaces of existing or future colonies. White populations were required not only to man the empire and control the 'natives', but also to prevent rival master races from investing and annexing colonial territories. Increasing attention was turned towards motherhood, and propaganda and educational campaigns targeted women as those with the prime responsibility for the rearing of the Imperial race. Since the birth and rearing of healthy children was a matter of major concern to the state, the responsibility for child-rearing was no longer an individual or private affair but a matter of national duty. The state assumed ever-increasing powers to intervene within the private sphere of the family and to maximize reproductive powers through a range of interventions, from compulsory schooling, provision of school meals and milk, family allowances and maternity leave, to restrictions on female and child labour, training of midwives and food hygiene legislation. This was all tied into a powerful ideology of motherhood that continuously emphasized women's sacred maternal duty and the need to avoid birth-control and 'race-suicide'. Young women needed to be taught how to choose a suitable future father and trained in the skills required to raise the eugenically conceived child; the correct forms of baby nutrition, of cleanliness and sanitation. Through such instruction, it was noted in 1903, women would be preserved for 'their supreme function, the procreation and preservation of the race'.[25]

The eugenic emphasis on the duties of the mother was frequently linked to a conservative attack on the 'new woman', who was pushing for greater rights, the franchise, and was 'deserting' her natural maternal function for educational advancement and professional training. Typically, the books and manuals on mothercraft and childcare assumed that all babies were male, and preferably 'virile'; the future soldiers and colonizers of the imperium. As the eugenic doctor and expert on childcare, Caleb Saleeby, wrote in his *Parenthood and Race Culture* (1909): 'The history of nations is determined not on the battlefield but in the nursery, and the battalions which give lasting victory are the battalions of babies. The politics of the future will be domestics.' For Elizabeth Sloan-Chesser, author of *Perfect Health for Women and Children* (1912), home was 'the cradle of the race ... Empire's first line of defence'.[26] In France millions of pro-natalist postcards were printed showing babies sitting on the barrels of fieldguns; these were described as the 'seeds' of future *poilus* or 'tommies'.

Race, Sport and National Fitness

The final aspect of white self-referential racism we shall consider, the techniques through which Europeans worked upon their own racial substance, concerns the spread of movements for the perfection of national physique through athletics, gymnastics and drill. From 1880 onwards the concern over racial degeneration, national efficiency, and military and imperial weakness began to find a solution in physical training and mass sports. England provides the best-known example of the trend, through the ethos of 'muscular' Christianity and the development of new team sports, particularly football, rugby and rowing, among the élite youth in the public schools and at Oxbridge. However, although each nation tended to have its own specific sporting culture, as with, for example, the nationalistic functions of skiing in Sweden or French cycling in the *Tour de France*, the underlying links between physical fitness, competitiveness and national efficiency were quite universal. Through team sport, youth learned the arts of obedience and command, withstood pain with stoicism, trained the will and, most crucially, developed an *esprit de corps* and heroic sacrifice on behalf of the school or nation. The heroic language of war, as well as of imperial conquest, was that of the playing field. Doctors played a key role in the national and international associations for football, swimming, cycling, rowing, athletics, gymnastics and skiing that proliferated across Europe, while the theory and language of physical training was elaborated as a eugenic and Social Darwinist discourse. The links between physical fitness and militarism were most explicit in the gymnastic and rifle clubs of France, Belgium, Germany (the *Turnen*), Bohemia (the *Sokol*), Denmark and Russia. Physical training and drill became a compulsory element in state schools, while youth movements, from the Boy Scouts to the *Wandervogel*, placed an emphasis on fitness, parading and nationalism.

The enormous expansion in international, mass spectator sports, exemplified by the revived Olympic movement, was accompanied by a growing feeling that success or failure in competition was a mark of the biological fitness of the race-nation. Major sporting events, like the international gymnastic competitions, provided arenas for the parading of national symbols (flags, uniforms, patriotic songs), synchronized and military-style movements, and splendid muscled bodies. The growing cult of the body, and in particular that of the super-male, diffused through newspaper photographs and film of famous athletes, established idealized aesthetic criteria for the perfect racial type. In contrast to the degenerate or neurasthenic type, debilitated and pathologically weakened by urban life, the sportsman's muscular physique exemplified not only physical fitness, but inner moral race characteristics, energy, will, stamina and purity. In Sweden, for example, skiing as the national sport carried deep cultural and symbolic meanings of manliness (connected to hunting and war), of heroism (linked to great polar expeditions) and of virtue (the image of snow, purity and the wilderness). Such connection between ideal white bodies and sport was later to receive its most famous representation in Leni Riefenstahl's film of the 1936 Berlin Olympics, in which the Greek aesthetic, the perfect body-type, was merged with that of the German Aryan.

The Influence of Social Darwinism and Eugenics

The remaining part of this chapter examines the extent to which Social Darwinism and eugenics spread geographically across Europe between 1870 and 1914, and how far they influenced a wider public and made an impact on political parties, government policy and legislation. This provides a useful case-study of the way in which scientific ideas percolated down into the wider society.

In recent years historians have undertaken a comparative study of Social Darwinism to show how the application of evolutionary theory to an understanding of society varied considerably from one nation-state to another, according to differing pre-Darwinian traditions in biological science and the social and political context prevailing in each country. To date we know most about Britain, France and Germany, the three nations in which Social Darwinism made the greatest impact before the First World War. But gradually, historians are extending their investigation to previously neglected states like Spain, Italy, Russia and Sweden. It appears that Social Darwinism, the general idea that contemporary society could be analysed as a process of struggle for survival between competing groups or individuals, was omnipresent throughout European higher culture in the later nineteenth century. To take just one example, Thomas Glick has shown that by the 1870s, battles over Darwinism were raging even in the backwaters of that most provincial of nations, Spain. Even in the distant Canary Islands controversy had filtered down to parish level, while a Valladolid secondary school teacher, Luis Perez Minguez, in an 1880 critique of *On the Origin of Species*, remarked that there was throughout Europe 'so dense an atmosphere of Darwinism that one can scarcely inhale anything else'.[27]

In the period from *c.*1900 onwards, a dense network of eugenic scholarship spread across Europe. Highly influential teams of scientists, working on the statistics of heredity and 'biometrics', Mendelian genetics, physical anthropology, psychiatry, public health, epidemiology, artificial insemination and serology were in constant communication through a network of correspondence, the exchange of learned papers, and colloquia. The First International Eugenics Congress in London (1912) was attended by delegates from Britain, France, Switzerland, Germany, Italy, Belgium, Spain, Greece and Denmark. Eugenic studies were also well advanced in Austria, Sweden, Norway, Romania, Serbia, Russia, Poland, Hungary, Holland, Portugal and Czechoslovakia. In many of these states scientists were establishing eugenic laboratories of criminal anthropology (Italy, Bavaria, Portugal, Poland) and eugenics entered the university curriculum.

Historians, among them Paul Weindling, have argued that the growth in late nineteenth-century society of a pervasive biological discourse or scientific language of race can be linked to the tremendous growth and influence of medical science. Right across Europe, there was a rapid expansion in the number of trained doctors of medicine and biologists, who became increasingly influential through their involvement in major areas of public policy and decision making, from sanitation, public health, crime and disease control, to the improvement of midwifery, childcare and diet. Michel Foucault, in an influential thesis, argued that modern states, from the eighteenth century onwards, began to develop *bio-power*, political technologies for the regulation of the life processes of entire human populations. The administration of life assumed two basic forms: firstly, the disciplining and optimization of the capabilities of the individual body, especially through the control of sexuality; and secondly, the regulation of the species body, of biological processes, propagation, birth, level of health, life expectancy and welfare.[28] Bio-power was indispensable to the development of capitalism and the modern state, the optimization of disciplined bodies and of healthy populations for the functioning of the economy, armies, police forces and colonial settlement. Strategies for the maximization of species power was an inherently racial project which was addressed, 'to the body, to life, to what causes it to proliferate, to what reinforces the species, its stamina, its ability to dominate, or its capacity for being used'.[29] Foucault's analysis would suggest that racism was an integral component of modernity, of capitalism and state power, and, as such, it might be predicted that racism would develop across Europe hand in hand with industrialization, urbanization and economic modernization.

But this is interpretation at a very generalized level. What were the political and legislative impacts of eugenics at the level of the nation-state? In order to answer this question it is helpful to distinguish between two main currents within the eugenics movement, on the one hand a highly conservative and implicitly racist type that emphasised negative eugenics, and, on the other, a more progressive form that was supported by liberal humanists, socialists and various brands of radicalism. Looking first at negative genetics, which lent itself to authoritarianism, this found its main ideological formulation through the germ-plasm theory of August Weismann (1834–1914) that was influential from the 1890s, and which was then reinforced by the rediscovery from 1900 of Mendel's theory. In general, both theories maintained that the hereditary component or germ (today we might say the genetic coding) could not be altered in any way by the environment. In the hands of eugenicists, who greatly exaggerated nature over nurture, this meant that inferior or degenerate types could not be improved or altered in any way by programmes of reform, education, rehabilitation or improved environment (housing, health, diet). Even if there were minor improvements these could not be genetically transmitted onwards to any offspring. Such a theory was highly conservative; it argued that reform programmes were a waste of time and money, since no amount of education or welfare could change the immutable hereditary material that determined behaviour. The germ-plasm theory tended to be adopted by those professional élites, particularly in Britain and Germany, who hoped to legitimate the *status quo*, the fixity of class, race and gender identities and inequalities, at a time of unusually rapid social, political and economic change. Such eugenicists shared a paranoid fear of decline and regression, rather than an optimistic vision of a future utopia. Eugenic discourse was peppered with terms of moral condemnation towards the 'degenerate' lower orders, terms that indicated the way in which the science of heredity was largely a translation into scientific language of traditional conservative, religious and class attitudes towards the 'undeserving', corrupt and immoral poor. The eugenicists' preoccupation with the sexual lives of the working class, their wish to eliminate 'hereditary' prostitution, primitive and uncontrolled libidinal drives and uncontrolled reproduction, was closely related to bourgeois respectability, sexual repression and the wider concern to moralize the poor.

Negative eugenics spread rapidly among large sectors of the European educated élites who, during the period 1870 to 1914, began to desert liberalism for a conservative or modernizing authoritarianism. This can be seen, for example, in the growing support for Bismarckian state socialism among leading eugenicists like Ernst Haeckel. This anti-liberal trend was partly rooted in a disillusionment with an earlier phase of social reform that, it was thought, had failed to make any impact on criminality and other forms of 'degeneration'. However, before the First World War, negative eugenics had a limited impact on the legislation of European states. Firstly, it can be noted that it took many decades for the eugenic movement to find an institutional base from which it could make an impact on national policies: eugenic associations were only established in Germany in 1905, Britain in 1907–8 and France in 1912. This delay is itself indicative of differences that divided and weakened the movement internally, and of the problems that eugenics faced in gaining wider public support. Before 1914 ideas or legislative proposals for premarital medical inspections, castration or sterilization of criminals or the 'feeble-minded', institutional segregation of 'degenerates', the enhancement of élite reproduction, and similar measures, were generally met with opposition on the grounds that they represented a dangerous threat to civil liberties. A widespread criticism of such eugenics was that it was dehumanizing and reduced people to the level of animal breeding stock.

The political constraints that prevented the implementation of eugenic programmes can be illustrated through the example of Winston Churchill, a keen advocate of the improved breeding of the British 'race'. During his term as Home Secretary (1910–11) Churchill circulated eugenic reports to the Cabinet, including a study by Dr Tredgold, *The Feeble-Minded: A Social Danger*, which in apocalyptic language attributed national decline to the 100 000 'criminals, paupers and unemployables, prostitutes and ne'er do wells', who were breeding at twice the national average. Churchill, who was influenced by the introduction of forcible sterilization of 'degenerates' in the State of Indiana, drew up similar proposals in a paper intended for Cabinet. He also advocated procedures that would have given the Home Office extraordinary powers to send 'mental defectives' to forced labour camps, 'segregated under proper conditions so that their curse died with them'. However, Churchill's views were extreme, even by the standards of the age, and his proposals met with strong opposition from Home Office officials, including one expert, Dr Donkin, who argued for a more 'humane' policy. Charles Masterman, a junior minister at the Home Office, told Churchill that such proposals were not politically acceptable given the climate of public opinion, while the Prime Minister Asquith refused to defend such ideas in public.[30] However, Churchill – who was one of the Vice-Presidents of the First International Eugenics Congress in 1912 – did contribute to the campaign that culminated in the only piece of eugenics legislation to be passed into law in Britain, the Mental Deficiency Act of 1913 . But, noted one commentator in 1914, compulsory sterilization of the kind that existed in the Unites States was politically impossible since 'public opinion in this country is not ripe for such drastic a proceeding'.[31]

In other European states the situation was similar. In France the campaign for a premarital examination law, which was attacked as a measure that would endow doctors with unwarranted powers, went on for many decades, only to pass finally into law in 1942 under the Vichy regime. It is significant that the leading German eugenicist, Ploetz, showed anti-Semitic, Pan-German sentiments in his diaries and private correspondence, and was sympathetic to Hentschel's published plan of 1904 for an Aryan racial utopia *Mittgart*, a breeding colony with ten women for every eugenically selected male. Yet, in public, Ploetz suppressed his racist views, recognizing that they would not be acceptable to opinion, and even attacked Hentschel for applying the practice of cattle breeding to humans. There was no eugenic legislation in Germany before 1914 and it was only after 1918 that a political climate arose that would enable sterilization and premarital examination laws to be passed in Denmark (1919), Norway (1919), Germany (1933), Sweden (1935) and Switzerland.

The second, more progressive current in European eugenics can be generally described as neo-Larmarckian. Larmarck's theory, in so far as it maintained that acquired characteristics could be inherited, lent itself readily to a more progressive environmentalism: social reform could have an impact on both the living as well as on their future descent. Many eugenicists regarded themselves as on the political left, and saw amelioration of the social and welfare conditions of the working class as a way of creating a future population which would grow increasingly perfect in physique and intelligence. Theories of Social Darwinism and a more negative eugenics made little impact in France before the 1920s and this has been ascribed to the entrenched position of Lamarckian theory. In no European state was there a deeper level of anxiety about degeneration and demographic decline than in France, a pessimism that arose from a birth rate which was much lower than that of its competitors, especially Germany. Perhaps in no society were feelings of national degeneration as entrenched as in France, yet, in a contradictory way, this did not lead to a powerful current of negative eugenics. The reason was simple enough; it was politically untenable to promote an élitist vision of selection, the elimination of the 'unfit', when France desperately needed to foster and protect its total population. This created a climate in which radical eugenicist and racist ideologues like Georges Vacher de Lapouge and Charles Richet remained marginal figures. The enormous loss of French life in the First World War further reinforced the emphasis on 'quantity over quality'.

Russian eugenics followed a rather similar development to that of France. During the pre-Revolutionary era Social Darwinism had made a big impact in Russia: in 1866 V. M. Florinsky published *The Improvement and Degeneration of the Human Race* and Galton's *Hereditary Genius* was translated into Russian in 1875. During the period 1900–14 numerous works appeared on evolution, and the hereditary aspects of alcoholism, crime and psychopathology, while I. A. Filipchenko taught the first genetics course at St Petersburg University from 1913 onwards. However, the full implications of a socialist eugenics was only to develop after the Russian Revolution. A specifically Soviet or 'Bolshevik' eugenics developed from 1920 which attacked negative eugenics, particularly American sterilization programmes, as bourgeois forms of dehumanization. For Marxist biologists, the concept of an immutable germ-plasm was unacceptable since it was difficult to reconcile with revolutionary and visionary principles of progress through scientific control of the environment. Soviet science thus tended towards various forms of positive eugenics which would improve the quality of the entire population. The rejection of negative and selective eugenics was, as in the case of France, linked to the demographic crisis that marked the First World War and its aftermath. War and famine led to a truly catastrophic collapse in population and in St Petersburg, for example, births exceeded deaths by 37 per 10 000 in 1910, while in 1920 deaths exceeded births by 484 per 10 000.

Finally, there remains the question of how far Social Darwinism and eugenics filtered down to affect popular attitudes and culture. The

evidence here is patchy and difficult to interpret. Many leading eugenicists were avid publicists: for example, the racial anthropologist Otto
Ammon went on extensive speaking tours, as did Ernst Haeckel and
Karl Pearson. Propagandists lectured to ethical, debating and philo-
sophical societies, to working men's associations, school and university
students, women's clubs, and medical and nursing associations. Leading
exponents, fired with an almost religious sense of the scientist's vocation,
were also keen to publish their ideas in a non-technical language and in
a cheap popular format. The French eugenicist Edouard Toulouse, for
example, reached a broader public through a series of 'how-to' texts that
were published by Hachette between 1908 and 1914. The eugenic message was also widely diffused through popular plays like the *Damaged
Goods* by Brieux, or Couvreur's *La Graine*. Pearson wrote to Galton in
1907, overjoyed at the spread of eugenics into popular culture: 'I hear
most respectable middle-class matrons saying if children are weak, "Ah,
that was not a eugenic marriage!".'[32] In 1910 the German Racial
Hygiene Society organized a stand on eugenics at the International
Hygiene Exhibition which was visited by over five million people. The
industrialist Friedrich Krupp gave massive funding for the populariza-
tion of Social Darwinism and in 1899 offered a famous essay prize on the
topic: 'What can we learn from the principles of evolution for the development and laws of the state?', which received 60 entries from Germany,
Austria, Switzerland, Russia and the USA. The culture of the European
middle classes was permeated with evolutionary and Darwinian language,
and the basic concept of the 'survival of the fittest' was passed on to
millions of university students and school pupils.

However, it seems highly unlikely that the general public, including
many of those who were well educated, either read or understood the
complexities of Darwinian theory or, even less so, the new Mendelian
genetics. It seems likely that popular notions of heredity, evolution and
race were drawn from a much older discourse of animal breeding. This
'pre-scientific' form of understanding is of considerable importance
since it has continued to influence popular forms of racism right down to
the present day. The works of European eugenicists were saturated with
ideas and analogies drawn from the world of the stock-breeder. Since
breeders of horse, cattle, sheep, pigs and dogs were able, through careful selection and the keeping of elaborate stock-books, to mould and
shape animals into a desired form, it was widely assumed that the same
could be done with human beings. Darwin, in *The Variation of Plants and
Animals under Domestication* (1868), assumed that the ideas and practices

of animal breeders could have a scientific status. The papers given at the First International Eugenics Congress in 1912 made endless reference to the field of animal breeding and the American Charles Davenport, one of the delegates, looked forward to a revolution when 'human matings could be placed on the same high plane as that of horse breeding'.[33] All Europeans during the period 1870–1914, whether located in agrarian or urban societies, would have had almost daily contact with horses as transport animals, while horse-racing, hunting and riding fed into a common language rich in the terminology of blood-stock and breeding. The systematization of animal breeding, the invention of the specialized thoroughbred horse for hunting, the rearing of birds and pedigree dogs with particular characteristics like 'loyalty' or even of national 'types' (the British Bulldog, the Alsatian, the Pekinese), was introduced during the later eighteenth and early nineteenth centuries. The language and metaphors of animal breeding, as Enrique Da Cal has shown, provide a key to the way in which the scientific racist ideas of the educated élite were transmitted into popular culture.[34] A common eugenicist rhetorical device was to point out that more care and money went into the breeding of horses than into the improvement of the human race. Common-sense and popular forms of racism after 1900, in spite of the advances of Mendelian genetics, continued to view human heredity as a blending of 'blood' and of parental characteristics. Unfortunately, many eugenicists continued to use the language of the stock-yard into the 1920s and 1930s, thus encouraging both a widespread popular belief in an impossible science (human characteristics could not yet be 'engineered' through selection) as well as a dehumanizing racist language that reduced minorities to the level of animals ('breeding like rabbits', 'half-caste', 'mongrels'). Thus popular language became increasingly infused, as did that of the educated élites, with medical, biological and organicist terms or metaphors that lent themselves to the spread of racist attitudes.

The period from 1870 to 1914 was an age in which self-referential forms of racism achieved an unprecedented level of elaboration. Although earlier societies certainly had rules that controlled who should marry whom, and aristocratic and royal lineages preserved their essential 'purity' of blood, never before had any society invented such a range of techniques and scientific theory and practices to ensure biological fitness. The wider movements to improve national efficiency and the economic, military and imperial strength of the 'race', such as public health, natalism, physical fitness and urban hygiene found acceptance across the political spectrum. Before the First World War eugenics, in spite of its growing influence, made little impact on legislation: in general, the most negative forms of intervention – compulsory sterilization, premarital vetting, segregation of the 'degenerate' – could make little impact as long as politicians and the general public viewed them as a dangerous threat to basic civil rights. Many Europeans shared the sentiment of the American I. P. Whitehead that under eugenic statutes, a 'reign of doctors will be inaugurated and in the name of science...the worst forms of tyranny practised'.[35] However, the widespread diffusion of Social Darwinist concepts, of a eugenic language of 'fitness', at all levels of society, did reinforce racist assumptions that the highest form of the human species was the white European. Social Darwinism also lent itself to an age of mounting nationalist tension and insecurity. Contemporaries certainly used the terms 'race' and 'nation' as interchangeable and the nation was viewed, quite literally, as a distinct biological group (Nordic, Aryan, Anglo-Saxon, Celtic, Alpine or Mediterranean types), one that carried essential characteristics in the germ-plasm or 'blood'. As Vacher de Lapouge noted, 'nations are as real as races, they are biological entities.'[36]

In the latter half of the nineteenth century much of the language of degeneration had been centred on the dangerous and threatening lower orders, the savage and animalistic 'race-within' of the common people, but after 1900 there was a shift towards Social Imperialism and similar forms of welfare nationalism that began to emphasize the racial unity of all social classes. The language of class-as-race appears to have subsided as new forms of corporatism, 'solidarism' or organic unity moved to the forefront. The emphasis was on co-operation between classes, rather than competition and conflict, the efficient working together of all for the greater cohesion and strength of the nation locked in struggle with other states. Nor was such a vision of nationalism confined to conservatives worried by the growth of socialism and concepts of revolutionary class war. Numerous eugenicists regarded themselves as socialists, from Alfred Ploetz, who supported the German SPD, to Karl Pearson or Fabians like H. G. Wells, the Webbs and Bernard Shaw. From the turn of the century, a peculiar form of socialism began to appear that rejected Marxist ideas of class struggle as dysgenic and emphasized the technocratic and biological engineering of the unified race-nation. Right across Europe after 1870, and affecting all shades of political opinion, we can see signs of a deep shift towards authoritarian forms of nationalism. The rising medical profession, through its claim that biological science was above politics, assisted this evolution. Increasingly, doctors laid claim to determine social policy according to the iron laws of natural science, laws that were deterministic and beyond any moral values or system of ethics, and, in doing so, they threatened liberalism and the rights of the individual. The 'demands' of nature, it was claimed, were paramount and the selfish interests of the individual should, if necessary, be sacrificed to the greater good of the 'race' and the quality of its hereditary substance or gene-pool. Eugenicists began to argue that forceable sterilization was quite acceptable since the state already held power over life, the right to inflict capital punishment or to order soldiers to sacrifice their lives, for the higher good of the community and national survival. Vacher de Lapouge commented: 'The individual is crushed by his race, he is nothing. The race, the nation, are everything.'[37] The intrusion of dehumanizing forms of racism into medicine and public welfare was exemplified in Germany by the growing use of the concept of *minderwertig*, of 'lesser value'.

However, as will be discussed in Part 2, it was the seismic shock of the First World War that was to produce the conditions under which such ideas could find a more receptive political environment in rising fascist and right-wing nationalist movements.

2

BLACKNESS WITHOUT BLACKS[1]

In this chapter we examine how it was possible for Europeans to have a racialized view of the black between *c.*1870 and 1914, even though the vast majority had had no direct contact with or ever seen a black person. On the whole our purpose will not be to examine in any detail scientific racist thought, or the works of physical anthropologists on the 'Negro', but rather the question of how and why anti-black stereotypes achieved such a remarkable power and universality in European culture and consciousness, and a key role in the construction of racial hierarchies. By the nineteenth century the black represented the paradigm of racial Otherness, the marker of that which was most physically, mentally and culturally different from the 'civilized' European. As the anthropologist Professor W. H. Flower noted in 1880: 'The African negro has, on account of his structure being better known than that of any other of the lower races, always been taken as the antithesis of the white man of Europe.'[2] Although anti-Semitic stereotypes, as we shall see, were equally entrenched within European culture, the black was the automatic touchstone of all that was biologically or somatically dissimilar, at the lowest level in the hierarchy of racial types, the bottom rung in a descending ladder of primitiveness, beyond which one was no longer a human being.

Stereotypes and Race

Historically stereotypes have played a fundamental role in the way that racial attitudes have been both structured as well as transmitted among both educated élites and a semi-literate or illiterate public. As social psychologists note, the external world of perception is so immensely complex that the individual, to avoid a kind of sensory overload, is bound to shape and control the chaos of stimuli through imposing simplifyng categories or patterns. The mental representations of the world that we all deploy are drawn from a 'vocabulary', a way of seeing, that is transmitted to us through socialization by parents and the wider society. Racial stereotypes, like so many other forms of prejudice (gender, class), have an extraordinary capacity to convey perceptions (and feelings) of the Other which bear little, if any, relationship to external reality. However, these highly distorted images, instead of being recognized for what they are, are understood as real-world entities. So powerfully can stereotypes substitute for reality that the racist can see in both black and Jew, even when they are directly perceived, qualities the very opposite of those that are being observed. Because stereotypes are generally part of a defensive mechanism, to protect established beliefs, they tend to serve a highly conservative function and can be transmitted from one generation to the next, or between classes, and geographically across society, with an astonishing durability. Stereotypes are central to an understanding of racism in Europe and their formation and dissemination, a rich web of signs and references, has been seen by Sander Gilman and others as crucial to the maintenance of prejudice within the wider society.[3] The term 'black', added to any particular context or observation – as in 'The [black] criminal escaped' – has generally carried a complex set of cognitive and affective associations. The mind's eye would not only summon up images of physical appearance (often grossly distorted), but blackness might also activate negative feelings, a mood, a range of preferences. Our aim here is to explore the ways in which the stereotype of the black came to constitute a universal feature of European culture, one that existed in all social classes and across the Continent, from the great cities of the West to the most underdeveloped, rural societies of the Mediterranean or Eastern Europe.

It needs to be made clear that contemporary writers often used the term 'black' as the most vague of categories that could include all darker skinned peoples, from Africa to India and New Zealand. During the Indian rebellion of 1857 officers, wishing to express contempt and loathing, consistently referred to Indians as 'niggers'. However, this expression was most commonly deployed by both race theorists as well as within popular discourse as a term for sub-Saharan Africans, referred to in English as the 'Negro' (in French *le nègre*, in German the *Neger*). This categorization did not bear much relationship to the enormous physical and ethnic diversity of African peoples, rather it was a kind of composite being, a caricature that was constructed by reference to exaggerated features, like a crude 'identi-kit' image that constantly used the same simple components. The definition used by the famous Swiss anatomist Georges Cuvier in 1817 is quite typical of the standard formulation: 'The Negro race is confined to the south of mount Atlas; it is marked by a black complexion, crisped or woolly hair, compressed cranium, and a flat nose. The projection of the lower part of the face, and the thick lips, evidently approximate it to the monkey tribe: the hordes of which it consists have always remained in the most complete state of utter barbarism.'[4]

European Expansion Overseas, Slavery and Anti-Black Racism

In order to understand the centrality of the black racial stereotype within European society something needs to be said, no matter how briefly, about the long history of white contact with Africans, the exploration of the Continent between the fifteenth and nineteenth centuries, the development of slave societies in the plantation economies of the Americas, the abolitionist movement, and the eventual partition of Africa in the 'scramble' from 1875 to 1912.

European contact with blacks increased dramatically from the fifteenth century onwards as the west coast of Africa was charted and settled. It is clear that highly negative stereotypes began to develop even before the slave trade and were closely linked to a Christian world-view that saw the African as the embodiment of all that was most heathen: they were typically described as 'a people of beastly living, without a God, law, religion, or common wealth'.[5] Europeans were both fascinated and repelled by the African's skin colour, a revulsion that was deeply ingrained in the negative symbolic connotations of blackness, the symbolism of fearful night, of death, hell, the devil, witchcraft, and all that was most evil and sinister. Africans were associated with all that was most savage and beastly, and this animality was already in the sixteenth century described in terms of the sexual potency of blacks, their lewd nakedness and the supposed size of the male penis. From the seventeenth century onwards the physiological distinction between apes and blacks was seen as indeterminate, and their closeness was seen in sexual terms as one of 'beastly copulation'. The contact with Africa accelerated just as the Reformation and Counter-Reformation was leading to a generalized phase of sexual repression within European society and a puritanical preoccupation with sin. The process of stereotyping was in part a projection onto the black of all that was thought to be most opposed to the central values of the Christian order. Significantly, anti-black prejudice was constructed through the inversion of every taboo that was held to define a civilized society: taboos against eating human flesh, of sexual intercourse with animals, of incest, of sacrilege and paganism.

However, it was within the slave societies of the Americas that anti-black stereotypes achieved their most systematic formulation. As Robin Blackburn notes, the eighteenth century saw the elaboration of a *systematic* slavery that saw levels of degradation and violence unknown in the older forms of diffuse, *ancillary* slavery practised by Spain and Portugal.[6] The slave population of the Americas increased from 400 000 in 1700 to 2.4 million in 1770. The plantation economies not only engaged in barbaric practices like whipping, branding and the sale of blacks as chattel, but also institutionalized the slave system through regulations and law. White planter societies felt extremely vulnerable: frequently outnumbered ten to one by the slave population, paranoid at the potential for undetected revolt, and aware that domination depended on a precarious line of psychological control or terror, slavers erected elaborate codes of repression. For example, the boundaries between black and white society were policed by strict laws that banned interracial marriages or which blocked the social ascent and economic challenge of mixed-race freemen by defining those with a single drop of African blood as black. By the eighteenth century the association between slavery and the Afro-Caribbean was so deeply entrenched in European culture that the colour black was taken as an automatic signifier of slavery.

However, the crucial period for the systematic racialization of blacks, the elaboration of ideologies of racial inferiority, came with the century-long movement for the abolition of slavery between *c.*1750 and 1850. The main drive towards the abolition of slavery in North America and Europe came from Quaker, non-conformist and humanitarian movements from the 1740s onwards which emphasized the Christian ideal of the fundamental unity of mankind and the equality of each soul before God. As the Reverend Andrew Eliot stated in 1774: 'The meanest slave hath a soul as good by nature as your's, and possibly by grace it is better.' Enlightenment thinkers, located within a more secular tradition, arrived at a similar notion of equality on the grounds that people of all races shared the same universal human nature, and had a similar potential for rationality and progress. Enlightenment philosophers, in theorizing aesthetics and perception, were perfectly aware of the nature of the Eurocentric values that painted the black as ugly and disgusting. Thus, as Herder emphasized (1797), there was no hierarchy of colour in nature: 'The naturalist does not postulate an order of merit among the creatures which he observes; all are of equal value and concern . . . The Black has as much right to consider the White a mutant, a born vermin, as the white has to consider him a beast, a black animal.'[7] Kant remarked in 1790 that the normative idea of the beautiful varied from one society and racial group to another. This relativist and sociological approach to difference was anathema to conservative, anti-revolutionary and pro-slavery ideologues. The planter Edward Long, for example, met this challenge by emphasizing the radical biological difference of blacks. Long, in his *History of Jamaica* (1774) put forward a defence of slavery in secular terms that reflected the new science of race: 'I think there are extremely potent reasons for believing that the White and the Negroe are two distinct species.'[8]

The transition towards modern forms of anti-black racism from *c*.1870 onwards was marked by a reversal of the century-long trend towards a humanitarian and liberal movement for slave emancipation. The abolitionist campaign had been a long-drawn-out affair: a large-scale, popular movement in Britain had achieved abolition in a widen-ing movement (1788, 1799, 1806, 1814–67), while in France surges in 1794, 1815, 1831 and 1861 were separated by phases of restoration. This long battle appeared to have been won definitively in Europe by the 1860s and the Confederate defeat in the American Civil War (1861–5) marked the beginning of what seemed to be a new era of universal human rights, an inevitable stage in the progress towards a future society of enlightenment and humanity. The abolitionist move-ment, that had triumphed everywhere in Europe, had succeeded in spreading a more positive image of the black: if he or she appeared to be in a savage state, backward, immoral and violent, this arose from environmental conditions, including the dehumanizing impact of slavery itself, rather than from any innate inferiority. Given the right conditions of emancipation, education and development, the blacks would eventually catch up and join the civilized white European. It came as a considerable surprise to liberal humanists after *c*.1870 to note a deep shift within European society towards a new form of intolerance and anti-black racism, a kind of lurch back to a previous age of feudal despotism and cruelty that was in defiance of the march of progress.

The Growth of Anti-Black Racism from *c*.1870

This watershed has been best documented for anti-black racism in the case of Britain, but it is likely that a similar shift towards a more intolerant and aggressive form of racism took place within other European colonial nations during the last third of the nineteenth century. In Germany, for example, the leading anti-Semite Wilhelm Marr, like so many of his contemporaries, was radical in politics up until the 1848 Revolution, and then moved distinctly towards an anti-liberal, authoritarian and racist position. Between 1852 and 1859 Marr travelled as a merchant in Central America, particularly in Costa Rica, and was accused by the Berlin Central Society for Colonization of being a 'slave trader'. In an article of 1862, *Towards an Understanding of the Events in North America*, which was seen as a defence of the Confederate South and of slavery, he stated: 'the Negroes are closer to beasts than to human beings.'[9] It is interesting to note that Marr's initial shift towards a racist position appears to have been generated within a colonial context, and that his anti-black racism pre-dated and provided the basis for his subsequent development of a racial anti-Semitism. This, as will be seen later, may have been a general feature of European anti-Semitism and can explain in part why Jews were racialized as 'black' or 'Negroes' through cross-reference or analogy to the black stereotype.

In Britain the sea-change towards intolerance can be noted as early as Carlyle's virulent tract *Discourses on the Nigger question* (1849), but the key phase came in 1862–7. The American Civil War (1861–5), widely reported in the British press, gave rise to deep anxieties about an imminent slave war in which blacks, reverting to their primitive instincts, would engage in bloody violence and rape. In 1863 James Hunt presented a famous paper, *On the Negro's Place in Nature*, to the Anthropological Society of London: in this he developed the thesis that blacks constituted a separate species from the European and that 'there is a far greater difference between the negro and the European than between the gorilla and chimpanzee.'[10] Hunt's diatribe was a compilation culled from the most vicious anti-black writers, but significantly much of it was drawn from 'scientific' pro-slavery racists in the United States. Misguided abolitionists, Hunt claimed, through their 'rosepink sentimentalism' and belief in the 'mental equality of the different races', had inflicted untold misery on the blacks since they ignored the 'anthropological science' which understood their true characteristics, the inherent needs and wants of Africans. Race science could show why it was that the black had achieved his highest form of

development and happiness in the Confederate States and the pre-
emancipation West Indies, where 'the negro is working in his natural
subordination to the European'.[11] Hunt marked a reactionary and post-
emancipation link between the unworkable nature of black freedom and
the eternal backwardness of black Africa by contrasting the 'paradise' of
American slave society with the horrors of Africa, its juju worship, cannibalism, sexual depravity and barbarism.

Hunt's was a minority voice in 1863, but his type of racism was given
added impetus by the Jamaican rebellion at Morant Bay in October 1865
which was crushed on the orders of Governor Eyre with savage brutality
and the execution of 439 men. As during the American Civil War, the
British press indulged in sensational accounts of black atrocities, horrible
mutilations, the drinking of rum and gunpowder from victim's skulls,
and (the classic phobia) the rape of white women. Morant's Bay revived
memories of the Indian Rebellion (1857), the most profound and bloodiest
of challenges to British colonial power, as well as of the ongoing Maori
Wars. However, the deep anxiety of the metropolitan public, a kind of
moral panic in relation to the 'black peril', had less to do with any direct
threat offered to them by a distant colony than with tensions in British
society and the 'race' threat offered by the working class. The age of
Victorian economic stability was on the wane while the middle class was
profoundly unsettled by the agitation for a universal franchise. Popular
radicalism, from the era of the French Revolution onwards, had made
a direct link between the figure of the chained black slave, depicted on
countless plates, posters and prints, kneeling in supplication, 'Am I not
a man and a brother?', and the condition of the British labourer, the
industrial slave in mill and mine. The violent suppression of a workers'
demonstration in Hyde Park in 1866 was compared by them to the
crushing of blacks and they proceeded to burn an effigy of Governor
Eyre.

In a mirror image of this language of freedom, which saw black and
white engaged in a common battle to break the chains of tyranny, the
conservative middle class viewed the threat from below as quite literally
a race war, a challenge by the 'dangerous classes' who were described as
'savages' and 'negroes'. Moves to prosecute the Governor of Jamaica were
countered by a campaign of the middle class that, as John Stuart Mill
noted, was 'living in a constant dread of the encroachment of the class
beneath, which makes it one of their strongest feelings that resistance to
authority [by blacks] must be put down'.[12] The elaboration of a modern
and aggressive racism from the 1860s was thus one expression of a

profoundly insecure bourgeois society that constantly played upon and interwove the rhetoric of race and class. The modern race science that began to naturalize difference and emphasize the radical biological gap between black and white lent itself well to the language of class. The challenge that was offered by the lower orders to bourgeois hegemony, the call for universal rights and equality, was blocked by an ideology which emphasized the inherited, biological inferiority and low intelligence of the working class/race.

As Thomas Holt has argued, the trend towards a virulent form of racism was founded on the very premises of liberal ideology.[13] The 'freedom' that was granted with the abolition of slavery in 1833 was grounded on the premise that plantation economies were less efficient when based on forced labour. Once slaves were free it was expected that they would naturally follow the rational order of the market economy and become more productive. However, the ex-slaves in Jamaica preferred to find a different kind of freedom by moving away from the plantations and setting up as small peasant proprietors who controlled their own land and labour. By the 1850s this shift was being interpreted as the failure of emancipation: the ex-slaves' movement into what was viewed as a primitive life in the hill country, a decline into idleness, feckless poverty and moral degeneration, represented an inevitable reversion back to the inherent qualities of the savage. As the Jamaican magistrate A. Trelawny commented: 'Their march back to barbarism has been rapid and successful.'[14]

By the late 1860s the predominant thinking among colonial officials and policy-makers in London was that black populations in the Caribbean, Africa and elsewhere – unlike the colonies of white settlement like Canada and Australia, which could be prepared for self-government – would have to remain under the 'benevolent guardianship' of their white masters. Here was the root of the pernicious racist ideology, still current today in relation to African nations, which maintained that blacks were incapable of invention, of elaborating democratic political or legal systems, of hygiene and all the other features of 'civilization'. Such progress could be achieved only under white tutelage, but once the hand of the European master was withdrawn, black populations descended rapidly into chaos, barbarism and animality. On a visit to Jamaica in 1885 J. A. Froude expressed anxiety at the prospect of an independent black society that would degenerate into a savage, jungle existence: 'nature has made us unequal, and Acts of Parliament cannot make us equal. Some must lead and some must follow ... '.[15] During the same period British missionaries in West

Africa began to report that many years of work to convert the Africans, to win them from cannibalism, thieving, lying, sexual perversion and paganism, had got nowhere against the 'hereditary fetishism of their race'.[16]

The Partition of Africa and Racism

Was the transition after the 1860s to a more virulent form of anti-black racism peculiar to Britain, or was it a phenomenon shared by Continental Europe? Part of the answer to this question can be found in the way that several nations (Britain, France, the Netherlands, Germany, Italy, Belgium, Portugal) had a major stake in the drive towards the partition and rapid economic exploitation of Africa between 1875 and 1912. During the age of the New Imperialism anti-black racist stereotypes were powerfully reinforced through a mass of official and informal propaganda, from school text books and a cheap popular press, to the work of missionaries and colonial exhibitors. Before examining this area in more detail, some note must be taken of the development of racism in the colonies and its impact on metropolitan societies. It was in the overseas empires that Europeans, either as permanent settlers or as more temporary administrators, judges, missionaries, soldiers, traders and engineers, had the most sustained contact with Africans. While, within Europe before 1914, anti-black racism, in the almost total absence of Africans, developed mainly in a theoretical form, the colonies (as with the earlier slave plantations of the seventeenth and eighteenth centuries) provided the terrain in which racism grew in its most powerful and virulent forms, as a racial praxis grounded in military conquest, systematic violence, land dispossession, forced labour and segregation.

Between 1875 and 1912 the seven rival nations – Germany, Italy, Portugal, France, Britain, Belgium and Spain – partitioned a whole continent, created 30 new colonies and protectorates covering ten million square miles of territory, and acquired 110 million new subjects. The process of colonization varied historically from one territory to another, but there were certain shared characteristics that can be illustrated by the German occupation of the Cameroons and Namibia (1884–1914). In the Cameroons the Germans had no hesitation in taking over enormous areas of the most fertile land, which was divided up into plantation concessions owned by various companies like The African Fruit Company and the German West African Company, controlled by financiers, bankers and speculators in Hamburg, Berlin and Bremen. The plantations could only be made profitable through an enormous labour input, but since the indigenous people were resistant to the harsh and intensive forms of work imposed by overseers, the plantation companies resorted to a system of forced labour and brutality. So atrocious were the working conditions that 16 per cent of men died on the Prince Alfred Plantation during 1913. Wealthy bankers, like Adolf von Hansemann and S. Bleichroder, invested in the German South-West Africa Company that took over a huge Namibian concession in 1885, an area of 240 000 square kilometres. The seizure of hereditary cattle lands, the building of railway lines and the development of mining eventually led to the Nama-Herero uprising of 1904–7. This drawn-out guerrilla war was put down with the utmost savagery and a systematic repression that can be rightly described as genocidal.

The picture was much the same throughout Africa, a disregard for native land-rights, the brutal use of superior technical and military power to impose the settlers' will, the dislocation of indigenous societies, and a low evaluation of African life. The unspeakable atrocities committed in the Belgian Congo represented the most publicized example of a more generalized and often unrecognized abuse of human rights. Although voices of opposition were raised in Europe, by Socialists, missionaries and humanist liberals, in condemnation of the worst excesses, in general European governments utilized a two-track deployment of state power between colony and metropolis that accepted forms of colonial repression and control ('native codes', legal segregation, banning of trade unions, absence of political rights, harsh penalties for minor offences, military violence . . .) that would have been found absolutely intolerable within the bounds of metropolitan society as a breach of fundamental human and democratic rights. Such official double standards meant that the general public remained largely ignorant of the appalling conditions in distant colonies or was won over to the self-comforting assertions of the civilizing mission.

A key point to note here is that most of those Europeans who were posted to Africa, whether as government officials, soldiers, teachers or company workers, lived and operated within a colonial system of values and practices that they often absorbed, or internalized, from the demeaning way that whites spoke to or treated servants, to public whippings and elaborate codes of segregation or racial abuse (*wog*, *nigger*, or French expressions like *bougnoul*, *raton* and *bicot*). From diaries and letters we know that many Europeans were, on first arrival in the colonies, initially shocked by the treatment of blacks, but admitted to a process of gradual habituation. But most crucial of all, colonial societies in Africa, as had the earlier slave societies of the Caribbean and the United States, elaborated the most stark racial ideologies to legitimate even the most brutal acts. For example, it was a commonplace perception, upheld by colonial medical science, that the black body showed muscular strength, but was 'deficient' in the refined sensory nervous system and brainpower of the European. Blacks, in an animalistic way, were far more resistant to pain and hardship: this meant that physical punishment needed to be more harsh to make any impact on their brutish being. In 1904 Leutwein, the Governor of German South-West Africa, in a report on the physical punishment of blacks claimed that 'with the leathery skin of the natives – the Hottentot as well as the Kaffirs – even 25 strokes cause but a slight sensation of pain'.[17] Similarly, it was thought that the native had far fewer needs and was 'happy' to survive on a frugal diet, thus legitimating lower wage levels.

Such deeply entrenched racial attitudes and assumptions were brought back into European society by returning ex-colonials. Many of those who served in the colonies, apart from rank-and-file soldiers drawn from the working class, belonged to an educated and trained élite (civil engineers, lawyers, army officers, doctors, administrators, company managers, professors) who, on their return to Europe, continued to be employed in important and influential positions, from which they could spread racist attitudes as educators, government officials or members of imperial leagues. It was precisely because ex-colonials had a detailed experience of Africa that they could lay claim to a special expertise in 'native management' and related matters, so that they carried particular weight in European society as advisers to colonial departments, leading politicians, government commissions and other policy-making fora. Perhaps the most deeply entrenched attitude which colonials brought back into European society was a horror of 'miscegenation' and of sexual relations between even the small number of blacks in Europe and white women. Although much research remains to be done on the scale and impact of ex-colonials within European society, including into the post-colonial era of the later twentieth century, what scattered evidence there is points to this circulation of imperial élites as a crucial element in the elaboration of racism in Europe. This process was to accelerate, as will be noted in Chapter 6, with decolonization and the 'return home' of many hundreds of thousands of settlers and officials who felt bitter at their displacement by Africans.

The remaining part of this chapter looks in part at the ways in which anti-black stereotypes were disseminated in popular culture after 1870 through the mass media, schooling, missionary propaganda and other channels, reaching into even those regions, peasant societies and provincial backwaters in which there was no black presence. However, the main emphasis is placed on the little known history of a small, but very significant, European-wide black minority presence during this early period, and what can be learned from this about changing white racial attitudes within European society. Particular attention is given to the direct exhibiting of blacks within the great international or colonial fairs, as well as in travelling shows, as providing an insight into the construction of racist messages that had a major impact on the viewing public.

The Black Presence in Europe

It is often assumed that the black presence in Europe is a relatively recent phenomenon, a product of post-1945 labour shortage and governmental recruitment of colonial immigrants. However, migration of blacks into Europe, particularly of slaves, had existed on some scale since the sixteenth century. In Lisbon in 1551 there were 9950 slaves, most of them Africans, comprising one-tenth of the city's population, while in Seville in 1565 there were 6327 slaves. Thus in the mid-sixteenth century the Iberian peninsula already had a black presence that was not to be exceeded for the whole of Europe until after 1914. During the eighteenth century similar permanent slave communities built up further north in the major Atlantic ports, from Bordeaux and Nantes to London, Bristol, Liverpool and Amsterdam. During this period the number of blacks probably reached a peak of 5000 in France, and 20 000 in Britain. There was even a distinctive community of blacks in the Caucasus mountains near the Black Sea, probably descendants of Turkish slaves, which survived into the Soviet era.

As the slave trade was gradually terminated so the inward movement of Africans that fed into the port communities was ended, and the black population that had settled permanently appears, over the course of the nineteenth century, to have gradually melded through intermarriage with Europeans and to have 'disappeared' as an identifiable minority. However, from the 1860s onwards the displacement of sail by steam led to the practice of shipping lines hiring cheap labour in the ports of India, Africa, Arabia and elsewhere, to undertake low skilled, but physically demanding, jobs like boiler-stoking. The non-European sailors that were abandoned by shipping lines in European ports, or who jumped ship, gradually began to settle and build up permanent port communities, several of which became the historic core of the oldest ethnic settlements surviving today, most notably in Marseilles, London, Cardiff, Liverpool, Amsterdam and Hamburg.

As colonial conquest and trade accelerated so did the number of Africans and black Americans coming into European ports. A sizeable and multi-ethnic community of Indians, Chinese, Somalis and Africans began to put down roots in London, Cardiff, Glasgow and elsewhere in Britain. There was a similar multi-ethnic presence in Marseilles, a major port of call for shipping passing through the Suez Canal. There were numerous black seamen in Hamburg by the 1890s, as well as in the Russian ports of Archangel, St Petersburg, Nicolaiev, Kronstadt and Vladivostok. United States' shipping records show that of 132 ships indicated as bound for Russia between 1798 and 1880, there was rarely one that did not have at least one black seaman on board. Of the 12-man crew of the bark *Chasca of Boston* that arrived in Cronstadt in 1869, nine were black Americans. Blacks would have been a not uncommon sight on the quays and in the streets and inns of all the major seaports of the Atlantic and Mediterranean coasts.

Inland from the ports of Europe blacks would have been a rare sight: indeed, it seems unlikely that the majority of Europeans, particularly those who lived in rural communities or small towns, and who rarely travelled beyond the provincial capital or region, would ever have seen a black person. However, the great cities of Europe did see the passage of a tiny but significant number of blacks after the 1860s, especially as the spread of railway lines and the commercialization of mass leisure (theatres, dance-halls, political meetings) made it possible for black actors, jockeys, boxers and students to circulate. During the colonization of Africa after 1870 young black men, who were regarded as particularly gifted by administrators or missionaries, were sent for training in Britain, France, Germany and Russia. Numerous black American abolitionist speakers went on tour through Europe in the 1860s, like T. Morris Chester who was received by the Tzar in 1867, and then travelled on through Denmark, Sweden, Saxony and England. The famous Shakespearean actor Ira Aldridge performed widely in Britain from 1825 onwards, before touring the Continent in 1852 and 1858, visiting cities in Belgium, Germany, Bohemia, Austria, Hungary, Poland and Russia. He again toured

Moscow and provincial Russia in 1861–6, and finally died on the road at Lodz in Poland in 1867.

African slaves had also been servants and entertainers in the royal courts of Europe since the thirteenth century and this fashion then spread into the nobility, as exotic symbols of wealth and status. Peter the Great of Russia, for example, procured a number of black servants, including the great-grandfather of Pushkin, Abram Petrovich Hannibal, who had been captured by slavers in Abyssinia in about 1700. In 1753 the philosopher David Hume remarked, 'there are Negroe slaves dispersed all over Europe'.[18] Although this fashion may have gone into decline in Western Europe after 1800 as the movement for the abolition of slavery gathered pace, the imperial Russian court continued to retain a permanent staff of about 20 black servants right down to the Revolution. A favourite subject of eighteenth-century portrait painters was of the noblewoman attended by her black servant, often a little boy, who served not only as a symbol of wealth, but also as a contrast to enhance the whiteness of the mistress's skin. This genre continued in French painting to the end of the nineteenth century, as in Edouard Manet's famous *Olympia* (1863), and throughout this period the black maid or servant continued to be a fashion accessory. In England, with the abolition of slavery in 1833, African servants were no longer so fashionable or as easy to acquire, but an identical role continued to be played by the thousands of black servants and *ayahs* (nurses) introduced by the British Raj from India and from South-East Asia.

Throughout Europe between 1870 and 1914 there was thus a small, but none the less significant black presence, largely confined to the major ports and cities. Although small in number, however, they would often have received considerable publicity as speakers, actors, musicians and sportsmen, and lectured or performed before large audiences of the European middle class. How did Europeans react to such a black presence? Here, we need to distinguish between two levels, the reactions of the middle class and aristocracy, and that of the working class. As far as the latter is concerned, the main zone of contact was in the major ports and, in general, the number of black Africans or Afro-Americans was far too small for them to be perceived as economic competitors or a social threat. Black Africans were, however, during this period only one group among the numerous ethnic minorities that could be found in European port settlements, from Chinese and Bengalis to Kabyles and Arabian Arabs. Indigenous hostility towards blacks was part and parcel of a generalized dislike of colonial seamen, regarded as inherently inferior. Just before the First World War, in 1910, French seamen in Marseilles went on strike against the employment of Kabyles by the merchant navy, while between 1910 and 1912 Italian immigrant workers in the oil refineries fought with North Africans brought in as strike breakers. In 1913 Kabyle workers came under attack again from Belgian immigrants in the coal-mines of Northern France. The Netherlands seamen's trade union in 1911 also objected to the increase of Chinese labour in Rotterdam and Amsterdam, which was being introduced by the shipping companies to undercut wages. This economically based hostility, which began to take on a racist tone, was a forewarning of a major wave of anti-colonial prejudice that was to develop during the First World War. However, the predominant reaction of the European working class on catching sight of the rare black person in the street or bar appears to have been one of curiosity, a naive fascination with skin colour and frizzy hair. The black British writer A. B. C. Merriman-Labor, in an account of his personal experience in late nineteenth-century London, noted that the most hostile reception came from white children in the street: 'bad boys will not hesitate to shower stones or rotten eggs on any passing black man . . . They will call you all kinds of names, sing you all sorts of songs', or from adults in working-class suburbs, like the factory girls that might shout, '"Go wash your face guv'nor," or sometimes call out "nigger! nigger! nigger!"'.[19]

From the diaries and correspondence of educated Africans and, in particular, of black Americans it is possible to piece together an interesting picture of middle-class and aristocratic reactions. In England there is evidence of hostility from the urban élites that had absorbed the prejudices of the Caribbean plantocracy or the ideas of race science. For example, the deep revulsion against black males having any relationship with white women came to the fore in 1833 when the great American actor Ira Aldridge, playing Othello in London opposite Ellen Tree, was subjected to a racist campaign in the press as 'the unseemly nigger' who, it was claimed, 'pawed' the white actress. When blacks faced discrimination, an objection to their presence in the same hotel, or as part of a mixed black and white couple in the street, this was frequently from visiting white Americans who brought with them the racist values of the South. Down to the 1860s visiting black Americans reported a general climate of tolerance in Britain, but from then onwards noted a distinct change in public attitudes towards an increasingly aggressive racism. This, as has been noted above, coincided with a general change towards a more negative racist ideology during the age of imperial expansion, Social Darwinism and nationalist xenophobia.

Elsewhere in Europe, outside the ports, the bourgeois response to the black presence appears to have been quite positive. In Russia the patronage of black servants and artists by the Tzar and the nobility provided them with a high level of social approval and protection. It was possible for such servants, whose children had access to education, to rise to high positions, like Michael Egypteos who attained high rank in the navy, or George Thomas who amassed a fortune through the ownership of hotels and restaurants. Ira Aldridge was lionized in St Petersburg and Moscow in the 1860s, while the whole town of Lodz turned out for his funeral in 1867. Pushkin's black ancestry never seems to have presented a problem as far as his social acceptance was concerned. Likewise, African students who arrived in Germany in the 1890s from the Cameroons, and then married German women and put down roots, achieved a respected position in society and suffered little racism before the 1930s.

What can we conclude from this apparent enlightenment? The evidence is patchy, but it can be surmised that the further east one moved in Europe from the seaboard, the more a black presence was limited to a tiny élite of educated servants and performing artists towards whom the public held quite tolerant ideas. Moreover, the Central and East European states (Poland, Austria, Hungary, Russia, Czechoslovakia) had little or no maritime colonial tradition, and few connections to a colonial praxis that could impinge on society through commercial interests, settler links and imperial propaganda. Hence the anomaly that the most autocratic or conservative of regimes, in Tsarist Russia, Wilhelmine Germany and the Austro-Hungarian monarchy, showed few traces of anti-black prejudice. This apparent toleration of Africans was barely distinguishable from the centuries-old courtly tradition that retained blacks as favoured 'pets' and exotic trophies.

Exhibiting Blacks in Europe

From 1870 onwards popular attitudes towards the black were significantly shaped by the great international fairs, a process of exhibiting that provided the framework through which most Europeans caught sight of the African 'in the flesh' and confirmed a sense of inherent white superiority. This practice was an extension of a much older tradition. For many centuries natives of Africa and the Americas had been captured and brought to Europe as objects of curiosity, but the exploitation of 'savages' in shows developed greatly during the nineteenth century as an aspect of travelling circuses, leisure gardens, music-hall spectaculars and other forms of mass popular entertainment. Between 1810 and 1815 a Boer farmer exhibited Saartjie Baartman, known as the 'Hottentot Venus', in London and Paris in a kind of freak-show and, even then, caused some scandal by the degrading way she was paraded because of her steotopygia, or prominent buttocks, and ordered to 'move backwards and forwards, and come out and go into her cage, more like a bear on a chain than a human being'.[20] Another nude black 'Venus' was paraded in 1829 at the ball of the Duchess Du Barry in Paris. The commercial possibilities of such spectacles was recognized by major circus and show-ground entrepreneurs, like the Americans Barnum and Bailey who toured both the United States and Europe.

However, the full potential for the display of live 'savage' peoples was developed furthest by the huge universal exhibitions and colonial and trade fairs that, following on from the first Great Exhibition at the Crystal Palace in 1851, proliferated throughout the cities of Western Europe. Between 1878 and 1914, during the height of the conquest and partition of Africa, exhibitions – frequently constructed on a vast scale – were an annual occurrence throughout Europe. Although the major locations were Paris (in 1867, 1878, 1887, 1889, 1891, 1893, 1900) and London (1886, 1892, 1897, 1899, 1903, 1908, 1924), international exhibitions were also held in Moscow (1872), Vienna (1873), Italy (1888), Germany (1891), Antwerp (1894) and Brussels (1897, 1910), as well as in major provincial cities like Glasgow (1901), Cork (1902), Wolverhampton (1902, 1907), Bradford (1904), Liège (1905) and Marseilles (1906). In the era before the significant spread of the cinema, such spectaculars were enormously popular and attracted huge gates. The Paris World Fair of 1889 was attended by 39 million people, that of 1900 by 50 million. Special cheap excursion trains were laid on to the Marseilles Colonial Exhibition of 1906 from all over France and Germany. Attendance by workers at the Franco-British Exhibition at White City (1908) was encouraged by employers, like Lever Brothers at Port Sunlight who laid on six special trains for 3500 workers. Through the international and provincial exhibitions literally millions of Europeans were to have a direct experience of Africans, an experience that provided the most powerful impetus to the diffusion of racial stereotypes.

Exhibitions and fairs, carefully planned and orchestrated stages for the 'selling' of imperialism, conveyed a complex of explicit and implicit meanings that related to white colonial triumph and racial superiority. One of the most popular forms of spectacle was the reconstruction of

famous military campaigns or battles in which white officers fought heroically in the arena with hordes of naked savages, with Ashanti, Dahomeans, Zulus, Shona and others. At the 'Savage South Africa' show in
Earl's Court (1899–1900) the public was presented with 'a sight never seen
previously in Europe, a horde of savages direct from their kraals', some
200 Zulu warriors. The Zulus re-enacted the famous massacre of the
Shangani Patrol in 1893, which – in the best traditions of public-school
heroism – went down patriotically singing 'God save the Queen'. However,
in such *tableaux vivants* the ferocious nature of the Zulu was always
eventually contained by the superior discipline and manliness of British
soldiers. In the simulated battles the inevitable defeat of the African was
invariably portrayed as a stage of racial progress, a Social Darwinian
triumph. The press review of 'Savage South Africa' referred to 'the
Matabele consent[ing] to bite the dust in deference to the hot fire of the
Maxims'.[21]

Such military re-enactments of the first stage of imperial conquest
frequently legitimated colonial might through crude sensationalism and
the most negative stereotypes of 'Darkest Africa', images of barbaric
practices, bloody human sacrifice, cannibalism, slavery and fetishism, that
it was the duty of the new masters to uproot. The Franco-British Exhibition of 1908, for example, displayed gruesome trophies like the war drum
beaten at executions. 'Devil worship', visitors were informed, 'is associated
with many of the curios. Sinister indeed is a triple-faced mask covered
with human skin flayed from sacrificial victims.'[22] Time and again
military expeditions and conquest, as well as propaganda on behalf of
the work of missionaries, was legitimated by such stereotypes, as with the
French campaigns in Dahomey in 1890 and 1892. In 1890 the mass-
circulation French illustrated press had given extensive and sensationalist
cover to human sacrifice in Dahomey, with images of snake worship,
decapitated heads on spikes and of human crucifixion. It was because of
this widespread public interest that Europeans flocked to see the newly
conquered Dahomeans who were exhibited in Paris in 1893. The Dahomean troupe were so popular that they continued to tour Europe and
America, and at the Paris World Fair of 1900 the Dahomean pavilion
was constructed in the form of a 'Tower of Sacrifice', decorated with
pikes and the 'actual skulls of slaves executed before the eyes of [King]
Behanzin'.[23]

The second standard element in the exhibitions was the emphasis on
the post-conquest phase of pacification and 'civilizing'. The military per-
formance, or the direction of the spatial layout, often moved sequentially

from the first stage of military conflict to one of containment, in which
the 'savages' were presented as humbled and pacified subjects who
responded with happiness to the enlightened direction of the colonial master. The very process of placing recently conquered tribes on display in
the European exhibitions was not unlike the ancient Roman parade of
peoples as trophies of war. The subjugation and pacification of the Zulu
was symbolized at the International Horticultural exhibition of 1892 in
London by a Zulu Choir who performed Rossini and Sullivan. The great
exhibitions, a vicarious tourist trip to the 'Dark Continent', accentuated
the zoo-like quality of human display by placing the Africans in compounds. In the 'villages' the domestication of the savage was represented
by the inclusion of African women and children engaged in peaceful
family life, usually open-air cooking, and in the transition to enlightenment and economic productivity represented by handicrafts, the weaving
and carving of objects that could be bought by the crowds. At the Paris
World Fair of 1900 visitors could watch Africans being schooled in
French by the Alliance Française. The Guide to the Imperial International Exhibition in London in 1909 emphasized the progressive and
productivist logic of colonialism in the civilizing of the human-sacrificing
Dahomenians:

> Order and decency, trade and civilization, have taken the place of rule
> by fear of the sword. France has placed its hands on the blackest spot
> in West Africa, and wiped out some of the red stain that made Dahomey
> a by-word in the world. Today Dahomey is a self governing colony of
> France, with a revenue which exceeds its expenditure, a line of railway,
> rubber and cotton plantations, exporting palm oil and copra, maize,
> nuts, dried fish, cattle, sheep, pigs and fowl.[24]

The major exhibitions were constructed on a truly vast scale, and in addition to the sites allocated to the various Dutch, French, British, Belgian,
Italian and Portuguese colonies and the displays of economic wealth and
tropical produce, provided a setting for the latest and most advanced
European technologies, from turbines to automobiles. The way in which
the exhibition grounds were laid out, in a complex of pavilions and
streets, was as a totalizing global experience, an encyclopaedia of every
land and people. The greatest racial and cultural contrast was established
between the primitive, mud-hut 'villages' of the Africans and the spec-
tacular displays of European technological achievement, symbols of
modernity, displayed in huge electrically lighted halls. Nor were such

contrasts accidental since exhibition designers began to plan layouts to correspond to a racial hierarchy, an evolutionary progression from the most 'primitive' people (Dahomeans, Hottentots, Ashanti, etc.), via intermediary racial categories (Arabs, Chinese, Indian) to progressively higher types, the white Dominions (Australia, New Zealand, Canada), and finally the United States and the various European nations.

Although there were the beginnings of anti-colonial protest at such exhibitions in inter-war Paris, in general we can speculate that the degrading and racist display of black people probably powerfully reinforced popular stereotypes of Africans as savages who were at the bottom of the human evolutionary chain, quite literally placed on show like animals in a zoo. Spectators fed monkey-nuts to a group of Congolese who were shown in travelling colonial exhibitions in Belgium. The animality of blacks, a dangerous savagery that created a *frisson* of horror and delight in white audiences, was emphasized by a symbolism of containment, of compound fences and of ring-masters, billed as great white hunters and animal trainers, who brought a touch of racial mastery to the show. The very first major display of Africans at the Paris Jardin d'Acclimatation in 1877 was organized by 'a foreign merchant whose speciality is furnishing interesting specimens to the zoological gardens of Europe and who is supplied ... by paying local hunters'.[25] The circus entrepreneur and creator of 'Savage South Africa', Frank Fillis, had recruited the Zulus among white farmers in Natal through an advertisement in the press: 'Wanted: horned animals, baboons, zebras, giraffe, koodoo, springbucks, hartebeestes, young Afrikander girls, good looking and to be slightly coloured.'[26] The skills of Fillis were praised in the London press: 'he has achieved some wonderful results in the training of the troupes of savages and, incidentally, of the horses also'.[27]

Although, with hindsight, the crude propaganda purposes of 'native' display can be readily discerned, it is interesting to note that even the most sensationalist exhibits sought to provide a guarantee of authenticity by providing them with a scientific gloss. As Annie Coombes has argued, exhibitions and museum displays had a close relationship with the developing discipline of anthropology, which had much to gain in prestige by becoming associated with the enormously popular displays. Before 1914 the 'armchair' anthropologists of Europe rarely carried out any kind of field work, and they welcomed the convenient arrival of Africans to carry out direct research. On the first display of exhibited Africans in Paris in 1877, the Anthropological Society established a committee to carry out investigations: armed with calipers, tape measures and cameras its members recorded the physical features of the natives who were, appropriately, paid with 'little trinkets'.[28] In return, the exhibitions, which laid claim to authenticity and the educational advantage of their displays, were able to gain considerable legitimation from the close association with physical anthropologists, invited to advise on displays and catalogues, and with famous 'explorers' like Stanley, who could lay claim to expertise. The great exhibitions thus provided a crucial bridge between the field of academic race science and popular forms of racism.

This linkage can be further seen in the development of related forms of 'showing' African peoples and their culture. Ethnological museums that spread throughout the major cities of Europe from the 1860s onwards, from London and Liverpool to Cologne, Dresden and Bergen, invented displays of artefacts, from spears and drums to clothing and 'fetish' statues, that were placed in an 'evolutionary' sequence, with the most primitive African forms at the bottom of the hierarchy. The partition of Africa led to a vast flow of such plundered materials into the museums of Europe. Anthropologists, missionaries and explorers, as well as commercial photographers in colonial Africa, made increasing use of the camera, especially the light and portable Kodak, to record the great variety of races and cultures. Such photographs were reproduced in vast numbers in the form of millions of postcards, illustrations to school text books, missionary publications and popular compilations like the *Harmsworth History of the World*. Such images, many of which were fakes claiming to represent cannibals, fetish worshippers, slaves, nude 'beauties' and other exotica of 'Darkest Africa', were invariably presented above texts that guaranteed their scientific and anthropological veracity as racial 'types'. Such accessible images, doubly convincing because of their apparent objectivity and reality, had an enormous impact on a wider public. In the whole range of representation, from exhibition catalogues to museum displays and postcards, there was an intense preoccupation with the minute description and recording of the African body, a way of looking that reflected the impact of physical anthropology and racial science on a broader popular culture.

Mass Culture and Race

The diffusion of racial stereotypes of Africans within European society occurred through a vast array of other channels, although the basic messages were the same as those already explored for the processes of exhibiting and display. This has been studied in most detail for Britain, where an astonishing range of materials, products and organizations spread jingoistic, colonial and racist texts and images between 1870 and 1914. John MacKenzie, for example, has studied this enormous range of sources of imperial propaganda in the diverse forms of advertising and packaging (tea, chocolate, soap), music-hall acts, missionary slide shows, juvenile literature (Henty, John Buchan, Rider-Haggard), school textbooks, youth organizations (Boy Scouts, Church Lads' Brigade) and colonial organizations (Primrose League, British Empire League).[29] Robert Roberts, in his semi-autobiographical account of life in the slums of Salford before 1914, recorded the impact of imperialism and ultra-patriotism on the local children, of Seeley's *The Expansion of England*, Kipling, Empire Day and the penny weeklies that diffused a public-school ethos of heroic combat with savages.[30]

There can be no doubt that Britain was unusual in the extent to which popular culture became steeped in imperial and racial values. The picture in Continental Europe is much less clear, in part reflecting the little research that has been carried out on this topic in countries like Hungary and Poland, but also the historic reality of a much lower level of involvement or interest in colonial matters. However, although each European state had its own quite specific national cultural traditions, it seems probable that anti-black racial stereotyping was a universal feature of European popular culture. William Schneider has shown how an unprecedented flood of information reached the French public on Africa and blacks, both through the great exhibitions as well as the mass press journals like the *Petit Parisien* and the *Petit Journal*, which both reached circulation figures of over one million by the 1890s. Those colonial states that were most involved in the great international exhibitions, notably Britain, France, Belgium and the Netherlands, also had the greatest diffusion of colonial images and texts in advertising, postcards, newspapers, children's books, comics and other ephemera.

As one moved east through Europe, away from the maritime states, there appears to have been a falling away in the sheer volume of racial propaganda. For example, Spain, Germany, Russia and Austria did not have a strong presence in the international exhibitions. Spain had lost most of her colonial territories by 1900 and participation would only have been a humiliating symbol of imperial decline and failure. German colonies in Africa, while extensive, were weakly developed and could not compare to the vast possessions of Britain and France, and so imperial displays could do little to show German great power status compared to that of her rivals. Both Russia and Austria, without a maritime colonial tradition, and oriented towards the land-locked areas of central Asia, had little interest in the exhibitions.

Recent research into the early history of the cinema provides the most interesting new insights into the processes through which vivid images of colonial peoples were diffused into almost every small town and village of Europe, from Spain to the Caucasus. Between the first public showing of a film by the Lumière brothers in a Paris café in December 1895 and the First World War cinema spread globally with an astounding speed. As a Belgian newspaper noted in 1909: 'Which illustrated newspaper, which book, which theatre can compare with the cinematograph as a propagator of ideas? A new film coming out from Paris will within three months be seen across the globe by 300 million spectators.'[31] So keen were the early film entrepreneurs to cash in on the public interest in images of black Africans that they either, like Georges Méliès in 1896, used black American actors to play out scenes, or they filmed the 'native villages' in the great exhibitions, as at Tervuren in Belgium in 1897, or Paris in 1900. From 1900 onwards British, Belgian and French companies organized expeditions specifically to shoot film in Africa, and this growing footage was increasingly utilized by Catholic missionaries, as well as by colonial associations, to promote imperial interests and the civilizing mission in thousands of small towns, village halls and schools. Some companies, like the Belgian Cinématographe des Colonies (founded 1908) were specifically dedicated to the genre of exotic travel and colonial film production. That such powerful moving images of black Africa were able to penetrate rapidly into even the most isolated rural areas of Europe was due to the activity of thousands of travelling projectionists, many of them descendants of the traditional fairground exhibitors and showmen. By 1902 such entrepreneurs had even reached into the Caucasus and Asia Minor, and by 1910 permanent cinemas had been established as far away as Baku (8 cinemas), Kazan (10) and Kiev (12).

Such geographical diffusion was aided by the rapid development of new cinema technologies. The Pathé-Kok projector, which sold 2000 on its launch in 1913, was able to reach into villages without electricity since a hand-cranked dynamo supplied the light current, while simultaneously turning the film mechanism. The rate of cinema expansion is partly reflected in the increase in cine-film production by the German AGFA factory from 111 000 meters in 1908 to 20 million in 1912. While it is safe to conclude that film, which had a novel and astonishing impact on the public, reached into every corner of Europe by 1914, we know little of the impact that moving images of black Africans had upon audiences. Yuri Tsivian argues that no matter where any film claimed to be located, 'it was often perceived as set in a non-descript macaronic universe', or what Michel Foucault would define as 'heterotopia', spaces lacking in cultural or geographic identity.[32] It seems likely that uneducated peasant or industrial workers would however, no matter how nondescript the images of 'primitives', have absorbed the traditional stereotypes of the African as a naked, spear-waving heathen, devoid of clothing, living in 'jungle' zones without even the most basic qualities of civilization. Indeed, as always, it was the intention of the film makers to emphasize such stereotypical representations either in the interests of increasing profits through sensationalism and the exotic (witch-doctor rituals, cannibalism), or in order to legitimate the colonial and missionary enterprise by demonstrating how necessary and enlightened European intercession was.

Occasionally, a rare glimpse is afforded of the impact of such stereotypes upon European popular culture. In the Cornish fishing town of Padstow an ancient tradition of guise dancing was transformed in about 1900 into an annual revel called the 'Darkie Day', in which locals blacked themselves up in the American minstrel tradition as plantation slaves and sang songs accompanied by ukulele and accordion. The 'Darkie Day' was still going strong in 1998 when it came under criticism from the Council for Racial Equality in Cornwall.[33] Photographs of the inter-war Lord Mayor's procession in Norwich show locals blacked up as naked savages, carrying spears and bows.

Anti-Black Racism in Germany

That racist stereotyping of blacks was generalized even within those European societies that had no direct involvement in colonialism, the phenomenon of what Sander Gilman has called 'blackness without blacks', can be explored in more detail with relation to the German-speaking lands. A study of Germany helps provide some answers to the question of how it was possible for the vast majority of people within a society to share quite marked and consistently racist attitudes towards a minority with whom they had no direct physical contact. The German case is valuable since it provides an insight into the ways in which popular racism was diffused in all areas of Europe, including the isolated rural areas of the major colonial powers, where there was no physical black presence. Suzanne Zantop has investigated the depth of the German

colonial fantasy in the period 1770–1880, the century before the acquisition of any overseas colonies.[34] The educated German élite throughout
this period devoured popular collections of travel and exploration, like
the 21-volume *General History of Travels by Sea and by Land* (1747–74),
studied African skulls and artefacts, and debated all the central issues
of plantation slavery, abolition and racial scientific theory. Leading
anthropologists, like Johann Blumenbach, Christoph Meiners and
S. T. Sommerring developed all the classic racial theories of black difference, cultural inferiority, low intellect and physical proximity to the
apes. The major philosophers, from Kant to Hegel and Schopenhauer,
speculated on the nature of the black race, while popular dramatists like
Kotzebue (in *The Negro Slaves* of 1796) and Kleist (*Betrothal in Santo
Domingo* of 1811) presented the isssues of slavery in the theatres of Berlin
and Vienna.

Nor did the classic anti-black stereotype remain restricted to the élites,
but became diffused more generally within German society. Daniel Defoe's
Robinson Crusoe (1719) gave rise to the proliferation of a vast number of
national variants and adaptations, known as 'Robinsonades', that appeared
everywhere from Switzerland, Silesia and Thuringia to Russia and Greece.
For example, Joachim Campe's *Robinson the Younger: A Reader for Children*
(Hamburg, 1779) had gone through 117 editions by 1894 and influenced a whole generation of late nineteenth-century colonialists. Robinsonades, in addition to scenes of cannibalism and black savagery, conveyed
the central message of the European hero who not only conquers the
tropical wilderness, but also brings a superior intelligence to bear on the
taming and education of Friday. In Heinrich Hoffman's popular nursery
story *Der Struwwelpeter* (1844) children who mocked a black boy because
of his colour were then punished by a type of St Nicholas, who threw
them into a giant inkwell from which they emerged even blacker. This
cautionary tale carried the ambiguous notion that being black was a
punishment, the inverse of a popular theme in advertising throughout
Europe, the wonderful powers of that soap which could even wash the
black white. Even before the establishment of African colonies, German
advertising made full use of black stereotypes as in the promotion of
chocolates (the *Sarotti-Mohr* from 1868), Liebig's soups, cigars and
other products using images of a degraded 'golliwog' type. The post-
emancipationist image of the compliant black was also diffused in
Germany, as it was throughout Europe, by the translation of Harriet
Beecher Stowe's *Uncle Tom's Cabin* (1853). The Hamburg animal trader
and zoo director Carl Hagenbeck organized a travelling show of exotic

animals and peoples, which he referred to in the standard pseudo-scientific way as 'anthropological-zoological exhibits', while the painter Paul Friedrich Meierheim in his picture *The Savages* (1873) captured a scene of blacks performing before a peasant or village audience. Perhaps the groups that had a bigger influence on the formation of popular attitudes towards the black than any other, both in Germany as elsewhere, were the Catholic and Protestant missions. Church organizations were able to provide a direct link between missionaries, who had a first-hand experience of Africa, and the most isolated parish schools and churches. Missionaries frequently emphasized the shocking paganism of Africa in order to increase support for their own activities, like Mallet of the Norddeutsche-Mission in Bremen who wrote in 1854 of the heathen that 'the devil has exercised unlimited dominion over them for so long that they have become his slaves and have sunk into beastly and hellish conditions.'[35]

This fragmentary evidence for pre-colonial and colonial Germany might suggest that anti-black stereotypes were far more prevalent in Europe than has been generally acknowledged. Research in this field for Central and Eastern Europe has been almost non-existent, but even in pre-Revolutionary Russia the degrading American stereotype of the black minstrel, 'sambo' or 'coon' type was used on posters to advertise the craze for ragtime music and dancing in the dying years of the Tzarist regime.

What were the functions, if any, of such racial stereotyping? Firstly, for the vast majority of Europeans blacks constituted a purely external Other. Schoolboys may have gained a vicarious thrill from adventure books that recounted the heroic deeds of white men battling with evil cannibals, but everybody knew that black people offered no fundamental threat to those who lived within the bounds of European society. There were no literary fantasies or paranoid anxieties relating to a 'black invasion' or a 'black peril' internal to Europe, as there were within colonial societies. Europeans were far too sure and arrogant in their immense racial and technological superiority to feel any danger from the arrows and spears of primitive peoples who were held to have no power of invention and no history. Some historians have argued that the European public was largely indifferent to imperialism and that colonialism played little part in domestic politics. This was not the case, however, for Western Europe in general and the German case can again be used to provide an excellent example of the logic of colonialism.

Germany, more so than Britain and France, experienced the enormous disruptive impacts of late and extremely rapid industrialization. The

conservative Bismarck, faced with the beginnings of the great Depression
(1873–96) and the rise of the 'red peril', utilized social imperialism as an
ideology of crisis management. Until the early 1880s Bismarck was
a reluctant imperialist, opposed to the high costs of official colonial
expansion, but changed ground when he began to recognize the potential
of imperialism for integrating a state torn by class differences, through
focusing attention on successes abroad. Official colonial expansion also
linked to an economic turning point marked by a rejection of liberalism
and free trade and a move towards protectionism and towards colonies
as captive zones of trade, settlement and raw materials. The German
drive into Africa was also inspired by a fear that other powers would
soon take all, leaving Germany out in the cold. The Partition of Africa
was based less on rational economic calculations than on perceptions of
'pegging out' a future stake. Thus stabilization of the social order was
closely linked to a 'New Imperialism' and, as Bismarck remarked, 'for
internal reasons, the colonial question . . . is one of vital importance for
us.'[36] Similar factors can be seen at work in both Britain and France after
1880.

In this dramatic shift towards an accelerated competition for empire,
for a stake in Africa, the creation of popular support for colonialism was
of major significance. And central to the 'selling of empire' was racism,
a message of inherent white superiority that was diffused in the vast
array of novels, boys' adventures, travel books, missionary tracts and
popular journals on Africa. A direct linkage between colonial economic
interests and the social imperialist strategy of winning over the working
class to colonialism can readily be established. The organization of works
outings to the great colonial exhibitions was undertaken directly by
commercial and imperial interest groups: for example, the executive
committee of the Franco-British Exhibition of 1908 had several leading
figures from the British Empire League, such as Sir John Cockburn, the
Earl of Derby, Viscount Selbourne and Lord Blyth. The Mayer ethnological museum in Liverpool encouraged educational visits by schoolchil-
dren and workers. On display were numerous artefacts from West Africa
that had been presented by Sir Alfred Jones, a powerful magnate with
interests in Africa and director of the Elder Dempster Shipping Line,
who encouraged his senior employees in West Africa to collect ethnographic materials which were shipped to Liverpool at no cost.

The dominant racial message that was diffused throughout the states
with a colonial stake was quite simple in its formulation: the indigenous
people were so inherently backward that they required the direct inter-

vention of the superior white race to bring them education, science, medicine and economic development. Although some literature contained traces of a Social Darwinism that justified racial extermination (the inferior blacks would have to make way for the white), the dominant discourse was that of the 'civilizing mission'. Colonial powers generally recognized the need to retain native peoples as the basic work-force, particularly in tropical areas where the climate made dense European settlement impossible. Where the modern form of racism differed fundamentally from the older Enlightenment and liberal ideology was in its claim that biological and hereditary characteristics of blacks and whites were so invariable and determinate, that the former could never be 'lifted' to the same level as the latter. This justified a future colonial scenario in which the European domination and 'guardianship' would continue indefinitely, since the African would always require the superior political skills, the inventiveness, energy and advanced culture of the white man. Although this racist discourse did not go totally unchallenged within European society, underlying the colonial policies of left and right, of Social Democrats and Marxists, as well as Conservatives and Liberals, was an unquestioning assumption of black inferiority.

3

THE RISE OF POLITICAL ANTI-SEMITISM

Some historians perceive hatred of the Jews to be an 'eternal' racism that, in spite of minor shifts in its formulation, can be traced back over two millennia as a central and abiding component of European culture. While such lines of continuity certainly can be found (for example in the mythical view of the Jew as deicide) what such an essentializing approach tends to overlook is the extent to which anti-Jewish prejudice itself changed radically according to the historic context. How a Catholic artisan and guildsman of fourteenth-century Toledo or Prague, situated within a feudal and pre-industrial age, looked toward his Jewish neighbours was grounded in a total world-view that was quite unlike the perceptions of a factory worker of the late nineteenth century, living within a capitalist and secular age. Through the many centuries of European history, long phases of quite stable and relatively unchanging anti-Jewish patterns of prejudice can be contrasted with more dramatic watersheds or short periods of crisis, when the traditional archetypes have tended to fragment under stress and pass through a major restructuring and reformulation, before those new ways of seeing, in turn, became stable and enduring. Such a point of transition emerged during the 1870s and gave rise to a type of anti-Semitic racism that was to remain dominant in its new formulations down to the present.

This transformation can be analysed as a shift from a centuries-old *anti-Judaism*, that was fundamentally religious in meaning and 'pre-modern', to a new *anti-Semitism* that, in keeping with a secular age, constructed Jewish difference through the biological and naturalizing categories of racial science. However, the racialization of anti-Jewish discourse, the

86

adoption by propagandists of a scientific language of difference, was one element within a complex ideology that was essentially an expression of the anti-modernist and anti-democratic sentiments of social groups faced with crisis (conservative Christians, decaying aristocratic land-owners, the *petite bourgeoisie*, small shopkeepers and artisans in decline) and which integrated a vast range of concerns, from xenophobia and radical nationalism to nostalgia for the passing of a traditional rural order. Anti-Semitism as a form of racism can only be made sense of if it is placed within this broader context.

This chapter is divided into two parts: firstly, anti-Semitism is con-sidered as an *ideology* that was formulated, primarily through print, by propagandists, writers, politicians, academics and other members of the educated élite. This generalized form of ideological anti-Semitism, like other currents of race science, could be found right across Europe and sharing the same basic themes and constructions, regardless of the spe-cific national, social, economic and political contexts. The second part then examines the social and political forms of anti-Semitism and the extent to which the ideological formulations filtered down and influ-enced the attitudes and behaviour of a wider public. Here, we need to look more closely at the specific national contexts. Since the general processes of modernization (from industrialization and urbanization to banking and agrarian reform) and the related crises of transformation varied enormously across Europe, so did the national and regional contexts within which anti-Semitism took root. The question of the varying national formulations of anti-Semitism and the depth of their impact on society from the 1870s onwards will be examined in relation to three geographic zones that exemplify the key types and range of anti-Semitic development, from the more advanced industrialized liberal democracies of Western Europe (Britain and France), through a central constellation (Germany and Austria), to the underdeveloped peasant societies and autocracies of Eastern Europe (Poland and Russia).

Anti-Semitism as Ideology

The first part examines the general features of anti-Semitism as an ideol-ogy, as a system of thought relating to the political, economic and social order. At one level of analysis, anti-Semitic works appear to be hope-lessly confused, contradictory, irrational, and therefore lacking in the internal consistency that historians of ideas normally expect to find within a 'rational' system of political thought. For example, Jews were seen as both the key agents of capitalism (bankers, stock-market traders) as well as of revolutionary socialist organizations that sought to overturn capitalism; Jews were hated for trying to assimilate into gentile society as well as for remaining apart; the Jews were accused of promoting scientific materialism that undermined religious faith and also acting as diabolic agents, a dark and occult force that remained loyal to the Talmud and to the 'blood libel', the ritual murder of Christian children. Underlying such apparent and often puerile inconsistency lay an inner unity and cohesion: as Stephen Wilson notes: 'It was a system of belief that provided a total explanation of a supposed state of cosmic and social decadence by identifying the Jews as the evil agents of that dislocation and decay.'[1] Anti-Semitism was highly attractive precisely to the extent that it could 'resolve' the contradictions and tangled confusions of modernity through oversimplifying, universal causes that could appear quite cogent to 'common-sense' opinion. It was able to provide a total explanation for every conceivable ill in modern society through the 'diabolical causality' of a great Jewish conspiracy that was, from behind the scenes, intent on achieving global domination through the control and manipulation of entire national economies and political systems. As Urbain Gohier explained in *The Jewish Terror*: 'Watchwords launched by the heads of the Jewish nation in whatever part of the world they find themselves are transmitted, heard, and obeyed immediately in every country; and countless obscure and irresistible forces immediately prepare for the desired effect, the triumph or ruin of a government, an institution, an enterprise, or a man.'[2]

The central characteristic of such a 'paranoid' ideology is that it could always 'prove' that any misfortune was the work of Jews, even in the absence of any evidence. Indeed, the very absence of proof was itself seen as an indication of the insidious and diabolic power of the Jews to suppress the truth, particularly through the ownership and control of the press by Jewish magnates and journalists. It was in the very nature of such 'paranoid' forms of thought that they were not open to critical evaluation by the normal standards of proof. Conspiracy theory enabled anti-Semites to present a single cause for every great and petty hatred in society, from dislike of modern art and feminism to fears of moral decline and degeneration. When the carpets of the anti-Semitic propagandist Edouard Drumont were soaked in January 1910 by the Seine in flood, he found the inevitable answer: upstream from Paris, he claimed, extensive deforestation had destroyed the natural cover and the retention of rainwater. This destruction was the work of greedy and ruthless Jewish entrepreneurs. This instance provides an example of the way in which modern anti-Semitism reformulated traditional and age-old stereotypes of the Jew as the rapacious and anti-social exploiter into a pseudo-scientific, rationalist discourse of natural causation that fitted in with modern secular perceptions of the world. The popular appeal of anti-Semitism was precisely the fact that it offered clear and simple answers to extremely complex and disturbing questions, from the causes of unemployment and economic depression to rising crime and immorality. As Michel Winock notes, herein lay the very modernity of anti-Semitism in that, in a new age of the 'masses', it knew how to capture the people's attention through providing a simplification and fictional *why* for the misfortunes of the world: 'An action cannot be grounded in too subtle or too nuanced an analysis of the living context; in contrast, it becomes a rallying cry if it is based on a universal causality and a mythological system of representation that allows people to bypass the rational approach.'[3]

Anti-Semitism developed as a coherent ideology during a period of gestation from c.1860 down to the late 1880s and, by 1890, could be found in the works of numerous ideologues and propagandists, from Wilhelm Marr and Otto Glagau in Germany, to Széchenyi and Istoczy in Hungary, Schonerer in Austria, and Drumont in France. The similarity in the key ideas across Europe arose from the fact that anti-Semitism was international in scope: major thinkers readily borrowed ideas from one another, while the First and the Second Anti-Jewish Congresses at Dresden (1882) and Chemnitz (1883) saw the direct contact of representatives from Germany, Austria, Hungary, Russia, Romania, Serbia and France. Anti-Semitism was fully formed as a system of ideas by 1890, and very little new was later added to the ideological formulations that remained largely unchanged between the late nineteenth century and the present day. In the following section the structures of this anti-Semitism are analysed with reference to five major themes relating to the economy, religion, nationalism, decadence and biological racism.

Economic Anti-Semitism

The Jews had been viewed by European society for many hundreds of years as a group that was peculiarly adept at moneylending and commerce, and forms of usury and economic exploitation that were regarded as both unethical and parasitic on the main body of hard-working Christians who generated true wealth through hard labour. This traditional type of anti-Jewish sentiment was reformulated to fit in with an age in which the vast expansion in finance capitalism, the growth of modern banking, stock-exchange activity, paper money and currency manipulation was associated with all the worst aspects of uncontrolled capitalism. Both conservatives and socialists attacked the rise of enormously wealthy magnates, the accelerating oppression and exploitation of the working class and peasantry, and the creation of 'unearned' fortunes through cunning manipulation of money markets, speculation and fraud.

Anti-Semitism drew much of its critique of contemporary capitalism from socialism and Marxism, but whereas the latter, in spite of hints of an anti-Jewish bias, interpreted exploitation fundamentally in terms of class interest and the relations of production, the former placed a much stronger emphasis on the primary function of the Jews. For the anti-Semites, the Jews were the key driving force behind all forms of rapacious capital-ism, able to exert a frightening and growing stranglehold over the world's economy through an international network of financiers. The perceived enormous wealth of Jews connected directly to their ability to monopolize the press, control public opinion, ruin and displace the ancient landed aristocracy, and, as *nouveaux riches*, to flaunt themselves as owners of great country estates and as patrons of high-society restaur-ants, theatres and social networks, from which they would have been previously excluded. This anti-capitalist position of anti-Semitism enabled it to make an appeal to diverse groups and interests that were losing out in the crisis of modernization, small peasants, artisans and landed gentry, who were going under, and members of the bourgeoisie, who lost money in the stock-market crashes like that of 1873 or found entry to the professions (law, medicine, journalism) increasingly competitive and difficult.

Religious Anti-Semitism

The religious roots of anti-Semitism were ancient. Traditional anti-Jewish prejudice had been inspired since the origins of Christianity by a world-view that had made the Jewish people, as Goncourt claimed, 'a race bespattered with the blood of a God',[4] and collectively guilty of the worst crime imaginable. Jews, it was thought, were commanded by their religion to subvert, abuse and defile everything that was held most holy by Christians, and the age-old persecution of the Jews was fuelled by rumours of symbolic inversion of the sacred, desecration of the host and the 'blood libel' or ritual murder of gentile children at Passover. Such traditional forms of anti-Jewish belief, far from disappearing in the later nineteenth century, were integrated into the new anti-Semitic movements. Where the potential mass audience was still most profoundly religious, as in the Catholic populations of rural France, Germany, Austria and Poland or Orthodox Russia, anti-Semitic agitators emphasized the old crude themes of Jewish diabolic intent. But, in general, religious anti-Semitism was marked by a major restructuring and the 'modernization' of its discourse.

Traditional anti-Jewish prejudice was tempered and moderated by the paradoxical belief that the Jews were an essential component of Christian eschatology in which the Second Coming of Christ depended on their conversion. The mission of the Church was the conversion of the Jews and orthodoxy maintained that after baptism the Jew became a full member of the Christian faith and community. This doctrine was at odds with modern racism which was built on the idea of radical difference: each race was so fixed in its essential characteristics that it was impossible for individuals to cross over the divide and assimilate into another group. While racism formulated radical exclusion mainly through biological and 'scientific' theory, religious anti-Semitism achieved an identical goal through cultural formulations and the precept that the Jew remained a Jew even after conversion. Baptism of the Jews was as effective, it was claimed, as 'trying to wash a blackamoor white'.

Emancipated and assimilated Jews in Western Europe during the course of the nineteenth century had become closely associated with a dynamic liberal culture that placed a high value on education, intellect, scientific thought and progress. The Church, which by the late nineteenth century was in crisis and facing the challenge of secularism, scientific explanation of the universe, socialism and militant anti-clericalism, portrayed the Jews as engaged in a war against Christianity, the agents of a subversive rationalist tradition that originated in the Enlightenment and the French Revolution. Anti-Semitism endowed Jews with an essential way of thinking, a 'corrosive intellect', that was materialistic and profoundly opposed to the Christian world-view and to spiritual values. Religious anti-Semitism was able to find a single scapegoat and explanation for the huge weight of complex, modernizing forces, from industrialization and urbanization to rural decline and the collapse of traditional hierarchies and values, that did, in reality, present an enormous threat to the Church. However, while the Church was in crisis by the turn of the century, it still held an enormous influence and used its considerable power over public opinion, through the pulpit, Church schools and Catholic mass-circulation newspapers, to disseminate anti-Semitism.

Degeneration and Anti-Semitism

A third strand in anti-Semitism relates to the theme of decadence and degeneration. As we saw in Chapter 1, European bourgeois society in the late nineteenth century was profoundly suffused with a sense of morbidity, decay and cultural pessimism. While modern racism began to analyse this in terms of Social Darwinism and biological deterioration, this anxiety also found expression through anti-Semitism. Traditional anti-Judaism had, since the pogroms of the Middle Ages, portrayed the Jews as a dangerous internal enemy which insidiously threatened the very life-force of Christian society through the poisoning of wells and the deliberate spreading of the plague. Increasingly through the nineteenth century, anti-Jewish discourse was peppered with images or metaphors of the Jews as a monstrous fungus, a parasitic growth that fed upon the healthy body of the host society, finally reducing it to an emaciated and sickly shell. This age-old paranoia was taken on board by modern anti-Semitism, but, once again, we find that the traditional formulations were increasingly expressed through a secular and scientific language. The Jew was viewed in biological terms as a race that carried tainted and diseased blood in its veins, a source of dangerous 'bacilli', of venereal disease and vague but horrifying germs, that threatened to infect European society. Exclusion of the Jews, the construction of a barrier against social contact and intermarriage, was expressed through a language of pathology that played upon the profound and often irrational anxiety of contemporary society towards sexual disease and 'degenerative' illness. The rather nebulous, and thus all-inclusive, concept of 'degeneration' also extended to the closely interlinking concepts of physical health and morality. The Jews were viewed as the major organizers of prostitution and the white slave trade, and anti-Semitic texts betrayed an exaggerated and lurid prurience, a heated sexual fantasizing about the Other, a mixture of sexual loathing and fascination, that equated Jews with moral corruption, physical deformity and disease.

Nationalism and Anti-Semitism

A fourth component in anti-Semitism was related to a deepening form of 'closed' or exclusionary nationalism that sought to define itself, the concept of a homogeneous and cohesive group identity, over and against the threat posed by an internal 'alien' presence. Throughout late nineteenth-century Europe nationalism assumed an increasingly conservative and aggressive form that was partly linked to the insecurities of deepening international tensions and anxieties about the security or integrity of the nation-state. Nationalist ideologies, rooted in romanticism and conservative traditionalism, emphasized the idea that membership of the homeland could only be acquired through descent from countless generations of forebears, from the ancient *Volk*, or people who carried the culture, language and spiritual values of the nation in their 'blood'. In opposition to xenophobic nationalism the Jews were seen as profoundly alien, a dangerous and subversive 'foreign' element lodged within the territory and fabric of society. Jews, it was thought, constituted a 'nomadic race' that had no roots, no sense of belonging, and since they clung to their own ancestral customs and religion, they constituted a 'state within the state'. In an age when patriotism and sacrifice for country was infused with powerful religious feeling, the Jew was perceived as a profound danger, a person who owed primary allegiance to his own race-nation. In particular, nationalist anti-Semitism targeted the Jews as 'cosmopolitan', members of an international network or 'nation' of Semites whose perfidious goal was the subversion, weakening and destruction of the homeland, through the control of global finance, the organisation of Marxist revolution, or the fomentation of destructive wars between states. The paranoid image of the Jew as the 'enemy within' was to find expression in countless spying panics, of which the Dreyfus affair was the most famous, or in challenges to the patriotism and reliability of Jewish soldiers during times of national crisis or war.

Although, for purposes of analysis, the various strands of economic, religious, degenerative and nationalistic anti-Semitism have so far been treated separately, in reality the standard discourse wove all these elements into a powerful, cross-referential matrix. Endless numbers of texts could be quoted to illustrate the typical 'flavour' and structure of anti-Semitic discourse, but here a single passage from a newspaper of 1891 will suffice to show how the themes of parasitism, destructive capitalism, global conspiracy and anti-nationalism were typically woven together.

The Rothschild leeches have for years hung on with distended suckers to the body politic of Europe. This family of infamous usurers, the foundation of whose fortunes was laid deep in the mire of cheating and scoundrelism, has spread itself out over Europe like a network. It is a gigantic conspiracy manifold and comprehensive. There is a Rothschild – a devoted member of the family – in every capital of Europe. Vienna, St Petersburg, Paris, London, Berlin, are each and all garrisoned and held for family purposes by members of this gang. This blood-sucking crew has been the cause of untold mischief and misery in Europe during the present century, and has piled up its prodigious wealth chiefly through fomenting wars between States which ought never to have quarrelled.[5]

Here the Rothschilds were seen as not only a hideous and monstrous growth, a parasite that reached across Europe, but also as the instigators of international conflict and war which, through putting nation-states at each other's throats, simultaneously weakened these societies while making huge profits at their expense. Such Jews could obviously have no sense of national identity, of patriotism or belonging.

Scientific Racism and Anti-Semitism

The fifth and final element to be considered is the specifically racist component in anti-Semitic ideology. The term anti-Semitism, which was a neologism probably first used by Wilhelm Marr in 1879 and which certainly gained currency in the same year through the foundation of the German Anti-Semitic League, was specifically racial in its formulation since it referred to the Semites, a group that was defined by contemporary scholars as a people of the Middle East who were biologically and linguistically quite distinct from the European 'Aryan'. The new term, which spread very rapidly into popular usage, marked a shift from traditional forms of anti-Jewish prejudice that were fundamentally religious, to a type that was based on scientific criteria. Anti-Semitism appealed much more readily to a secular age in which historical and social phenomena were interpreted through a rational and scientific approach that included physical anthropology, material culture, evolution, geography, climate and linguistics. Racial anti-Semitism facilitated an ideological position, freed from the restraints of Christianity, that erected a radical barrier between immutable groups that were locked into their physical and mental differences. Drumont, in *La France Juif* (1886) – a work of enormous influence that by 1914 had attained 200 editions – presented history as an endless conflict between the enthusiastic, heroic, disinterested Aryan and the money-grasping, scheming, clever and deceitful Semite. He reflected the new thinking in describing his work as 'an ethnographical, physiological and psychological comparison of the Semite and the Aryan, these two personifications of races that are distinct and irremediably hostile to each other'.[6] The Belgian anti-Semite Picard also wrote in 1892 of this essential biological difference:

> Of race one can say that it is IRREVOCABLE. . . . It is not altered by any change of milieu; it persists: it is always there, like one of those mineral poisons, which, once introduced into an organism, can never escape analysis. . . With whatever disguise a Semite living among us may masquerade, he will remain himself, in his body, and more so in his soul. Should he interbreed with one of us, his Semitic blood will affect all his issue; we know enough about heredity for this point not to be insisted upon.[7]

Racial anti-Semitism showed a profound ambiguity towards the Jews. The Jews of Europe in the late nineteenth century could be divided, in a rough and ready way, into two main types: in Eastern Europe the Orthodox, Yiddish-speaking and highly traditional Hasidic Jews, often living in ghetto conditions of considerable poverty, were immediately recognizable by their dress, culture and language. By contrast, in Western Europe emancipation and upward social mobility had led to a remarkable integration of Jews. Many had converted or abandoned all signs of Jewish observance, and were completely indistinguishable in physical appearance and culture from their fellow British, French or German citizens. Anti-Semitism delighted in its gross caricatures of the so-called *Ostjuden* or Orthodox Jews who moved westwards in their hundreds of thousands in the 1880s to escape Russian persecution. The Orthodox or 'ghetto' Jew enabled anti-Semites to deploy the most grotesque, traditional images of the Jew as an immediately recognizable physical type, invariably dirty, repulsive, hook-nosed and yellow-skinned, like Dickens' Fagin who, distinguishable by his kaftan and red beard, 'seemed like some loathsome reptile, engendered in the slime and darkness through which he moved: crawling forth, by night, in search of some rich offal for a meal'.[8]

By contrast, what was profoundly disturbing to anti-Semites about the integrated Western Jews, was that they could not be spontaneously identified in a crowd, and it was this very invisibility that rendered the Jew a far more dangerous and frightening presence, operating secretively and destructively within the bowels of society. Richard Wagner described the assimilated Jew as a master of disguises, 'a plastic demon', and 'His physiognomy and form changes. He conceals himself, he slips through the fingers like an eel. Today he wears Court livery and tomorrow drapes himself in a red flag . . . one doesn't recognize him; unnoticed he invades all circles.'[9] The modernizing Jew was, ironically, far more disliked than the Orthodox and highly traditional Jew; an antipathy that arose from the fact that it was the assimilating Jews, highly educated and ambitious, who presented a major challenge to the Gentile domination of both the universities and employment in the professions (particularly in medicine, the law and journalism), in banking and commerce, the civil service and political office. The contradiction between an anti-Semitism which attacked Jews for their refusal to abandon tradition and to assimilate and an anti-Semitism that attacked the Jews for denying their ancient roots and modernizing was resolved by the usual conspiracy theory. The French anti-Semite Gougenot de Mousseaux claimed in 1869 that the split between Orthodox and Reform Jews was a cunning strategy for world domination: the first group, the 'indestructible nucleus of the nation' would retain the Talmudic way of life, while the latter were sent out as emissaries to penetrate and subvert the Gentile world from within.[10]

The problem faced by the anti-Semites was how to 'contain' the Jews, how to halt and reverse the gains made possible by emancipation, and to find techniques that would enable the identification of the 'invisible', their symbolic marking, and their exclusion from the nation and *Volk*. The problem here was that the modern Jews, those that offered the greatest challenge, could no longer be readily identified through religion. The growth of a racial anti-Semitism from the 1870s onwards was in part an attempt to reconstruct and reassert ethnic hierarchies that were rapidly distintegrating, to rebuild and reinforce breached defences that would keep the enemy outside. Scientific racism presented itself as a rational technique of identification: the Jew might try to disguise himself as one of 'us', by conversion, change of family name and other 'ruses', but his true nature was irrevocably stamped in biology, to be revealed by the scalpel, the microscope and the anthropologist's callipers.

However, the prime logic of racial anti-Semitism, to demarcate the Jew as irredeemably Other, could find expression through cultural and literary forms, as well as biological science. For example, in a macabre short story by Oscar Panizza, *The Operated Jew* (1893), the grotesque anti-hero, the Jew Itzig Faitel Stern, posseses all the most exaggerated and absurd qualities of the traditional anti-Semitic stereotype: he is deformed and twisted, bow-legged and diseased, has thick black locks, fleshy lips, a hooked nose, yellowish goggle eyes, speaks with a nasal twang and 'a rich amount of saliva', and presents the spectacle of a 'monster', a 'dreadful piece of human flesh'. Stern spends his fortune on a complex and painful 'psycho-physical operation', a medical transformation or plastic surgery, that will transform him into a good German: his twisted bones are broken and reset by surgeons, his hair bleached golden by drugs, his Yiddish accent removed by speech therapy, and his 'Jewish blood' is totally replaced through a transfusion of blood from strong peasant women. Itzig, now Siegfried Freudenstein, 'passes' as a Gentile and marries a blonde German girl. But at the wedding feast he gets drunk and grotesquely reverts to 'racial type', his nasal voice returns, his face becomes sensual and fleshy, his eyelids droop, his hair begins to curl and changes from blond to red, then to dirty brown and jet black, and he begins 'clicking his tongue, gurgling, and tottering back and forth while making disgusting, lascivious and bestial canine movements with his rear end'. The bride and guests flee from the 'counterfeit of human flesh'. Apart from the strong undertow of sexual prurience, the horror of miscegenation and racial pollution, the story is a powerful assertion of the inescapable physical and psychological difference of the Jew – a difference that is constructed through a naturalistic vocabulary and 'scientific' racial scrutiny.[11]

So far we have looked at anti-Semitism mainly in terms of ideas, but intellectual history alone can tell us very little about the wider causes of anti-Jewish racism and how and why particular social groups were drawn towards such sentiments. What was distinctive about the new form of anti-Semitism that emerged from the 1870s was not only its ideological 'shape', but the fact that these ideas were elaborated simultaneously by ever-widening circles of ideologues and political propagandists until they became a common currency. The following exploration of the map of anti-Semitism, based on the three 'constellations' of Central, Eastern and Western Europe, begins with an examination of the Central area represented by Germany and Austria. Both countries shared similar features of late but rapid industrialization, fragile liberalism, rising German nationalism, a remarkable ascent of Jews into financial and professional circles, and the organization of the most significant anti-Semitic political parties prior to the First World War.

Anti-Semitism in Germany and Austria

Contrary to expectation, the number of Jews in Germany was not particularly high, rising from 512 153 in 1871 to 615 021 in 1910, figures that, as a percentage of total population, actually represented a decline from 1.13 per cent to 1.07 per cent. Within Austria (leaving aside the sprawling multi-ethnic Habsburg Empire), Jews numbered about 180 000 in 1910 or 2.5 per cent of total population. Despite these relatively low, and even stagnant numbers, anti-Semitism between 1870 and 1914 was in part fuelled by growing Jewish visibility, a perception of a rapid increase in numbers and power, and anxiety that they were set to 'conquer' the Germanic peoples. The visibility or prominence of the Jews arose from three factors. Firstly, there was a growing internal migration of Jews from poor, rural areas into the major cities, where they often became concentrated in slums. Secondly, political persecution of the Jews in Russia and desperate poverty in Eastern Europe led, after 1881, to an enormous westward flow of Jewish refugees. Although only 70 000 were allowed to settle in Germany – most of the diaspora of 2 750 000 Jews crossed the Atlantic – there was a deep anxiety that Jews would pour over the borders from Poland and Russia where 75 per cent of the world's Jewish population was located. The Jewish population of Vienna grew dramatically from 6000 in 1857 to 175 318 in 1910, most of them refugees from Galicia. The Eastern Jews, with their distinctive dress and language, appeared as a barbaric throwback to the most primitive anti-Semitic stereotypes. In 1879 the influential historian Treitschke warned of the dangers of an invasion of Posen by 'all the filth in Polish history. There was nothing German about these people with their stinking caftans and their obligatory lovelocks, except their detestable mongrel speech.'[12]

However, for the anti-Semite, by far the most threatening Jewish presence arose not from the impoverished and alien *Ostjuden*, but from the 'rise' of the highly westernized assimilated Jews. The period from 1850 down to 1871 had been a 'golden age' for German Jews; they were widely tolerated and, even before the German Emancipation Law of 1869 removed all limitations, they had taken full advantage of new-found acceptance and opportunities in order to forge ahead. The Jewish community, with its highly literate culture, achieved a remarkable degree of upward social mobility through educational achievement and entry into the professions, particularly medicine, law, journalism and finance. The dynamic rise of the Jews led to their 'over-representation' in many sectors, where they constituted a percentage that was much higher than their presence in the overall population. In Prussia for every 100 000 Jewish males 519 went into higher education, while for Catholics and Protestants the figure was 33 and 58 respectively. The competition from Jews, at a time of over-provision of graduates, led to an anti-Semitic backlash in student and professional associations, and moves to impose quotas or a total exclusion.

During the course of the nineteenth century the Jews, in their battle for emancipation, had become closely allied with political and economic liberalism, the advance of parliamentary democracy, the extension of civil rights, equality before the law, and overall values of rationalism and progress. In Central and Eastern Europe it was the historic weakness of the bourgeoisie, linked to late industrialization, that had given the Jews such a prominent role as modernizers, as investors and industrialists. During the late nineteenth century the Jews came under increasing attack as the symbol of modernizing forces, of the rapid industrialization and urbanization that appeared to be destroying traditional society. Unlike Britain and France, where the industrial revolution had started much earlier and evolved gradually, Germany and Austria were affected by an accelerated and more traumatic pace of change. Germany, in particular, faced the tensions and upheavals produced in a traditional society by an almost unprecedented advance in new technologies, backed by capitalist finance. The anti-Semitic political parties that began to appear from 1879 onwards were able to recruit among urban groups that were in crisis as a result of the stock-market crash of 1873 and the following economic depression that lasted until 1896. Typical victims of change were the small shopkeepers of Berlin and Vienna who blamed their problems on Jewish-owned department stores and retailers, or the artisans and self-employed who could not compete with large-scale, industrial enterprise. Anti-Semitic propagandists shared much of the socialist critique of capitalism as an exploitative and inhumane system, but crucially blamed the Jews, rather than class relations, for the crisis which they were undergoing.

An interesting example of the links between economic modernization and the growth of populist anti-Semitism can be found among the peasants of Hessenland. German agriculture prospered between 1850 and 1870, but by 1871 Hessenland was undergoing a transition to capitalist forms of farming, linked to the penetration of railways and access to urban markets. The peasants who clung to the old open-field system faced depressed agricultural prices, indebtedness, bankruptcy and the loss of mortgaged lands. Jews played a major role in the region, as they did throughout Central and Eastern Europe, as cattle dealers, traders and moneylenders. Otto Böckel, the so-called 'peasant king', from 1885 began to establish an electoral base in Hesse through an anti-Semitic movement that blamed the 'evil' Jews for the farmers' plight and mobilized the peasantry through the use of modern propaganda techniques. Böckel established his own newspaper, organized mass meetings, torchlit rallies and songfests, set up credit co-operatives and legal advice centres, and built up a network of grass-roots activists through anti-Semitic clubs, the *Reformverein*. Through such modern and innovative techniques of mass party organization Böckel was able to gain a sensational victory in the 1887 election at Marburg.

The possibility of such mass politics was crucially dependent in Germany and Austria, as in so many other European states in the late nineteenth and early twentieth centuries, on the extension of the vote and, in this respect, modern anti-Semitism can be integrally linked with the extension of parliamentary democracy. Karl Lueger, the famous mayor of Vienna who so impressed the young Adolf Hitler, was able to build up a power-base in the city through a demagogic and opportunist anti-Semitism that appealed to the 'little man', the artisans, shopkeepers, clerks, teachers and minor functionaries who felt most threatened by Jewish competition. It was precisely this group, the 'five-florin men' who had been enfranchised in 1882 and who held the key to the control of Vienna, who were cultivated by Lueger's skilful populism.

Modern anti-Semitism was not, however, a phenomenon that found support solely among those groups that were facing economic and social crisis from the advance of industrial and financial capitalism. Of equal importance was the growth of reactionary and defensive forms of nationalism that appealed strongly to thriving and successful members of the middle and upper classes, to academics, lawyers, editors, writers, doctors and businessmen. In Germany from 1879 there was a distinct sea-change towards a conservative, 'closed' nationalism as Bismarck, faced with economic crisis, the rise of the Social Democratic Party and potential revolution, opted to resolve internal problems by channelling growing tensions into aggressive nationalism and social imperialism. It is no coincidence that at the very moment that German society was mobilizing against external dangers, it should also turn against the Jews as an alien, internal threat to national solidarity. A widespread view was that emancipation had been granted to Jews on condition that they become totally assimilated into society and an integral part of the nation, yet the

Jews, it was felt, showed a perverse tendency to retain their religious and cultural identity and sense of apartness.

Anti-Semitic writers marked a shift from an assimilatory discourse which insisted on the total 'disappearance' of the Jews through religious conversion, intermarriage and other forms of integration, to a racial language that emphasized the radical non-Germanness of Jews for which the only solution was physical exclusion or expulsion from the nation. Adopting the ideas of French racists like Gobineau and Drumont, or the *volkish* and anti-modernist romanticism of German nationalists like Paul de Lagarde and Julius Langbehn, and the Anglo-German Houston Stewart Chamberlain, the whole of history was interpreted as a constant race-warfare between the blond, heroic and inventive Aryans and the parasitic, cowardly and destructive Jews. The ideal of a strong and spiritual German *volk* was associated with an ancient bloodstock and organic community which was rooted in the soil, the forests and landscape. It was precisely the life of the peasantry and of venerable cathedral cities, so powerfully evoked in contemporary Romantic literature and arts, that was thought to be most threatened by the corrosive forces of capitalism, industrialism and the soulless materialism orchestrated by cosmopolitan Jewry. In the late nineteenth century the boundaries of the German 'race' were increasingly seen as identical with the boundaries of the nation, and this aggressive national-racism fed into the Austrian pan-German movement led by the anti-Semitic agitator Georg Ritter von Schonerer, and into the Pan-German League.

Historians are in disagreement as to the impact of anti-Semitism on German and Austrian society before the First World War. The various German anti-Semitic parties (the German Reformers, the German Socialists, and the Christian Socialists), having reached a peak with 16 seats in 1893 and 3.3 per cent of the vote, were in decline by 1896 and by 1914 – after 30 years – had not achieved one of their declared aims. Too many historians, looking for the roots of Nazism, have badly distorted our understanding of the past by selecting out all the most extreme examples of anti-Semitism from before the First World War, while neglecting the considerable forces arrayed against it. In Germany and Austria before 1914 *political* anti-Semitism was restricted in scope by a number of factors. Firstly, the dominant forces of conservatism, wedded to authoritarianism and traditional élitism, were horrified by the growth of the new forms of populist anti-Semitic mobilization and the activities of rabble-rousing demagogues were seen as dangerous and as distasteful as Socialism. More crucially the Wilhelmine state, as well as Austria under the rule of Emperor Franz Josef, upheld the rule of law in the defence of Jews and deployed its power to contain and restrict anti-Semitism. For example, the Civil Service Decree of 1892 forbade state officials, and especially teachers, from being active in the anti-Semitic parties, while between 1893 and 1915 the public prosecutor brought 537 individuals to trial for anti-Semitism. The enormously powerful Social Democratic Party, while it had individual members tainted by hostility to Jews, maintained a solid opposition to anti-Semitism and prevented it taking deep root in the working class. Many members of the middle class only confided their anti-Semitism in private letters and diaries, a sure indication that the open expression of prejudice was still felt to be socially unacceptable in educated circles.

In spite of this limited success of anti-Semitism, which surged and declined with the onset and end of the great depression of 1873–96, there exists a broad consensus among historians that all the essential ideas of inter-war anti-Semitism were already fully developed between 1870 and 1914 and also widely diffused into German and Austrian culture. Before 1914 it seems likely that specifically scientific and biological forms of racial anti-Semitism were made almost universally available (although not necessarily accepted) by the middle-class and working-class 'intelligentsia', through a vast array of propaganda sources, from newspapers and novels to the activities of nationalist organizations like the Pan-German League, the Navy League, the Agrarian League and the Army League. Evidence for the relationship between elaborated forms of racial anti-Semitism and popular culture can be provided by Otto Böckel's farmers' movement in Hessenland. In a pamphlet of 1887, *The Jews, Kings of Our Time*, which became a classic of anti-Semitism, Böckel set out to expose appalling cases of Jewish usury and exploitation of the peasantry. In his *volkish* idealization of rural life, the 'way of our ancestors', and of the destructiveness of the Jews, he presented the latter in pseudo-scientific terms as 'a tenacious, ancient race that is remote from our own and that cannot be disposed of through baptism or mixed marriage ... an alien race that thinks differently, feels differently, and acts differently from us'.[13] However, Böckel, who had a superb feel for the culture and mentality of the peasantry, modified the more sophisticated and overtly racist language that he directed towards an educated middle-class audience for a more populist discourse when he addressed the peasantry. In his campaigning newspaper the *Reichherold*, he replaced a scientific form of racism with one that appealed more to the traditional Christian anti-Judaism of the farmers. The rhetoric of anti-Semitic ideologues could take on a pseudo-scientific or naturalistic expression without having to be formulated in a technical way: for example, in 1893 the Bavarian Catholic priest and politician Georg Ratzinger stated with Social Darwinian overtones: 'Parasitism can no more be tolerated in commercial life than in nature. If it is not stopped, it will overrun all other higher forms of life.'[14] A further example of the way in which racial anti-Semitism filtered downwards from 'high' into popular culture by an almost invisible, but powerful osmosis is provided by Hitler's account in *Mein Kampf* of his early days as an unemployed down-and-out in Vienna.

The fragmentation and ineffectiveness of organized political anti-Semitism in Germany and Vienna prior to 1914 led its opponents to underestimate its force. In 1906 the Socialist leader Bebel remarked of anti-Semitism: 'It is consoling that it has no prospect of ever exercising a decisive influence on political and social life in Germany.'[15] Anti-Semitism was, however, slowly finding its way into the organizations of students, teachers, judges and other professional groups; into the Protestant and Catholic Churches; nationalist leagues; as well as into a myriad of propaganda outlets, from novels and newspapers to theatres and popular clubs. Anti-Semitism was endemic, not so much as a set of abstract ideas or intellectual choices, but rather as a complex of feelings, prejudices and thoughts such that the simple word 'Jew' immediately triggered a set of associations, of hostility and revulsion, ranging from fears that German identity was endangered by 'cosmopolitanism' and revolutionary socialism to deep anxieties about parasitic capitalism, materialism, feminism, homosexuality, social reform, treachery, miscegenation and racial degeneration. In an inverse direction, the radical anti-Semitic propagandist Theodor Fritsch was capable of making lengthy speeches without once mentioning the Jews by name, by utilizing a standard lexicon that was known to all. The word 'Jew' thus became a metaphor for everything that was most 'un-German' and it was this 'mind-set', entrenched within culture and language in the late nineteenth century, that was transmitted forward into the First World War and an apocalyptic era of mechanized killing, revolution and the radical dislocation of all economic and social certainties.

Anti-Semitism in Eastern Europe

During the last two decades of the nineteenth century most educated opinion would have immediately associated the most violent and pernicious anti-Semitism not with Germany, Austria and France, but with Tzarist Russia, where a wave of bloody pogroms first erupted in 1881–2, and then on an even larger scale in 1903–6. Turning to an analysis of the East European constellation of anti-Semitism, attention is concentrated on Imperial Russia, which included 'Congress Poland' that was annexed by the late eighteenth-century partitions, although similar conditions could be found in Romania, Bulgaria, Serbia and Hungary. Jews were largely excluded from the heartland of the Empire, including Moscow and St Petersburg, where they made up 0.1 per cent of the population. In 1881 the four million Jews of Imperial Russia were concentrated in the Pale of Settlement (2.9 million people or 12.5 per cent of the total population) and in Polish territories (1 million people or 13.8 per cent of the population). By 1897 numbers had increased to 5.2 million, or half of the world's total Jewish population, concentrated in one of the most poverty-stricken and underdeveloped areas in Europe.

As in Germany, anti-Semitism grew in response to the profound economic and political tensions of modernization, as market forces penetrated the almost feudal agrarian society, while a late and explosive industrialization in the major cities led to mass inward migration and the creation of a volatile proletariat. However, the situation was quite different in that anti-Semitism was barely influenced by the ideological and scientific racist forms that emerged in Western Europe, but was expressed in terms of the traditional Catholic and Orthodox anti-Judaism of an ignorant, superstitious peasantry. The 1881–2 pogroms, while linked to a crisis of modernization, had more in common with the collective murderous assaults of Medieval or pre-industrial Europe than they did with the type of political anti-Semitism found in the West. The archaic structure of anti-Judaism can be shown by the fact that outbreaks of violence were invariably fuelled by traditional religious beliefs in the eternal role of the Jews as persecutors of Christ, perpetrators of the most evil acts of desecration and subversion of the Christian order.

Enlightened West European opinion was appalled by the resurgence of Medieval forms of irrational prejudice and rumour, that Jews had poisoned the wells of Christians or engaged in the infamous 'blood libel', the ritual murder of Christian children at the Passover and the use of their blood to bake *matzoh*. Pogroms frequently erupted during the celebrations of Holy Week, a time of popular revelry and mass drunkenness, when religious parades through the streets reminded people of the role of Jews in killing Christ. The infamous 1903 massacre at Kishinev, a town of 147 000 people with a volatile ethnic mix of Jews (50 000), Bulgarians, Serbs, Greeks, Macedonians, Albanians and Germans, followed on from the murder of a boy which was presented by both the Greek Bishop and the anti-Semitic newspaper *Bessarabia* as a ritual killing. As Jews celebrated Passover on Sunday 19 April a mob of labourers, carpenters, draymen and peasants began two days of looting and murder that left 47 Jews dead, 424 wounded and 1300 houses and shops burned or gutted.

What motivated such outbursts of collective rage? In the isolated rural areas and small towns the Jews performed a traditional role as commercial middlemen, as traders, shop and innkeepers, and moneylenders. Under the quasi-feudal *arenda* system in Poland Jews operated as agents of the lords, taking over the commercial running of estates and distilling vodka, which was a noble monopoly. Orthodox Jews were absolutely distinct from Christians, in their Yiddish language and appearance (black coats, beards, white stockings, *peyes* side-locks) and no intermarriage took place with Gentiles, but in spite of the sharp ethnic divide between each community the daily trading contacts were reasonably amicable. Farmers recognized that Jews played an important and useful economic function. However, the growth of a money economy and the penetration of modern commercial practices into the countryside drove increasing numbers of peasants into debt. Although the great majority of Jews were as poor as the Poles and Russians with whom they lived in a symbiotic relationship, deepening economic crisis led growing numbers of farmers to see the Jews as the instigators and profiteers of the deeper processes of capitalist transformation that were in reality beyond their control. As tensions mounted, the peasants were able to articulate their hatred through age-old proverbs, such as, 'Every Jew a thief', 'Every Jew is a usurer', 'You torture me like Jews tortured our Lord', or 'A baptized Jew, a domesticated wolf and a painted maiden are equally worthless'.[16]

However, the most explosive tensions and related pogroms were urban phenomena, a result of the most profound economic transformation. The more traditional the economy, the more important was the role of the Jews in the absence of an indigenous bourgeoisie capable of developing modern commercial and financial systems. In the more enlightened atmosphere that predominated in Russia after 1857 Jews made rapid advances in the towns, becoming more visible through their economic role, the opening of stores, warehouses, banks and factories. In Odessa, for example, Jews grew from 14 000 in 1858 (14 per cent of the total population) to 140 000 in 1897 (35 per cent of population), and by the turn of the century owned half the large stores, trading firms and shops; 35 per cent of factories; and controlled 70 per cent of the export trade in grain. The Jews, in such a situation, easily fell victim to a major pogrom in 1905 during which a lumpen-proletariat of extremely poor dock workers, day labourers and rural migrants indiscriminately murdered 800 men, women and children.

The traditional interpretation of such bloody pogroms is that they were deliberately orchestrated by the Tzarist government which, by making the Jews a scapegoat, was channelling the explosive and revolutionary forces in Imperial Russia away from the regime. There can be no doubt about the virulent anti-Semitism of the Imperial court, the flavour of which is conveyed in a letter from the reactionary Minister of the Interior, Pobyedonostzev, to Dostoyevski in 1879: 'The Yids...have invaded everything...They are at the root of the Social Democratic movement and tsaricide. They control the press and the stock market. They reduce the masses to financial slavery. They formulate the principles of contemporary science, which tends to dissociate itself from Christianity.'[17] However, the evidence suggests that the government played little part in deliberately fomenting pogroms since the Tzar and his ministers showed a profound fear of popular, mass actions, whether of left or right, that might get out of control. At the local level senior government officials and police officers did show some complicity in violence by their failure to act quickly and effectively against rioters.

Despite the fact that the autocracy viewed all political action and violence as a prerogative or monopoly of the state, the last decade of the nineteenth century did see the growth of new forms of political anti-Semitism in both Poland and Russia that were parallel to the development of mass political organizations in Western and Central Europe. Firstly, in Galicia (Poland) – where the rural population could vote for the first time in the 1890s – the Union of the Polish Peasant Party, founded in 1892 by the clergyman Stojalowski, mounted a strong anti-Semitic and national populist campaign. But more important in the long run was the National Democratic Party (the 'Endeks') founded in 1897 under Roman Dmowski. As will be seen later (Chapter 5), Dmowski whipped up a virulent anti-Semitism campaign after 1903 as a means of uniting Poles, formerly split by the Partition, into a national community by targeting Jews as an internal enemy.

In Russia reactionary and pro-monarchist forces found little space, within an autocratic system that rejected any form of independent political movements, whether of the left or of the right, to organize politically for the defence of a regime that was in terminal crisis. The basis for a large-scale political anti-Semitism only appeared with the crisis of 1905, the catastrophe of the war with Japan, and the Tzar's signing of the October Manifesto (30 October 1905) which opened the way to the dismantling of autocracy. Conservative élites, who felt profoundly threatened by industrialization, the penetration of Western competitive society, the dissolution of traditional peasant communities and the rise of revolutionary socialism, went on the offensive against the Jews by founding the Union of Russian People (November 1905) and a range of anti-Semitic leagues, unions and societies known collectively as the 'Black Hundreds'. The 'Hundreds', which tried to establish a mass political base among a decayed aristocracy, urban thugs, reactionary priests and a medley of 'little people' (shopkeepers, cabmen, traders, migrant peasants) who were suffering from unprecedented economic crisis and dislocation, called for the expulsion or 'extermination' of the Jews and orchestrated a wave of assassinations, violent strike-breaking and pogroms. Between late October 1905 and September 1906, the Black Hundreds helped to incite an unprecedented wave of violence and some 650 pogroms in which 3100 Jews were murdered.

Russian anti-Semitism was quite different from that in Western Europe. Firstly, before the collapse of autocracy in the Revolution of 1917, it was not possible to organize the same scale of political movements and parties that had appeared in the West after the 1870s, as the franchise was extended and parliamentary systems became more open. Secondly, very few Russian thinkers or ideologues attempted to develop the kind of scientific racism that was found so widely diffused in the West. A very small number of anti-Semites did have access to the works of German and French racists; for example in 1891 Ivan Aksakov invoked Darwin, claimed that money grubbing was a 'characteristic of the Semitic race', and asserted that Jews possessed innate racial characteristics.[18] Michael Menshikov and Tolstoy were influenced by the Anglo-German racist Houston Stewart Chamberlain. Educated élites did attempt to introduce Western forms of scientific racism or anthropology, but the endeavour remained very restricted since secular and scientific thought could have little appeal in such a traditional society in which a potential middle-class audience was so numerically weak. Anti-Semitic agitators also found to hand, in attempting to mobilize mass opinion, an enormously powerful, traditional and mainly religious form of Jew-hatred that saturated popular culture and which could be so readily mobilized. For example, a rabid tract that was printed in 1906 by the Black Hundreds on a secret printing press in the Police headquarters in St Petersburg, declaimed: 'Whenever those betrayers of Christ come near you, tear them to pieces, kill them.'[19]

Slavophile nationalism provided a much stronger ideological expression of anti-Semitism than scientific racism. Not dissimilar to the romantic, irrational *volkish* form of nationalism in Germany, it provided a sense of an organic, spiritual Russian community, deeply rooted in the native soil and *narod*, which resisted the 'putrid West' with its dangerous forces of materialism, atheism, corrosive rationalism, scientific technology and universal values. Anti-Semitic writers like Dostoyevsky and Danilevsky, in their belief that the Slav's historic destiny was to triumph over a decaying West, were motivated by a racist ideology. However, anti-Semitic hatred formulated in religious, ethnic or 'archaic' Medieval terms was just as capable as more 'modern', scientific forms in inciting large-scale violence. Russia also had a major impact on the formulation of modern anti-Semitism in Western Europe and the United States through the infamous forgery, *The Protocols of the Elders of Zion*, which diffused the powerful myth of a Jewish conspiracy for world domination.

Within the 'Eastern constellation' a brief mention of Hungary is important since it demonstrates the extent to which the potential for anti-Semitism could be constrained by social and political factors. By 1920 Hungary had a large Jewish population of 473 355 or 5.9 per cent of the total population, of which 45 per cent were massively concentrated in Budapest, where they constituted 23.2 per cent of the city population. As in Poland and Russia, Jews held a key economic position in commerce and finance as well as in the professions (50 per cent of all lawyers, 60 per cent of doctors, 34 per cent of editors and journalists). It was this geographic concentration of Jews, as well as their relatively large numbers in certain professions or sectors of the economy, that created a high level of visibility and the impression among non-Jews that their numbers were much greater than they were in reality. However, despite this classic Eastern position of Jews, there was a very low level of political anti-Semitism before the First World War. The ruling Magyar élites, concerned at being outnumbered within a complex, multinational Hungary, welcomed an alliance with the urban Jews who showed a West European pattern of assimilation, spoke Hungarian, regarded themselves as Magyars, and embraced Reform Judaism and modernization. Although Istóczy founded the National Anti-Semitic Party in 1883 and won 13 seats in the Hungarian Parliament, the government took a firm stand against anti-Semitism and the movement, deprived of oxygen, collapsed within a few years.

Anti-Semitism in Britain and France

Lastly, we turn to the West European constellation, exemplified by Britain and France. Although each of these nations was quite distinctive, what they had in common was a long history of state formation and an early, and more gradualist, industrial revolution, so that they were more mature and stable in their transition to liberal democracy than many countries further to the east. The number of Jews was small; by 1900 about 200 000 in Britain (or 0.5 per cent of total population), and a mere 75 000 in France (0.2 per cent of population), in the latter case only one-tenth of the German and one-hundredth of the Polish ratio. Thus, despite a flurry of anti-Semitic activity in Britain that centred on opposition to the arrival of 150 000 East European Jews after 1881, and in the French case corresponded to the height of the Dreyfus Affair (1897–1900), both – as mature parliamentary and liberal democratic states – were able to contain the threat of political anti-Semitism which, by 1905, had gone into retreat.

Britain can be looked at first and most briefly, since this represented the more straightforward of the two. Although Eastern Jews had been arriving in Britain as early as the 1840s, a dramatic increase in the number of refugees from Russia, Poland and Romania began in 1881, in response to persecution and economic misery. The concentration of extremely poor and highly distinctive Yiddish-speaking Jews in the East End of London, led to a growing campaign from 1886 onwards for immigration controls. Both trade union leaders and back-bench Conservative politicians expressed growing concern that the immigrants were competing for housing and undercutting wages at a time of growing unemployment. After a period of agitation lasting some 20 years, an Aliens Act was passed in July 1905 which introduced a modicum of control. Some historians argue that the campaign for controls was not specifically hostile to Jews; it just so happened that they constituted the majority of immigrants. However, a strong current of anti-Semitism can be detected within the British Brothers' League, a right-wing organization that agitated for controls, and in the statements of propagandists like Arnold White. The latter, the anonymous 'Special Correspondent' of the *Standard* derided the 'filthy, rickety, jetsam of humanity, bearing on their evil faces the stigmata of every physical and moral degradation'.[20] In a rather different key, the Boer War came under strong attack from radical anti-imperialists like the famous economist J. A. Hobson who claimed that conflict had been deliberately fomented for their own profit, 'by a small group of international financiers, chiefly German in origin and Jewish in race', a view shared by a Trades Union Congress resolution in September 1900 which condemned a war intended to 'secure the gold fields of South Africa for cosmopolitan Jews, most of whom had no patriotism and no country'.[21] Studies of English Literature after 1870, of writers like Trollope, Buchan, Kipling, G. K. Chesterton, Shaw, H. G. Wells, Hilaire Belloc and others, reveals a culture saturated with anti-Semitism and which regarded the Jew as the embodiment of cosmopolitan forces that were corroding and poisoning the traditions of Englishness and national identity.

However, there is a danger in concentrating upon the statements of the most notorious anti-Semites like Joseph Banister and Arnold White, since they remained isolated voices that had a marginal impact. On the whole, British society remained wedded, at all social levels, to traditions of tolerance for persecuted political and religious minorities. Public anti-Semitic statements were felt by the educated, middle classes to be disreputable or, as we would say today, not politically correct. In the lengthy parliamentary debates on the Aliens Bill, MPs went to great lengths to avoid the word 'Jew' or carefully dissociated themselves from attacks on the 'Jewish race', while even the most anti-Semitic press commentators concealed their identity behind pseudonyms like 'Old Londoner' and 'Stepneyite'. Arnold White found it difficult to encourage working-class witnesses to appear before the Royal Commission on Aliens, noting 'the disinclination of every Englishman worthy of the name to harass the persecuted Russian Hebrew'.[22] Political anti-Semitism remained a marginal issue, one that barely found a purchase outside the confines of the East End of London, and throughout the period between 1870 and 1914, in stark contrast to the Continent, the only known case of collective violence was a highly unusual anti-Jewish riot in South Wales in 1911.

There was also a surprising absence in the research and writings of British physical anthropologists, eugenicists, Social Darwinists and other 'race scientists' of any attempt to elaborate a specifically biological theory of Jewish racial identity. Robert Knox, in *The Races of Men* (1850) did devote some space to an analysis of the Jews as a non-Caucasian race, as 'African and Asiatic, not European', but later physical anthropologists showed little interest in this field. This was not a reflection of any under-development of race science as a whole, since Britain was a leader in Darwinism and eugenics, but rather of the relatively secure position of Jews within the society. In the absence of a significant anxiety about Jews as an internal threat to British society, most racial science, including eugenics, was more preoccupied with the dangers of class. As the left-wing scientist Lancelot Hogben remarked: 'In Germany the Jew is the scape-goat. In Britain, the entire working class is the menace.'[23] Once again it can be seen that the development of racial ideology did not stem from the impact of science and ideas, but rather the reverse, race science was structured as an expression of underlying national attitudes and preoccupations. Many Jews were prominent within the Eugenics Society and leading eugenicists, perhaps reflecting the wider religious philo-Semitism of England, even admired the traditional marriage endogamy, sex hygiene and 'unconscious' eugenics of the Jewish people. As a great imperial power British thinking on race was much more centred on colonial subjects (Africans, Indians, Asians) than it was on a tiny, and generally tolerated, internal 'Other'.

The French Jews, profiting from the first act of emancipation in Eur-ope (1791), were by the 1880s highly integrated, upwardly mobile and successful in education, the professions and business – the exception being the Orthodox Jews of Alsace-Lorraine who retained a distinct, trad-itional identity. As in Britain, this gradual absorption and acceptance of Jews into French society was thrown into confusion by the immigration of 'backward' East European Jewish refugees, especially into Paris. But, unlike Britain, the influx of Yiddish-speaking Jews from Russia, Poland, Romania and elsewhere coincided with a profound political crisis that reached its peak in the Dreyfus Affair. In the autumn of 1894 Captain Alfred Dreyfus was accused of passing military secrets to the Germans, a charge that reflected both a climate of paranoid nationalism, as well as a consistent theme in European anti-Semitism which viewed the Jews as a treacherous internal enemy. The anti-Semitic writer Maurice Barrès wrote: 'I need no one to tell me why Dreyfus committed treason ... That Dreyfus is capable of treason, I conclude from his race.' The 1895 programme of La Jeunesse de l'Union Nationale defined its aim as: 'the struggle against the Jew, the foreigner of the interior, completely refractory to all assimilation, irreducibly opposed to our traditions, our customs, our mentality and our interests.'[24]

It was only during 1898–9 that the 'Affair' became a major event, splitting France into two warring camps. As Eugen Weber has shown in

Peasants into Frenchmen, the process of welding France into a unified nation-state in line with the promise of the Jacobin Revolution was still gathering pace under the fragile Third Republic. The process of transition to a modern, secular and capitalist society was challenged from a number of directions. Firstly, there were the highly conservative forces, particularly of the Catholic right, which detested the values of the Enlightenment and of the 1789 Revolution which were at the core of the Republican tradition, marked by anti-clericalism, atheism, egalitarianism and universalism. The Church lamented the passing of an ancient France, a golden age of peasant stability and simple faith, of tradition, established hierarchy and organic unity. The Assumptionist *La Croix*, which had a daily circulation of up to 170 000, engaged in an intense anti-Semitic campaign in which the deep insecurity of Catholics, faced with secularism, Socialism and the erosion of religion, was vented on the Jew as the diabolic instigator of 1789, of capitalism and all-things modern, from the liberal laws on divorce to the invention of the crematorium. Secondly, anti-Semitism became the voice of the 'little people', the poor, the unemployed and the frightened *petit bourgeoisie*, who were able to find a simple and readily identifiable cause for all their hardships. The small savers who lost their money in the crash of the Catholic Bank, the Union Générale, in 1882; the small shopkeepers unable to compete with large Paris department stores; the hand-workers made redundant by mechanization; the peasant forced to sell cattle to middlemen at low prices – all such groups that fell victim to the growth of anonymous, large-scale organizations and new market relations tended to moralize the inhuman forces of capitalism, to seek out those malign individuals who were held personally responsible for their suffering and insecurity. Drumont, who reached a huge audience through his best-seller *La France Juive* and his newspaper *La Libre Parole* (circulation 200 000) presented himself as a defender of the oppressed against the Jew, depicted as a bloodsucker, as a capitalist exploiter, a bloated spider at the centre of a web of international financial institutions.

A popular and radical form of 'socialist' anti-Semitism began to make a significant impact on French politics during the opposition movement centred on General Boulanger (1886–8), which threatened an authoritarian *coup d'état*. Although Boulangism collapsed in farce, it was succeeded by a variety of proto-fascist organizations led by demagogues, like Jules Guérin who established the Ligue Antisémitique Française in 1897. The Ligue, which had some 5000 to 11 000 members, engaged in street-level violence, as did the followers of the extraordinary Marquis de Morès, an adventurer who, in his cult of 'action' and deployment of gangs of muscular La Villette butchers, unemployed workers, criminals and ex-anarchists, was an early model for the fascist thugs who appeared in the 1920s. At the height of the Dreyfus Affair in early 1898 anti-Semitic agitators helped trigger some of the 69 riots that took place throughout France.

The battle that raged in 1897–9 between Dreyfusard and anti-Dreyfusard forces was far more than a conflict over anti-Semitism. The Dreyfusard intellectuals, led by Emile Zola, recognized that the conservative and Catholic forces that were ranged against the Jews were essentially in arms against the secular Republic and the values of 1789. The emancipation of the Jews in 1790–1 was a key symbol of the Revolutionary tradition, the values of universal individual civil rights, citizenship and equality before the law, and hence any move to drive the Jews back into the ghetto was read as an attack on the whole Republican edifice. It was through the mainly ideological war of the Affair that the Dreyfusards welded together a defensive Republican movement that united Socialists and the liberal bourgeoisie in a stable bloc that remained intact until the debacle of 1940. In 1899 the Waldeck-Rousseau government decided to 'liquidate' the Affair and the popular anti-Semitic leaders were arrested. By 1902 the tide had turned against conservative reaction and anti-Semitism and the majority of French people – as in Britain – remained wedded to the values of liberal democracy, order, moderation, legality and respect for the rights of minorities. In March 1905 the visit by Wilhelm II to Morocco, during which he claimed a right to 'peaceful competition' in the French sphere of influence in Africa, sparked off an intense phase of nationalism in which public attention was drawn away from the internal enemy (the 'Jew') towards external dangers and imperial competition.

While the maturity and stability of French political institutions stood firm against the political crisis of the 1890s, French anti-Semitism was rather different from that in Britain in that it found expression in a highly sophisticated literary form and racial theory. Since, as has been noted, anti-Semitism was quite marginal in Britain it never attracted the central interest of major thinkers, but rather that of lesser and uninfluential figures like Arnold White. In France, by comparison, racial anti-Semitism was formulated in a much more powerful way by brilliant and original thinkers or by gifted propagandists. Ernest Renan, one of the most influential voices in late nineteenth-century France, interpreted history through the racial opposition between Aryans and Jews. Drumont, although not an original thinker, was a gifted propagandist who was able to fuse elements of traditional religious anti-Judaism (the blood libel, deicide, diabolism, poisoning of Christians) with contemporary, biological, racial anti-Semitism, making a powerful concoction. Advanced scientific theories of heredity began to inform the work of racists like the anthropologist Georges Vacher de Lapouge, the sociologists Gustave Le Bon or Jules Soury, who wrote of the absolute biological gap between races. 'Raise a Jew in an Aryan family from birth', wrote Soury in 1902, 'and neither the nationality nor the language will modify one atom of the genes of a Jew, and consequently, of the hereditary structure and texture of his tissues and organs.'[25] Although political anti-Semitism had been largely defeated in France by 1905, French writers had succeeded in elaborating radical and sophisticated forms of racial anti-Semitism that had a major impact throughout Europe and which were also to resurface with the rise of fascism in the 1930s. This was in line with the controversial thesis of Zeev Sternhell that the ideological roots of European fascism are to be found more in the France of the 1890s than in Germany or Italy.[26] Where Central Europe differed from France was not in the elaboration of a more radical form of racial or ideological anti-Semitism, but rather in the greater potential for aggressive nationalism. German unification was late and incomplete and the Empire was threatened by encirclement from Britain, France and Russia. But by 1905 German political anti-Semitism was in decline and, although it is easy to locate pre-1914 exterminationist statements (as in Russia, France, Britain and elsewhere), there was nothing distinctive about German racism, a 'deutscher Sonderweg', or 'special German path of development', that would indicate an inevitable road to the Holocaust. As will be seen in Part 2, what was to change all this was the revolutionary impact of the Great War.

PART 2

1914–1945

The First World War marked a crucial watershed in the development of European racism, a process of change that was closely linked to the unprecedented anarchy, violence and psychological trauma of the first 'total' war. What appeared to many contemporaries to be the terminal cataclysm of Western civilization witnessed the collapse of the German, Russian and Habsburg Empires, and precipitated civil war and revolution in Germany, Russia and Hungary. The Bolsheviks established a revolutionary regime that was determined to extend Communism to the rest of Europe as well as to ignite the flame of a universal, colonial revolt. Predictions of the inevitable collapse of capitalism seemed to take on substance as economic crisis and mass unemployment took on global proportions. In Germany an early phase of nationalistic euphoria and confidence in certain victory gave way, by the end of the war, to profound pessimism and right-wing nationalists, humiliated by the Treaty of Versailles, searched for scapegoats that would save the honour of the Fatherland, the dark forces within German society that were held responsible for the infamous 'stab in the back'. The mass slaughter and profound psychological trauma of mechanized warfare released a potential for violence that fed into tough ex-servicemen associations or paramilitary organizations like the Free-Corps. Fascism took root in Italy from 1919 onwards, before spreading its influence into Weimar Germany and inspiring authoritarian and ultra-nationalist regimes in Poland, Hungary, Romania, Spain, Portugal, and elsewhere.

The First World War, a huge fault line in European history, did not, however, coincide with a major shift in the strictly scientific formulations of racism. The rediscovery of Mendel's theory of heredity in 1900, along with the identification and mapping of human blood groups from 1905 onwards, did lay the basis for a modern science of genetics that was beginning to subvert the foundations of race-science by the 1930s (see Chapter 6). But, in general, this challenge came too late to reverse the influence of racial anthropology or to arrest the advance of Nazi racial anti-Semitism. With a few exceptions, the race-science elaborated between 1870 and 1914 by physical anthropologists and eugenicists, the categorization of quite distinct 'races' arranged on a ladder of biological difference, remained dominant until the end of the Second World War.

Race-science, which was primarily an ideological construct, continued to be driven by the specific political contexts of the inter-war period. While fascist and ultra-right nationalist regimes began to develop virulent forms of racism, aimed mainly at the Jews, the Soviet Union and the international Communist movement, despite being tainted with racism, offered a counter-ideology that emphasized the fundamental rights of all oppressed peoples, including the blacks of Africa and the United States of America. Unlike the pre-1914 period when ideas of 'race' had provided an almost universal way of interpreting history and society, during the inter-war period the meanings of race became far more contested. This was especially true of the new generation of anti-colonial nationalist and revolutionary leaders, like Kenyatta, Nehru, Gandhi, Nkrumah, Padmore, Ho Chi Minh and Messali Hadj, who, as students and migrant workers, organized and militated against racism inside Europe.

The First World War saw an unprecedented recruitment of black colonial troops and workers into the war industries and the front-line, and after demobilization the first large and permanent settlements of non-Europeans appeared in France and Britain. Chapter 4 centres mainly on European reactions to this significant black presence and the first extensive and direct contacts with the 'savage' within the heartland of the white 'Civilized Order'.

4

ANTI-BLACK RACISM IN AN AGE OF TOTAL WAR

Black Soldiers and Workers, 1914–18

During the First World War both Britain and France recruited an enormous number of 'colonial' or 'native' workers, soldiers and sailors from their respective Empires and moved them into the European theatre of operations. France, which had a long tradition of imperial native regiments, and which was most desperate to find replacement manpower for the millions of Frenchmen called to the front, had the least hesitation in calling on the 'patriotism' of its subject peoples. In all, France mobilized some 300 000 colonial workers and 600 000 soldiers from Senegal, Indo-China, Madagascar, China, Algeria, Tunisia and Morocco. Likewise, the British deployed 138 000 Indian troops, as well as workers from the West Indies, West Africa, South Africa and China. If this number is added to the 200 000 black labourers and soldiers brought in by the US Army, then the total of black and Asian men in Europe was in the region of one and a half million. Europeans were confronted directly, within the boundaries of their own societies, with an unprecedented number of 'racially distinct' people and it is this contact which provides a rich source of historical evidence about early 'race-relations'. Nor was contact restricted to the War of 1914–18 since, although France, Britain and the USA repatriated the majority of colonials and black GIs after the Armistice, many tens of thousands stayed on and created the first large ethnic minority settlements, both in ports from Cardiff to Marseilles, as well as in French industrial towns from Lyons and Paris to Lille and Metz. This process of post-war settlement led to the first manifestations of large-scale, popular racism. For example, the demobilization of British soldiers and sailors coincided with a wave of race riots in British ports in 1919, while the French occupation of the Rhine with black colonial troops during 1919–24 stirred up an extremely vicious racist campaign in Germany.

The deployment of black and Asian soldiers and workers into Europe during the First World War was accompanied by the injection of highly racist practices and attitudes from colonial and ex-slave societies, particularly from the USA, into a European society that, on the whole, showed widespread popular tolerance or even friendship towards minorities. Where there was a long tradition of native regiments, as with the British Sikh and Gurkha or French North African battalions, commanding officers, who were always white, often held a paternalist attitude towards 'their' men, who were viewed as 'big children' whose intelligence was too low for them to act as officers or to understand the complexities of modern tactics. But, when trained to respect white authority, the commanders could be proud of their endurance and courage: racial myths of native savagery, especially the use of the knife or bayonet by Indians, Algerians and Senegalese in hand-to-hand fighting, were deliberately cultivated and used as propaganda to intimidate the Germans.

However, more negative racial attitudes were far more prevalent among white officers who brought into the European theatre the prejudices and violence of colonial societies, from Algeria and South Africa to Australia, or the 'Jim Crow' practices of the American South. White colonial societies, and the colonial officers who controlled black units in Europe, were, in general, strongly opposed to the deployment of native troops and workers in the metropolitan territory. As noted earlier, colonial powers tended to operate a twin-track system of state regulation, in which the extremely repressive apparatus intended to maintain an iron grip on colonial subjects, from systematic police and military violence to the denial of basic legal and political rights, stood in stark contrast to the more liberal climate in Europe and the respect for the rule of law and individual rights. Colonials generally believed that control over the millions of 'natives', the 'thin white line' that protected settlers from being slaughtered and overrun, was fundamentally psychological: if the black population for an instant became aware of white self-doubt or anxiety, or could challenge the symbolic markers of European supremacy with impunity, then rebellion would inevitably follow. Settlers reacted strongly against any attempt by 'home' governments to introduce liberal or humane reforms into the colonies since it was felt that European politicians, ignorant of the hard realities of colonial life, had no understanding of the importance of the 'special measures' required to keep the native 'in his place', and that any tampering with the system threatened to put a match to the tinder-box. It was in this context that colonials feared that black troops or workers moved into Europe would become infected by the more liberal attitudes of metropolitan society, be treated with equality by whites, break down the barriers of segregation, and – ultimate of horrors – enter into sexual relations with European women. This 'taste of freedom', along with contact with trade unions, left-wing and anti-colonial nationalist movements, would, it was feared, have a profound effect on the political consciousness of the blacks who on demobilization would bring these subversive influences home and undermine the racial order.

A South African officer, outraged that French ladies had served tea to white soldiers after black recruits, and in cups previously used by natives, exclaimed: 'When you people get back to South Africa, don't start thinking that you are whites, just because this place has spoiled you. You are black, and will stay black.'[1] It was also feared that blacks would not only learn sophisticated military skills that could be used in colonial rebellion, but that the act of fighting, killing and defeating Germans would subvert the concept of white racial invulnerability. The South African government accepted that blacks should only be recruited as labour, not as combatants: as the *East Rand Express* remarked: 'The empire must uphold the principle that a coloured man must not raise his hand against a white man if there is to be any law or order in either India, Africa, or any part of the Empire where the white man rules over a large concourse of coloured people.'[2] Such fears that native contact with European society would prove to have a dangerous, radicalizing impact turned out to be justified. Demobilized troops and workers provided a powerful impetus to the emergence of nationalist, anti-colonial movements throughout Africa and Asia, and black political consciousness was also raised in the USA where a wave of post-war lynchings tried to put, as white racists proclaimed, 'those military, French-women-ruined negro soldiers' back in their place.[3]

In order to contain the dangers of political and moral corruption and to prevent the breaking of the mental chains of subservience, the French, British and American commands introduced colonial segregationist and racist practices into Europe, practices that had an impact on public opinion. Black regiments and labour battalions were strictly segregated from contact with British and French society: for example, it was standard practice for Algerian, Senegalese, black American, Indian, South African and other colonial units to strictly control or ban off-duty visits to town centres and bars, and, in particular, to block invitations to French homes. American officers brought with them all the worst practices of the racist Southern states, including savage beatings of blacks by Military Police and peremptory hangings for charges of 'rape'. Colonel Linard of the US Army drew up a circular, the *Secret Information Concerning Black American Troops*, which was distributed to French army officers and local government officials, warning them of the need to avoid giving offence to white Americans by breaking segregationist practices and spelling out the dangerous consequences for the United States of blacks returning home infected by egalitarianism. The circular advised officials that the French should not eat with black officers, shake them by the hand, strike up any friendships, or permit contact with women. Far from trying to moderate the racism of American officers to fit the more tolerant climate of French society, Americans publicly lectured the French on the need to 'respect' Jim Crow values and to collaborate in their implementation. Some Americans legitimated this by reference to scientific racism, like Major J. N. Merrill, commander of the black First Battalion, who held that all blacks were 'rank cowards' who, if they fought well, only did so when individuals had a high percentage of white blood. Anthropology, he claimed, had shown through 'the measurements of the cranial capacities and facial angles...the negro race...has reached a state that will not improve and cannot improve.'[4] Similar attitudes could be found in colonial units. The South African command kept black workers in guarded compounds and prohibited entrance to shops 'unless under European escort'. Likewise, the French Army tried to isolate colonial workers from social contact with French civilians by segregating them in camps under strict militarized regimes. African soldiers on leave were not allowed to accept invitations to stay with French families, while in 1916 the army command issued instructions that female nurses were to be withdrawn from hospitals for injured colonial troops to prevent the development of 'liaisons'.

How successful were the armed forces in their segregationist aims and did the colonial racism of the military élites have any impact on European society? The letters and autobiographical record left by colonial and black American soldiers show an unmistakable pattern of open acceptance from the French and British working class, a friendly welcome that was experienced with a sense of euphoric astonishment by those who had grown up inured to the arrogant insults, violence and institutional racism of white colonial society. There are endless testaments like that of the American soldier who wrote to his mother: 'These French people don't bother with no color line business. They treat us so good that the only time I ever know I'm colored is when I look in the glass.'[5] What appears to have been a genuine level of open tolerance by the French public was reinforced by the fact that black troops were fêted as gallant fighters, come to risk their lives in defence of the French empire and the mother country. North Africans were welcomed into many French working-class homes and the military authorities were unable to prevent close relationships developing between black troops and European women.

Black and white soldiers inevitably came into close contact at the front and, through the shared hardship and danger of trench warfare, built up a sense of mutual respect and camaraderie. In 1918 about 50 West Indian limbless soldiers, convalescing in a military hospital in Liverpool, came under a violent, racially motivated attack by white soldiers who had served in South Africa, but were defended by 'some of the British Tommies who had fought side by side with these coloured soldiers in the trenches'.[6] Similarly, French civilians intervened to protect black French subjects from assault by American military personnel. Such incidents illustrate the wide gap between colonial racism, which was deeply entrenched in senior military and administrative personnel who had served in the colonies, and the European lower middle and working classes who, in spite of the racist stereotyping of blacks in the media, appear to have been quite open-minded and ready to assess blacks directly and individually, according to their personal and human qualities.

However, this generalized tolerance within the European working class did come under strain during the course of the war in the field of labour relations and it was here that the first indications of popular anti-black racism can be located. This took on a particularly marked form in France, where the majority of black workers were located in labour battalions that supplied labour for the docks, quarries, mines, forestry work, or in the munitions, chemical and gas industries. The trade unions objected that colonial workers were being deployed to undermine wage levels and from the spring of 1917, as French society entered a deepening war crisis, African workers were subjected to increasing street-level assault, and eventually to large-scale riots like those in June 1917 in Dijon and Le Havre where crowds of up to 1500 people attacked local Moroccan barracks and killed 15 people. Women frequently demonstrated against colonial workers on the grounds that their deployment enabled husbands and sons to be replaced and then dispatched to the front, where they risked death or injury. Africans were also accused of strike-breaking activities, taking over 'women's work', or being a burden on scarce resources and eating the 'bread of French workers'. Sexual competition over women was a frequent cause of violence in bars, and Frenchmen perceived colonial workers as libidinous primitives and malingerers who, in the absence of husbands and fiancés who were risking their lives at the front, posed a predatory sexual threat to the honour of French women.

Demobilization and Inter-War Racism

Economic racism continued on an extensive scale in Britain immediately after the end of the war, as tens of thousands of colonial and white seamen and soldiers were demobilized and found themselves in competition for housing and employment in the major ports. A series of major race riots erupted in South Wales (Cardiff, Newport and Cadoxton), Liverpool, London, Glasgow and Tyneside. Shipping lines had greatly increased their employment of cheap colonial labour from the 1870s, but instead of returning them on homebound ships as required by law, they were frequently abandoned in British ports where they congregated in squalid lodging houses or settled permanently and married local women. During the war thousands of black seamen were recruited, often facing great danger at sea, but with the Armistice, 20 000 men were demobilized and stranded in British ports.

White sailors, backed by their unions, demanded that the shipping lines give priority of employment to European seamen, while black sailors, many of whom were British subjects, protested that in spite of their enormous sacrifice in the defence of Empire, they were being denied equality of treatment. As the Secretary of the African Races Association of Glasgow wrote to the press in 1919: 'Did not some of these men fight on the same battlefields with white men to defeat the enemy and make secure the British Empire?'[7] In Cardiff, Liverpool and Glasgow large crowds of up to 2000 people, often led by ex-servicemen who deployed military tactics, laid siege to the black dockland ghettos, destroying lodging houses and shops. During riots in London a black seaman, William Samuel, was told by a police sergeant: 'We want you niggers out of our country this is a white man's country and not yours.'[8] Much of this rioting took place against a background of extreme labour unrest and turbulence during which the government, frightened by Bolshevism and the imminence of Communist-inspired revolution in Britain, deployed 12 000 troops and six tanks into 'Red Clydeside', and three battalions, tanks, and a battleship and destroyer into Liverpool.

During the inter-war period both the French and British governments followed identical policies in trying to repatriate all black soldiers and workers or, where African labour was still deployed, as in the merchant navy, to place them under the most strict surveillance or segregationist practices. In general, the presence of 'inferior races' was viewed as a threat to European society through miscegenation, criminality, the transmission of disease, and the formation of alien and unassimilated communities that endangered the 'national way of life'. By 1920 the French authorities had, for example, rounded up and repatriated all but 5000 of the 300 000 Algerians who had seen war service, while immediately after the 1919 Riots, the British government repatriated many hundreds of seamen. However, many black seamen and immigrant workers from the colonies were French or British subjects and since they had, as passport holders, rights of entry and of settlement, in practice it was difficult for the authorities to impose strict racist controls without breaking the law. However, both imperial powers succeeded in introducing mechanisms of racial subordination and control that reconstituted, within a European context, the segregationist and racial categories of colonial regimes.

British shipping owners, faced with recession and declining profits, reinforced on-board racial divisions between British sailors on standard articles or contracts and low-paid men on Asiatic articles. These divisions were then carried over into interracial dockside communities in which shipping lines and local police, backed by the India Office, collaborated in attempts to segregate black seamen from Europeans and from contact with trade unions. In 1925 the government introduced the *Coloured Alien Seamen Order*, quietly achieved by Order in Council and without public debate, which exposed even black seamen who were British subjects to official registration (fingerprinting, identity photographs), police harassment and enforced deportation. Likewise, French colonial governments, worried by migrant worker contact with the Communist Party and anti-colonial, nationalist movements in the metropolis, pushed hard for severe restrictions on labour migration, as well as the establishment of special police intelligence units to infiltrate immigrant communities, segregated hostels and clinics, and a system of enforced deportation. The founder of the special police and 'welfare' apparatus, the senior colonial official Octave Depont, legitimated control and segregation with the paternalist argument that North Africans were like 'big children' who needed protection from the corrupting ways of Parisian society. Natives, he claimed, both needed and liked strong leadership: 'Our surveillance is not for them a form of subjection, but a protection – better still, a state of happiness.'[9]

In both France and Britain such measures were initiated by colonial, labour or police ministries and departments that were imbued with imperial assumptions of racial hierarchy, labour discipline and control, such as the British India Office, the Colonial Office and the British Board of Trade, and the French Ministry of the Interior, the department of Algerian Native Affairs and the Ministry of Labour. The imposition of policies of racial subordination and control in Britain and France, enforced through administrative orders that were implemented without any parliamentary debate or control, were justified to the public through concerted propaganda campaigns. The authorities created a climate of opinion that would readily accept the necessity for special controls and policing through the dissemination of highly racialized images of black immigrants as primitive 'invaders' who threatened European society through the transmission of dangerous microbes, criminal activity (pimping, drugs, gambling), by the sexual danger presented to women and children (rape, molestation), and the proliferation of squalid ghettos. Laura Tabili has argued that the recolonization and racialization of black minorities in inter-war Britain was largely the work of state agencies and employers' organizations, acting in collusion with local police, town-hall officials and trade union leaders. The same dynamic of racialization, in relation to Maghrebian immigrants, can be found in inter-war France. The origins of both racist propaganda, as well as institutional racist practices, can be traced to élites, rather than to any initiatives or antipathy arising from the British or French working class.[10]

Fear of Miscegenation in Britain and France

The linkages between European racial science, colonial institutional racism and the diffusion of racial prejudice in metropolitan society can be shown through the profound anxiety, even paranoia, that attached to the idea of racial mixing or miscegenation. This was such a central and continuous preoccupation throughout the period from 1900 to the Second World War that it will be examined in more detail for the insight that it can provide into the general processes of racialization of European society.

From an early stage in the development of slavery and plantation economies in the Americas, the control of large black populations by numerically tiny and vulnerable strata of white masters was, in part, achieved by the rigid control of sexual boundaries and the prevention of mixing between the two sides. The more racist the colonial regime, then, in general, the more marked the legal or customary restrictions on intermarriage, as in the apartheid system of South Africa or the segregationist and lynch-law practices of the American South. The economic and political rationale of such racial stratification is clear: to prevent the majority black population slowly achieving a degree of equality and upward social mobility, and 'flooding' the white élite, it was essential to prevent intermarriage and the appearance of a mixed-race descent that was interstitial, ambiguous and a threat to the demarcation of clear racial boundaries.

So entrenched were such values within white colonial societies, through socialization, the maintenance of powerful taboos, religious doctrine, and the general cultural and social codes of correct speech, symbolic distancing and avoidance of physical contact, that the very idea of proximity to the black body was associated with feelings of profound loathing, contamination and staining, of dirt and disease. Reflecting the 'double standard' of patriarchal European societies, particularly strong revulsion was felt towards sexual relations between a black man and a white woman (less so between a white master and a black servant), since such 'appropriation' of the European female was regarded as the most powerful challenge to the status, honour and the most intimate foundations of white male hegemony. The history of colonial societies is rife with the brutal beatings and murder of 'natives' for 'overstepping the mark', making supposed slights and petty challenges to the symbolic order of white racial and sexual superiority. This was the central theme, worked out with deep psychological insight, of E. M. Forster's novel *A Passage to India* (1924). Periods of internal crisis within colonial regimes, stoked by fear of imminent black revolt and the uprising of servants within the domestic space, were frequently accompanied by the so-called 'Black Peril', powerful currents of panic and racial paranoia that were driven by unfounded rumours of the systematic rape of white women as an instrument of incipient race war.

During the nineteenth century it was a widely accepted practice within the British, French and Dutch empires that European soldiers or administrators should regularly cohabit with native 'concubines', often in stable unions that led to the formation of mixed-race families. However, from about 1880 onwards a deep shift within Western European societies towards a more puritanical and sexually repressive code, linked to a cult of manliness and 'muscular Christianity', was eventually translated into a strict regulation of sexual relations in the colonies. While earlier colonial regimes had largely tolerated white sexual relations with black women, often through prostitution, even such 'irregular' contacts, let alone marriage, were increasingly regarded as immoral, a source of 'pollution' and degrading to the Europeans sense of prestige, founded on segregation and a deepening apartheid. For example, the 'Crewe Circular', a Colonial Service directive of 1909 on 'Immoral relations with native women', threatened severe penalties against any officials who engaged in concubinage. During the early 1900s all southern and central African colonies legislated against sexual intercourse between black men and white women. Under the Southern Rhodesian Immorality Act of 1903, a black man resorting to a white prostitute could be imprisoned for five years. By the turn of the century, it was widely believed that colonial hegemony was crucially dependent on the maintenance of a white 'moral power', self-discipline, and the upholding of a correct social and spatial distance between Europeans and blacks through strict rules of segregation and etiquette. The taboo against interracial sex was also reinforced, as has been seen, by race-science which demonstrated that miscegenation inevitably brought about a process of physical and moral degeneration.

A major concern that arose with the growing numbers of black males who entered Europe from the turn of the century was that without the constraints of the colonial regime, the repressive laws, codes of practice and the threat of violence that normally contained the bestial instincts of the native and prevented him from associating with white women, the black would be unchained, a dangerous libidinal force set loose in the heart of 'civilization'. Moreover, it was felt that European women, not realizing the dangers offered by 'natives', would naively break the codes of segregation and encourage physical contact. In 1899 the British press showed widespread disgust at the way in which English women flocked to get close to 'near-naked blacks' appearing in the *Savage South Africa* show: these women were not only, it was claimed, 'degrading themselves', but 'seriously weakening the Empire', since colonists knew how crucial it was to keep 'natives who are worse than brutes when their passion is aroused . . . in subjection by a wholesale dread of the white man's powers and that dread is being dissipated daily by familiar intercourses at Earl's Court'. Following this *Daily Mail* campaign, the Earl's Court management barred women from entering the native 'kraal'. Worse was to come with the marriage of one black performer, 'Prince Lobenguela', to a Miss Florence Jewell: 'There is something inexpressibly disgusting', commented the *Evening News*, 'about the mating of a white girl with a dusky savage', while *The Spectator* noted, 'Miscegenation has long been regarded by the Anglo-Saxon races as a curse against civilisation.'[11]

There are endless incidents of this kind dating from the First World War and inter-war period as the numbers of black people increased enormously in Britain and France. Negative reactions to black intermarriage and sexual relations were especially marked among ex-colonial officials, army personnel and police officers, who brought into European society the racist attitudes of colonial society. Precisely because such officers and administrators claimed to have a special knowledge of native society and the 'primitive mind', they were able to carry particular weight with both government and public opinion, using their expertise to influence policy. During the race riots in Liverpool in 1919 black men were blamed for associating with white women. Sir Ralph Williams, former governor of the Windward Islands, wrote to *The Times*: 'To almost every white man and woman who has lived a life among coloured races, intimate association between black or coloured men and white women is a thing of horror . . . What blame . . . to those white men who, seeing these conditions and loathing them, resort to violence?'[12] During the inter-war period eugenicists and race-scientists, several of whom had visited South Africa, wrote at length on the psychological problems and 'vicious tendencies' of 'half-caste' children in the interracial port settlements of Cardiff and Liverpool, while the Chief Constable of Cardiff called for the introduction of legislation to prohibit interracial marriage on the lines of the South African Immorality Act of 1927.[13]

The French press, in similar vein, showed an almost obsessive concern with African immigrants, particularly the Algerian, as a sexually overcharged animal, a rapist, molester of children, vector of syphilis, and a threat to the purity and honour of French womanhood. When an unemployed and mentally ill migrant worker from Algeria killed two women in Paris in November 1923, it led to a widespread moral panic, crowd attacks on Arabs and calls for stricter immigration controls. A deputy from the Paris region wrote: 'thousands of natives are terrorizing certain regions of France, certain sectors of Paris. They wallow in poverty, adding to the vices of the lower depths of the city those which they carry in a state of gestation. Libidinous crimes are on the increase, rapes, abductions, while armed robberies are beyond count.'[14]

Such racist perceptions did not, however, remain the monopoly of an educated élite. Politicians, journalists, novelists, colonial administrators, academics and a host of others from the French and British bourgeoisie had tremendous power to influence public opinion, as well as specific policies, relating to African migrants. They did so as the proprietors or editors of newspapers, as members of government, as senior officials in the police or in key ministries, as experts on health and tropical disease, missionaries, film directors – indeed all those that had their hands on the levers of state power or of cultural and educational expression. It was from this higher level that racist ideas and stereotypes filtered down into the wider society.

Fear of Miscegenation in Germany

The powerful reaction against miscegenation was not confined only to the great imperial powers, Britain and France, but also developed in the infant colonial powers of Germany and Italy. Debates in the German Reichstag in 1904 on the systematic genocide deployed against the Nama and Herero peoples of Namibia were formulated in a dehumanizing rhetoric which described Africans as 'labouring animals', 'human material' and, in an inversion of reality, as 'blood thirsty beasts in the form of humans'.[15] A shift, similar to that in British, French and Dutch colonies, occurred in the first decade of the twentieth century towards more radical forms of racial demarcation, the maintenance of Aryan racial purity and the criminalization of interracial marriage. Under pressure from the 'respectable' colonial middle class of Windhoek, disapproving of 'back-country' marriage between German farmers and native women, the colonial government issued an imperial ordinance outlawing interracial marriage in 1905.

Similar codes followed for German East Africa in 1906 and Samoa in 1912. The latter ordinance, debated in the Reichstag, decreed that mixed marriages consecrated prior to the new code, were legitimate and the children of such unions were juridically 'white', while marriages entered into after the ordinance were illegitimate and the children deemed 'black' and inferior: a perfect example of the arbitrary invention of racial categories. This measure, which caused some anxiety among Catholic conservatives, documented a major shift towards secular racist assumptions since the modern state was arrogating to itself the right to undo a sacrament on the basis of physical or biological features rather than on the grounds of religious belief, and it denied the humanity of indigenous peoples. All political parties, from the Liberals to the Socialists (SPD), agreed that miscegenation represented a danger to the racial purity of the German nation, while *Mischlinge* (half-breeds) were inevitably unhealthy and corrupt, 'harmful to the national and racial interest'.[16] The outlawing of marriage with black natives bore a distinct parallel with the growing anti-Semitic belief that conversion to Christianity could not remove the essential racial characteristics of the Jew. However, while dehumanization of black people, genocidal practices and racial ordinances could pass into law before 1914 (an indicator of the large gap between colonial and metropolitan racial fields), no such measures could conceivably have been introduced at this time against the Jews in Germany.

Race War and the 'Horror on the Rhine'

During the course of the First World War Germany, an infant colonial power and unable to recruit native soldiers or labourers into the European theatre as had France and Britain, attacked the Allies for fomenting a kind of 'race-war' and, in a dangerous inversion of Social Darwinian principles, utilizing inferior 'savages' as an instrument to undermine superior white stock and Western civilization. German propagandists dwelled on the unspeakable brutality of black soldiers who, it was claimed, returned from the front with trophies of decapitated German heads, fingers and ears. Field Marshal Hindenburg wrote in his 1920 memoirs: 'Where there were no tanks, the enemy set black waves upon us. We were helpless when they broke into our lines and murdered or, worse, tortured the defenceless. Human indignation and indictment is directed not at the blacks who carried out such atrocities, but at those who brought such hordes to German soil allegedly to fight in the war for honour, freedom and justice.'[17] The eugenicist Ernst Haeckel, shocked by the scale of slaughter in the 'barbarous war of annihilation', exposed the cruel destruction of young German soldiers, 'tortured and maimed in inhuman fashion by the "hyenas" of the battlefield, the barbarian Indians and the cruel Senegal negroes', and lamented the fatal loss of their future breeding capacity, and superior racial and hereditary potential. England, by 'mobilizing all the different races of man', was endangering not only Germany, but 'the white race as a whole. For the cultural and psychological differences that separate the highest developed European peoples from the lowest savages is greater than the differences that separate the savages from the anthropoid apes.'[18] German appropriation of the racial moral high ground, the emphasis on the deeper unity of the white race confronted with lower, primitive forms, was countered by the French claim that mobilization of all races, regardless of 'colour', and their treatment as equals upheld the universal principles of liberty, equality and fraternity.

The propaganda on a black-white 'race-war' was to assume international proportions during the occupation of the Rhine by French colonial troops between 1919 and 1923. The German government, convinced that the deployment of black 'savages' was a deliberate revenge and humiliation, mounted an elaborate propaganda campaign which presented black troops as diseased animals who roamed the Rhineland in packs, gang-raping German mothers and virgins, infecting the nation and polluting the Aryan race. The *Hamburger Nachrichten* claimed that the African who 'occupies a lower rung on the evolutionary ladder' was brought into Europe and 'systematically trained to desire that which was formerly unreachable for him – the white woman! He is urged and driven to besmirch defenceless women and girls with his tuberculous and syphilitic stench, wrench them into his stinking apish arms and abuse them in the most unthinkable way!'[19] Official funding was secretly given for the publication of obscene postcards entitled 'Die Schwarze Schmach', depicting a gorilla raping a German woman, also of posters and atrocity leaflets, translated into English, Spanish, Portuguese, French, Italian, Dutch, Swedish, Danish, Finnish, and even Esperanto, which were distributed globally through German export companies and expatriate associations. A lavish Bavarian film, again titled 'Die Schwarze Schmach' (1921), which played to full houses in Stuttgart and elsewhere, showed a squad of Senegalese soldiers who stopped the car of a young couple in the woods and raped the fiancée, infecting her with a venereal disease and preventing her marriage – thus symbolically destroying her role as mother and pure racial progenitor. The local press, including the Socialist newspaper, found it sincere and to be recommended. A stage version drew full houses in Munich.

What is most interesting about this propaganda campaign, detailing atrocities that an Allied investigation at the time proved to be groundless and prurient fantasies, was the enormous international support which it received, both among socialist, feminist and liberal circles, as well as on the conservative right. The astonishing alacrity with which the educated European middle class, apart from a small minority of doubters, accepted such crude rumours and propaganda provides detailed evidence of the universality of anti-black racism, a profound and disturbing sexual *angst* entrenched within the psyche of 'white civilization'. E. D. Morel, founder of the Congo Reform Society that had campaigned against Belgian atrocities and first Secretary of the left-wing Union of Democratic Control, interpreted (as did many Socialists and Communists) the deployment of black troops as an instrument of capitalist oppression, pitching unwitting natives against the trade unions, the strikes and revolutionary organizations of the European proletariat. But Morel, in his *Daily Herald* reports of April 1920, and a widely translated pamphlet, *The Horror on the Rhine* (1920), elaborated, in close detail, the most prurient fantasies of black atrocities. The sex impulse, claimed Morel, is in tropical Africa 'a more spontaneous, fiercer, less controllable impulse than among European peoples ... in the absence of their own women-folk, they *must be satisfied upon the bodies of white women*', which they did by roaming the countryside in armed bands, 'their fierce passions hot within them'.[20] Similar obsessive concerns with the black sexual danger were voiced throughout Europe in protest campaigns, petitions and resolutions by the National Conference of Labour Women (London), the Association of Dutch Women for Social Welfare, the Women's International League for Peace and Freedom, the League of Swedish Socialist Women, the Italian Anti-Slavery Society and similar organisations in Austria, the USA, Germany, Peru, Argentina, Canada and New Zealand. The Italian Prime Minister, Francesco Nitti, felt a great 'sensation of disgust and horror', not only at the savage rape of women and boys and by local municipalities that were compelled by the Allies to 'furnish German women for houses of prostitution, to gratify the lust of negroes', but even more so at the French breach of the unwritten rules of civilized Europe by occupying ancient cathedral cities, 'among the most cultured on earth ... The Rhine cities which contain the greatest masterpieces of Gothic art now lodge negroes who come from mud huts.'[21]

The visceral horror of the black body, of its potent sexuality and of miscegenation appears to have been almost entirely restricted to the European middle class, a reflection of the puritanism, repression and libidinal control of bourgeois society, as well as of a more elaborated racial ideology among educated élites. Within the zone of occupation on the Rhine the local German population was more friendly towards black than towards white French soldiers. The African-American writer

Claude McKay, visiting Hamburg and Berlin in 1923 at the height of the Rhine controversy, was given a friendly reception among the populace, 'in hotels, cafés, dancing halls, restaurants and trains, on the river boats and in the streets'.[22] The German propagandists tried to conceal the fact that many women had affairs with black troops and even married Annamese, Algerian, Malagasies and Senegalese, returning with them to their home country. Several hundred mixed-race children were born of such unions in Germany. Likewise, in Paris during the inter-war years, social contact was close between Algerian immigrant workers and working-class women in the factories, cafés and dance halls of the industrial suburbs. In 1930 some 700 women were married to Algerians while a further 5000 were cohabiting in stable unions. One French woman wrote a letter to the press recounting how the arrival of black American soldiers in a rural community had, after an initial reaction of fear that was shaped by stereotypes of savage cannibalism, given way after a day or two to deep sympathy for the affable troops who were so kind to the local children. This kind of evidence tends to show that the European working class, although sometimes entering into economic conflict with black minorities over scarce resources of housing and employment, were much more open and pragmatic in their relations with non-Europeans, unlike the middle classes whose attitudes and behaviour were more doctrinaire and determined by both class and racist assumptions.

The Nazis and Anti-Black Racism

There exists a vast body of research on anti-Semitism in Nazi Germany, but relatively little has, until very recently, been written on racial attitudes towards blacks during the period that Hitler was in power. The National Socialists were obsessed by notions of racial purity, and after coming to power in 1933, implemented a huge programme of sterilization, euthanasia and (later) genocide to achieve their aims of eliminating 'inferior' groups that threatened the German racial stock. However, this programme, while it assumed an exterminationist or genocidal form in relation to Jews, did not seek to eradicate black people, a difference in racial strategy that can be linked back to basic contrasts in Jewish and black racial stereotypes and to Nazi plans for a future colonial empire. The traditional racist image of the black was of a profoundly inferior type, ape-like, low in intelligence, driven by instinctual urges. Such a being posed no fundamental threat to the superior and masterful

European, as long as he was segregated within the colonial sphere as a pliable source of unskilled labour and prevented from interbreeding and 'polluting' the Aryan. By contrast, for racists, the Jews posed a huge threat because of their intelligence, their ability to organize an international network of financiers and revolutionaries bent on the subversion and enslavement of the German race. A key component in German anti-Semitic thought was the idea that the Jews made an instrumental use of race and deliberately plotted miscegenation between Aryans and inferior racial groups so as to undermine German stock. This racial logic was perfectly illustrated by Hitler's interpretation of the Rhineland occupation as a diabolic Jewish conspiracy to weaken the German race-substance. The Jew, he claimed, 'as a matter of principle always keeps his male line pure. He poisons the blood of others, but preserves his own ... It was and is Jews who bring the Negroes into the Rhineland, always with the same secret thought and clear aim of ruining the hated white race by the necessarily resulting bastardisation, throwing it down from its cultural and political height, and himself rising to be its master.'[23]

The core of Nazi colonial policy, which between 1933 and c.1941 showed strong continuity with that of Weimar, was to reverse the 'infamous' Treaty of Versailles, which had led to the appropriation of Togoland, the Cameroons, South-West Africa (Namibia) and East Africa. German propaganda, much of it aimed at international opinion, set out to disprove Allied claims of repressive German colonial policies, and this included paternalistic and protectionist measures taken towards the few hundred 'German Negroes' who were settled in Germany. During the long inter-war phase of Germany's 'colonialism in waiting', these black Germans were nurtured as an instrument of plans for the future reconquest of Africa, an empire that would be based on an apartheid-like system of strict racial segregation and the protection of the native in his 'traditional' culture. However, this posed a problem for Nazi racial policy of how to prevent this 'favoured' group, which was specifically excluded from sterilization programmes, from interbreeding with Germans, and this was largely achieved by concentrating them into large groups which could be readily segregated. The African groups were deployed in travelling shows (*ambulantes Negerdorf*) or as the cast for lavish colonial propaganda films like *Carl Peters*, *Ohm Krüger* and *Germanin*. The African Germans, who tended to be well educated, highly integrated and, in many cases, born in Europe, were thus forced to act out the role of semi-naked jungle savages.

As early as 1922 the colonial administration distinguished these protected 'German Negroes' from the 'real Negroes', the black occupation troops, and it was the latter's offspring, the so-called 'Rhineland Bastards', that became the main target of eugenic policies. These children, who numbered from 600 to 800, were viewed much more negatively as a living symbol of German defeat and humiliation. The infants became the centre of attention for the expanding ranks of race-scientists: one author claimed that according to Mendelian Laws, 'the German race will be polluted for centuries to come', while the visiting Swedish eugenic 'expert', the pastor Liljeblad, stoked up fears by estimating that such 'half-breeds' would number 27 000 by 1934. In 1933 Dr W. Abel of the *Kaiser Wilhelm Institute for Anthropology, Human Genetics and Eugenics*, carried out research on 27 children in Wiesbaden, claiming to demonstrate the usual flaws of the 'half-caste', particularly early psychoses and low intelligence. Abel went on to act as a race evaluator of the 'Special Commission 3', which in 1937 discreetly sterilized some 400 children.

Italian Fascism and Anti-Black Racism

In contrast to Germany, it has often been claimed by historians that Italian society was quite unreceptive to racism and that Mussolini's regime, resistant to biological racial doctrines, only went through a late conversion to official anti-Semitism in 1938 in order to seal the alliance with Nazi Germany. However, a number of historians have argued that the transition to political anti-Semitism was opened up by an earlier phase of colonial conquest and anti-black racism. Following on the conquest of Libya in 1932–3 Mussolini called on the Colonial Minister to take a tough line against miscegenation, and similar steps were taken after the brutal campaign in Ethiopia (1935–6). In line with other colonial powers, the Duce sought to eradicate *madamismo*, the common practice by which officers and civil servants cohabited with native women, and a law of April 19th 1937 imposed a sentence of between one and five years prison for such liaisons. The aim behind this was not to penalize white sexual relations with black prostitutes, but to prevent the birth of 'half-caste' children who would, it was thought, pollute and weaken the Italian race. The elaboration of biological race doctrine and legislation within the colonial context opened the way to the introduction of racial anti-Semitism in mainland Italy from 1938 onwards.

Inter-War Mass Culture and Racism

Lastly, this chapter looks at the revolutionary changes in mass culture during the inter-war period and the way in which this led to the diffusion of black stereotypes throughout Continental Europe. Historians of propaganda have shown how there was strong continuity between the themes of racism diffused in the age of the 'New Imperialism' prior to the First World War (see Chapter 2) and those of the inter-war period. For example, great international exhibitions, like those at Wembley in 1924–5 and in Paris in 1930–1, continued to show the 'domestication' of so-called primitive peoples. The genre of the boys' adventure story in which intrepid white heroes fought with cannibals and evil medicine-men remained ever-popular, although the old stereotypes were given a fresh impetus through new forms of mass consumerism and popular culture, like the comic-strip and film presentations of *Tarzan*. Edgar Rice Burroughs, in his first story, *Tarzan of the Apes* (1911), describes how the infant son of Lord Greystoke, shipwrecked on the West African coast, was raised by apes, and then effortlessly exerted his mastery over both the jungle and its primitive black inhabitants solely through his hereditary qualities as the son of a white aristocrat. 'With the noble poise of his handsome head upon those broad shoulders, and the fire of life and intelligence in those fine, clear eyes, he might readily have typified some demigod.' By contrast, blacks are constantly described as cannibals, witch-doctors and rapists, like Luvini who tries to assault Jane, a 'huge fellow, with a low receding forehead and prognathous jaw. As he entered the hut with a lighted torch which he stuck in the floor, his bloodshot eyes gazed greedily at the still form of the woman lying prone before him. He licked his thick lips and, coming closer, reached out and touched her.' Once again the compulsive obsession with miscegenation was transferred over into popular culture.[24]

Particularly interesting in the changing representation of black people was the role played by the new phenomena of jazz and dance. New forms of black American music and dance, the rag-time and the 'cake-walk', had already spread widely throughout Europe from the 1890s onwards, and had inspired classical composers like Debussy. But this was a mere foretaste of the jazz-craze and 'negromania' that took off from 1917, following the arrival in Europe of black regimental bands, like the Harlem Hellfighters and the Seventy Black Devils. During the 1920s, a young generation who wished to forget the horrors of war, and to caste off the prudery and stifling restraint of their Victorian elders, found a perfect expression in the 'hot' rhythms, the erotic physicality of the Charleston. During the 1920s controversy raged in Europe over jazz and served as a battleground for the definition of black art, the 'primitive' and latent racism.

The reactions of conservative Europe, as well as of emergent fascism, were fairly predictable: jazz, with its wild cacophony and exuberance, unlike anything in the repertoire of classical or popular music, was seen as profoundly decadent, an expression of dark instincts, of the black savage dancing and howling round jungle-fires to the throb of drums. Critics, like the German Arthur Rundt, saw jazz in racial terms: 'It is the animal freedom, to which the Negro, having landed in the teeming jungle of the World, gives keen expression... It is... the rhythm of America mirrored in the blood of the colored man.'[25] *Le Figaro*, reviewing Josephine Baker's famous erotic dance act in *La Revue Nègre*, described the show as a 'lamentable transatlantic exhibitionism which makes us revert to the ape in less time than it took to descend from it'.[26] Baker's tour of 1928–9 through Vienna, Budapest, Yugoslavia, Denmark, Romania, Czechoslovakia and Germany caused uproar and widespread condemnation of the naked and 'lewd' displays of the 'Congo savage'.[27] Even before Hitler came to power Wilhelm Frick, the Thuringian Minister of the Interior, issued a decree in September 1930 entitled 'Against Negro Culture – For German Nationhood' to suppress jazz, since it threatened to 'undermine the moral strength of the German nation'. In March 1933 the new Nazi government immediately banned jazz from the radio as a debased 'Judeo-Negroid' music, a form of 'musical decadence' that represented the 'disintegrating effects of cultural Bolshevist-Jewry'.[28]

However, not all Europeans' reactions were negative. Parisian intellectuals and artists, who were also drawn to African sculpture, lionized the American dancers and jazzmen, regarding them as the symbols of a dynamic and refreshing African spirit that challenged the exhausted and tight-laced culture of the West by, in the words of one critic, the 'return to the beginnings of the world, to the simplicity of the jungle'.[29] However, the avant-garde, in associating Africa with primitivism, inadvertently provided a fresh impetus to racial stereotypes by associating jazz with exotic images of the jungle savage. The French artistic directors of *La Revue Nègre* shifted Josephine Baker's show away from its background in the minstrel/plantation traditions of the American stage towards an 'African' programme of naked, eroticized brown bodies performing to 'jungle music'. In 1926 the semi-nude Baker appeared at the Folies Bergères wearing a suggestive skirt of bananas and, during her 1928 tour of Europe was attacked as 'degenerate' and 'pornographic' in Budapest and Vienna and was banned in Munich as a danger to public morals. Black performers like Josephine Baker fulfilled a highly ambiguous role: while through her rise to stardom and wealth in France she made a strong claim to black status and equality, she at the same time shaped her performances to conform to pre-existing French stereotypes of Africa and to a public demand that thrived off associations between black people, the jungle, bananas and apes. Such representations had more than a superficial import, the mere surface glitter of popular entertainment, since they underscored the almost universal assumption that Africans, racial primitives, would always remain backward and would never rise to self-government, but be eternally dependent on the kindly but firm hand of their white colonial masters.

The universality of racialized stereotypes of the black in inter-war Europe can be shown through the way in which it informed even Soviet culture, the regime which was most committed to the struggle for universal black rights and against colonialism. The official position of the Soviet Union was to support the doctrine of revolutionary internationalism and the struggle of all proletarians, regardless of creed or colour, united in the fight against capitalism and imperialism. The Communist International, in its support for anti-colonial, liberation movements in Africa and elsewhere, promulgated an egalitarian doctrine that served as a powerful bulwark against racism and fascism throughout Europe. Black writers and artists, like Claude McKay and Paul Robeson, were given a triumphant reception that was not merely the reflection of official Communist propaganda, but also of a genuine popular warmth. But Soviet intellectuals, as did many socialists in Western Europe, betrayed an incipient racism. In 1922 Meierhold, adapting a novel by Ilya Ehrenburg to the stage, complete with jazz band, depicted a sinister plot by American capitalists (here with undertones of anti-Semitism) to conquer Europe by colonizing it with Africans. But this plot was overturned by revolutionary heroes tunnelling from Petrograd to Wall Street, thus saving Germany, Austria and Britain in the nick of time from the horrors of cannibalism. This play was staged at the height of the Rhine crisis, during which the middle class throughout Europe fantasized about Western civilization being swamped by blacks. Maxim Gorky, one of the most influential ideologues in Russia, depicted jazz as a capitalist conspiracy to brainwash and control black Americans, and this dangerous music was now acting as a subversive force within Soviet society. This was a thinly disguised cover for the crudest racial stereotyping. 'Listening for a few minutes to these wails', claimed Gorky in 1928, 'one involuntarily imagines an orchestra of sexually driven madmen, conducted by a man-stallion brandishing a huge genital member.'[30]

Finally, in terms of black representation during the inter-war period an enormous impact was made through the cinema, which revolutionized popular entertainment and reached a vast and growing audience. In Britain the number of cinemas increased from 3000 in 1926 to 5000 in 1938, with annual ticket sales of 1000 million by the latter date. Nor was cinema restricted to the picture palaces of the more urbanized societies: film reached every corner of Europe, down to the travelling shows that visited village halls from Tuscany to the Polish *stetl*. The extraordinary visual power of film quickly made it a key factor, along with radio, in the diffusion of news and propaganda, and both Hollywood and national film production provide a valuable insight into racism and the representation of both blacks and Jews. Early Hollywood productions had often been crudely racist in form, like D. W. Griffith's notorious *The Birth of a Nation* (1915), which depicted the long pursuit of an innocent white girl by a lust-maddened and brutish black man, until she escaped dishonour by flinging herself down a cliff – a scene that led to its being banned by the French government in 1923. However, by 1925 European states were introducing legislative measures to restrict Hollywood domination, to nurture their own national film industries, and through offices of censorship, they were laying down strict guidelines on questions of morality and ethnic or racial representation. British censors were particularly sensitive to the impact of film on colonial audiences and banned pictures showing 'white men in a state of degradation amidst native surroundings', or 'equivocal situations between men of one race and girls of another race'.[31]

Down to 1914, a date coinciding with the completion of the partition of Africa, the main emphasis in the depiction of empire had been on the heroic and violent conquest of black savages. This was a staple in boys' adventure literature, as well as in the simulated battles of the great colonial exhibitions. During the inter-war period both France and Britain, worried by the rise of Pan-Africanism, Communism and other challenges to colonial rule, played down the frontier theme of military conquest and laid more emphasis on the peace, democracy, welfare and economic advance that benign imperial rule was bringing to the benighted savage. A favoured topic in many films was the story of how dedicated, or even saintly, doctors, braving every hardship in the jungle or outback, fought against superstition and the 'mumbo-jumbo' remedies of witchdoctors, finally winning over the illiterate natives to the benefits of European power and technology through demonstrations of the efficacy and superiority of Western medicine. Rapid advances in epidemiology after 1900, the control of malaria, typhus, typhoid and yellow fever, made the Western doctor a powerful symbol of the civilizing mission and of the legitimacy of colonial rule. In the French film *Itto* (1934), set in Morocco, a doctor saved the newborn son of the heroine from diptheria and she then persuaded him to prevent an epidemic through the inoculation of local children. A battle then ensued between superstitious anti-French rebels, misled by sorcerers, who tried to sell the vaccine for ammunition, and the local women, who eventually rescued the precious medicine. In the Axis co-production *Germanin*, directed in 1943 by Goebbels' brother-in-law, a heroic doctor, Professor Achenbach, was working in German East Africa to find a cure for the dreaded sleeping sickness when British officers destroyed his medical station. The professor continued his search for a vaccine in the IG Farben laboratories, returning to Africa in 1923 to a triumphant demonstration of an effective cure and of German superiority as colonizers over the British.

Through such films, in which Africans were invariably portrayed in 'ethnographic' sequences through native ritual, chanting crowds, dancing and beating drums, European directors conveyed a uniform message of white racial superiority. The backward native was trapped in the eternal horror of the 'Dark Continent', incapable through his low intelligence and racial sloth of ever improving his situation without the kindly, but firm directing hand of his white masters. This paternalistic, colonial ideology was massively promulgated through school textbooks, by missionaries and the popular press, so that hardly a child in Europe could not but feel a warm glow of altruism at the good works that 'we' personally were bringing to the poor savage. As one school text commented, in defiance of the extreme paucity and underfunding of indigenous education in the colonies: 'France wants the little Arabs to be educated like the little French children. This shows how our France is bountiful and generous towards the people she has conquered.'[32] However, this inter-war racism was, as long as black people kept in their subordinate role, relatively benign and paternalistic, bent on the protection of 'our' natives rather than, as the next Chapter shows, on the more violent and exclusionary strategies that inspired anti-Semitism.

5

ANTI-SEMITISM IN THE NAZI ERA

Any investigation of racial anti-Semitism in Europe during the second quarter of the twentieth century inevitably has to come to terms with what is probably the most intractable and most controversial of historical debates, that relating to the Holocaust. The recent libel action by the British historian David Irving, a 'Holocaust denier', against Deborah Lipstadt, is just one example of the way in which the issue of the mass killing of the Jews continues to arouse heated controversy, and to impact on contemporary ideological and political issues. A single chapter cannot possibly do more than to touch upon this immense and complex field: the approach taken here is to be deliberately selective and to present a particular interpretation, without giving full space to the countervailing arguments or theories. Inevitably, attention will focus on Germany as the epicentre of state racism, a genocidal strategy that was 'exported' to most of Continental Europe by the Third Reich. The structure of German anti-Semitic ideology is explored through Hitler's *Mein Kampf*, a typical 'populist' summation of inter-war racism.

How such a paranoid vision could ever have been translated into praxis, the barbaric legislation and killing apparatus of what Burleigh and Wippermann have called the 'Racial State', was significantly the responsibility of educated élites, of both key political players, as well as of 'race experts', from highly respected university professors of anthropology, medicine and eugenics, to legal experts and engineers.[1] The elaboration of genocide was, like all forms of modern racism, generated in a primarily top-down process. This is not to deny that there was no complicity by many hundreds of thousands of 'ordinary' middle- or working-class people. A diffuse, but deeply entrenched, popular anti-Semitism prepared the grounds for the widespread toleration of the gradual, but fatally deepening processes, the legal and political measures that opened the way to Auschwitz. However, as the very secrecy of the procedures surrounding the 'Final Solution' indicates, extermination was never initiated or approved by a wider public, nor did the Hitler regime seek a popular mandate for systematized killings that were always concealed under a language of euphemisms and codes.

The second part of the chapter goes on to examine anti-Semitism in other parts of Europe, particularly with regard to Poland, France, Italy, Hungary and the Soviet Union. Indigenous forms of anti-Semitism in these states were frequently tied into xenophobic nationalism and to right-wing, authoritarian regimes or political movements, but no matter how abhorrent and repressive this racism was, it did not assume a genocidal impulse. The extension of genocide into other European states was only made possible under the unique condition of Nazi conquest or hegemony, and with the active collaboration of small fractions of national élites that would, under normal peacetime conditions, have had no impact on mainstream politics or government policy. The transition towards systematic annihilation of the Jews was not an inevitable consequence of a deep, historical exterminationist ideology within German or European society, but rather of a political crisis that enabled a fanatical minority to seize power and to construct a German racial state, and to impose this on conquered satellites.

The Rise of the Nazi Movement

As was shown in Part 1, the decades before 1914 saw the spread of Social Darwinism and eugenics as well as the deepening of new, racialized forms of anti-Semitism. Eugenics, as the science of improving the biological well-being of the national stock, was not necessarily overtly racist: many of its exponents were Jews or Socialists, Social Democrats and Liberals. However, the core of Nazi ideology – which emerged from the chaos and slaughter of the First World War – represented a pulling together of the two strands of eugenics and anti-Semitism into an extremely potent and dangerous concoction. The distinctive feature of the period from the late phase of the First World War, through the Weimar Republic (1919–33) and down to the coming to power of Adolf Hitler in January 1933, is less the originality of racist ideas (there was little that had not already been said before 1914), but rather a profound political, social and moral crisis that enabled such virulent forms of anti-Semitism to spread within society and, finally, to receive a concrete expression in the Nazi racial state (1933–45).

Before examining Hitler's anti-Semitism, a few, brief comments about this background of military collapse and crisis, the general context in which Nazism began to thrive. Apart from a few exceptions, like the controversial thesis of Daniel Goldhagen in *Hitler's Willing Executioners*, most contemporary historians agree that the key to the crisis in German society that culminated in the Nazi dictatorship and the Holocaust can be located in the events of the First World War.[2] Firstly, it appeared to many Germans, Hitler included, that the defeat of 1918 had not come about by military means – the heroic and revered army had, it was claimed, stood firm – but because of the infamous 'Stab in the back', the treasonous subversion of the Reich by a combination of worker strikes, Bolshevik-inspired revolution, liberal defeatism and an international Jewish conspiracy. It was much more convenient for the military High Command, as well as a wider public, to search for scapegoats than to analyse the deeper causes of crisis within the failings of the traditional, authoritarian system or to accept any degree of responsibility.

The bitter and sour feeling of unwarranted defeat added to the humiliation of the terms imposed by the Allies through the Versailles Treaty. Germany lost 13 per cent of her territory, all her colonies, nine-tenths of her merchant fleet, and faced enormous reparation costs and a reduction of the armed forces to 100 000 men. The enormous economic costs of the first 'total war' had severely damaged infrastructures, lowered the standard of living, and indirectly led to the hyperinflation of 1922–3 that created a general panic and wiped out savings. Large sections on both the political right and the left mobilized for civil war, organized illegal proto-fascist paramilitary units or Communist workers' councils, and showed a contempt for parliamentary democracy which undermined the legitimacy of the infant Weimar government, 'a republic without Republicans'. Powerful conservative forces, including the army command and industrialists, fearing a revolution 'from below', were willing to give support and financial backing to extreme right wing or proto-fascist movements like the Fatherland Party, the fascist Schutz und Trutz Bund, the Free Corps and the German Workers' Party that resorted widely to violence.

Among the millions of demobilized soldiers, many of whom returned to unemployment and the soup-queue, was a particular kind of ex-serviceman who provided a ready source of recruitment for fascist paramilitaries. It has been argued that many of these men had been traumatized by the appalling conditions of modern trench warfare and inured to the dehumanizing conditions under which hundreds of thousands were reduced to mere objects of flesh. Life became cheap, the normal sensibilities to pain and suffering numbed, and the brutalized Free Corps units organized to crush the Spartacist revolution, or the brown-shirt thugs of the Nazi Party, injected into peacetime society extraordinary levels of casual violence. The fascist ex-servicemen were, above all, inspired by a virulent form of nationalism, and conditioned by years of militarization, which emphasized the importance of individual and heroic self-sacrifice on behalf of the higher value of the German *Volk*. The so-called *Volksgemeinschaft*, or national community, was imbued with an extraordinary emotional weight, a feeling that can only be described as quasi-religious in intensity. The disorientation and trauma that accompanied the collapse of the Reich found widespread expression in a sense of impending doom, of an apocalyptic vision of a terminal world crisis in which the German people were threatened with extinction. A distinctly paranoid view of an international 'Judaeo-Bolshevik' conspiracy, a Marxist-inspired race-war, intent on the destruction of the superior Aryan, was not only the pathological expression of a few mentally disturbed individuals, but was shared extensively across the right, from aristocratic conservatives in the High Command like General Ludendorff, to the rank-and-file fascists, like the unknown army propagandist, Adolf Hitler.

Racism in Hitler's *Mein Kampf*

One of the clearest documentary sources of the radical and potentially exterminationist anti-Semitism that emerged in 1918–23 can be found in *Mein Kampf*, dictated in prison during 1924. This text is not examined here because of the later importance of the *Führer* and its seminal role in the elaboration of the Holocaust, but precisely to the extent that it is a representative text, a fairly mediocre and typical expression of the paranoid prejudices of the 'little man', the street-fighting toughs of the Free Corps and other ex-soldier paramilitary organizations that pullulated after 1918. The memoir is particularly revealing of the way in which the scientific and political anti-Semitism of élites, relayed through newspapers, books and pamphlets, was picked up by *petit-bourgeois* or working-class activists and reconfigured into a crude populist blend.

Hitler, through his years of unemployment in the workers' hostels of Vienna (1906–13), in Munich and as a corporal during the First World War, had his roots in a lower-class milieu, while at the same time he had the education and *petit-bourgeois* origins that enabled him to read and absorb current racist texts and to recast them into a simplified, but powerful form. *Mein Kampf* provides a classic example of the way in which modern racist ideas, elaborated by intellectual élites, were diffused generally within society by an intermediary tier of opinion formers, what Gramsci would term 'organic intellectuals', from school teachers and priests to trade unionists, journalists, barkeepers, police officers and minor officials. Very little of what Hitler has to say is in any way original, rather he presents a potpourri of the eugenic and Social Darwinist thinking that had become generalized within German society.

Although *Mein Kampf* is an incoherent, repetitious and bombastic work, it is possible to detect within the verbiage a fairly coherent, if profoundly irrational, set of ideas. Hitler's thought started from the premise of a hierarchy of races, in which the Aryans (or Germans) occupied the pinnacle, the most advanced human type and the embodiment of superior moral, aesthetic, martial and cultural values. In line with so much nineteenth-century racial thought, Hitler interpreted the whole of history and contemporary international politics in terms of race conflict: 'The racial question gives the key not only to world history, but to all human culture.'[3] The driving force behind historical change was not class conflict, but rather a perpetual Social Darwinian struggle for racial dominance in which the weaker would inevitably go under and the higher type triumph. In this struggle, which for Hitler was redolent with the language of warfare, of martial strength and heroic self-sacrifice, the human spirit found its highest expression and ultimate meaning through the duty of guaranteeing the survival of the race. By fighting to ensure the victory of the highest form (the Aryans), the individual ensured a form of progress beneficial to all mankind, the long-term domination of the most advanced civilization and culture and the defeat of repulsive sub-human races. There was little here that had not already been elaborated by late nineteenth-century racists.

Hitler did not make it clear why it was that the Jews should wish either to enslave the Aryans or to exterminate them, except that they were driven by a 'diabolic' and destructive intent, a secular version of the age-old Christian anti-Semitism that regarded the Jews as engaged in an evil conspiracy to subvert and destroy Christian society. At a more Social Darwinian level, Hitler also believed that it was a Law of Nature that any group would be driven to try and assert its own dominance in the struggle for survival with other races. The evil and depravity of the Jews did not lie in their religion, but rather in their physical being, in the 'blood', and, as such, could never be expunged or modified by education, reform or any act of will. In this sense, they were inexorably driven to play out and fulfil their racial 'fate'. The Jews, in attempting to destroy the higher races, deployed a number of strategies, of which the three chief modes were international capitalism, revolutionary Marxism and biological race-war.

A central ingredient in the political anti-Semitism elaborated after the mid-nineteenth century was a belief in an international conspiracy of Jewish capitalists to exploit and enslave the national working class, as well as to undermine or destabilize national economies through their control of stock-markets, banks and other financial institutions. One of the most sinister ways in which subversion and weakening of the nation and *Volk* was achieved was through the deliberate fomentation of war, so that 'healthy' states would be thrown against each other in mutual destruction, while the Jews amassed huge profits from armaments sold to both sides. During the First World War the Jews had come under attack as shirkers and speculators, a treacherous fifth column, and Hitler echoed this in his claim that German war production had fallen almost entirely under Jewish financial control. British anti-German foreign policy that culminated in the First World War was controlled not by the government or national interest, but by Jewish finance which 'desires not only the complete economic annihilation of Germany, but also her complete political enslavement'.[4]

The second threat offered by the Jews arose in the form of Marxist Communism. Hitler saw in the Russian Revolution, and the ambition of the Comintern to spread revolution on a global scale, a deliberate conspiracy of Jews, mobilizing the power of barbaric 'Asian' or racially inferior Slav hordes gathered in the East to crush Germany. For him, as for many other anti-Semites, the proof for this could be found in the dominant role of Jews in the Bolshevik Party and in revolutionary movements in general. Karl Marx was a prophet who 'recognized in the morass of a slowly decomposing world the most essential poisons' and concentrated them 'for the swifter annihilation of the independent existence of free nations on this earth. And all this in the service of his race.'[5] It was the Communist organization of strikes and revolutionary movements in 1917–18 that had weakened Germany internally and led to the military defeat of 1918. The contradiction between Jews as both the masters of capitalism as well as revolutionaries bent on the destruction of German capitalism was resolved by Hitler through a distinction between subversive, Jewish international capital and the German national economy, which was to be protected in its 'economic independence and freedom'.[6]

However, the fundamental and most terrifying threat for Hitler, and the one that subsumed even the dangers of finance capitalism and Marxist revolution, was that presented to Aryan racial purity and strength: 'All really significant symptoms of decay...can in the last analysis be reduced to racial causes.'[7] The most devastating of all Jewish strategies was the attempt to destroy the racial substance of the German *Volk*. In line with contemporary eugenic science and race-biology, Hitler emphasized two ways in which the destruction of the Aryan race was being engineered. Firstly, the Jews encouraged all forms of hereditary disease and decay that undermined and enfeebled the national stock, from alcoholism and tuberculosis to birth control, abortion, the moral corruption of youth and the spread of venereal disease. Hitler, like many anti-Semites in an age when a profound fear of syphilis constituted a dark personal obsession, claimed that the Jews were the key organizers of international white slavery and prostitution. Venereal disease, a 'terrible poisoning of the national body', a 'mass contamination', resulted in hereditary degeneration, insanity and sterility. Birth control and family restriction was a 'Jewification of our spiritual life and mammonization of our mating instinct [which] will sooner or later destroy our entire offspring'. Hitler's rambling text was peppered with biological metaphors that presented the Jew as a physical embodiment of 'filth' and disease, a parasite that,'like a noxious bacillus keeps spreading as soon as a favourable medium invites him'.[8]

The most terrifying prospect of all for Hitler was, however, the prospect of racial mixing and an irreversible degeneration. At the core of Hitler's obsessive racism was the idea, a central concept in the modern racial theory that developed from the mid-nineteenth century onwards, that the hybrid offspring of parents from a high and a low race would be 'a medium between the level of the two parents'.[9] Interracial offspring would always constitute a weaker and inferior type and if the process of mixing was too extensive, it would eventually irremediably damage the master race. The exhortation against miscegenation carried all the teleological weight of the ultimate commandment: 'Blood, sin and desecration of the race are the original sin in this world and the end of a humanity which surrenders to it...The stronger must dominate and not blend with the weaker, thus sacrificing his own greatness' and peoples who 'bastardise themselves . . . sin against the will of eternal providence'.[10] Such passages in *Mein Kampf* echoed the best-selling novel of Artur Dinter, later Nazi *Gauleiter* of Thuringia, *The Sin Against the Blood* (1917), which adopted the stockbreeding theory of telegony, according to which one 'bad crossing' was sufficient to damage all subsequent offspring. In the novel a German woman, seduced by a Jewish army officer, was racially polluted so that even her child from a later marriage to the Aryan hero continued to show 'Semitic' traits. The diabolic plot to undermine the German race was, in Hitler's view, achieved in two ways. Firstly, Jewish marriage regulations tolerated a partnership between women and Christian males, a systematic policy deployed to 'poison the blood', while Jewish males 'practice the severest segregation', thus retaining racial purity and strength.[11] Secondly, the Jews deliberately encouraged miscegenation between Aryans and the lowest forms of racial life, as with the post-war deployment of French black troops into the Rhineland.

Hitler, following contemporary racial science, believed that such racial pollution of Aryan stock could not be reversed or 'bred-out' from future generations. Since such miscegenation had been going on since the Thirty Years' War, the terminal collapse of the Aryan race was perilously close; indeed, the defeat in the First World War was ultimately due to such biological deterioration. However, in a desperate race against time, it was still possible to reverse the process of degeneration since the nation still possessed 'great unmixed stock'. What was required was a eugenic race-breeding programme which would identify the pure Germans and ensure the proliferation of Aryan children, while at the same time banning miscegenation and destroying the reproductive capacity of the Jews. In order to justify this racial project Hitler deployed a pseudo-scientific and eugenic discourse: borrowing from the field of 'race-hygiene' that was disseminated widely in German culture, he outlined plans for the 'volkish state' to deploy the 'most modern medical means', including sterilization or euthenasia programmes aimed at the diseased, 'crippled' and 'cretins'; 'racial commissions' to certificate Aryan marriages; and the scientific 'breeding of absolutely healthy bodies'.[12] Hitler, who showed little understanding of genetic theory, had no hesitation in legitimating totally irrational ideas through a discourse that claimed ultimate scientific validity: in 1942 he told Himmler: 'the discovery of the Jewish virus is one of the greatest revolutions that has taken place in the world, the battle in which we are engaged today is of the same sort as the battle waged, during the last century, by Pasteur and Koch. How many diseases have their origin in the Jewish virus!'[13]

Some historians have noted that the language and symbolism of fascism was closer to that found in religion than rationalism; but a religion founded less on the Judaeo-Christian tradition, than on the sanctification of nature and the nation. As Mark Neocleous comments: 'In fascist thought the "laws of nature" are simultaneously scientifically verifiable and mystified. The resulting *biological mysticism* appears to have both the status of science and the power of religion.'[14] This was the central message developed and popularized in the early twentieth century by Ernst Haeckel and the Monist League. What was strongly conveyed through the language of *Mein Kampf* was a particular emotional and messianic charge, an apocalyptic feeling that the fate of the human race, or at least of its most sublime forms, was hanging in the balance and that the resolution would depend on a desperate war with the most cunning and powerful of enemies, the Jew.

Although the overall combination of ideas in *Mein Kampf* was unique to Hitler, the key concepts outlined above were not, it should be emphasized, the ramblings of a lunatic, but could be found widely dispersed both within German and European society. Just one example of this widespread and paranoid anti-Semitic vision can be provided by the notorious forgery, *The Protocols of the Elders of Zion*. This text, which was elaborated and diffused by Russian proto-fascists from 1897–8 onwards, found a global distribution after the First World War, was translated into numerous languages, and found widespread acceptance even among European educated élites. This bizarre and delusional text, which outlined a Jewish conspiracy for global domination, including the fomentation of Marxist revolution, found even a degree of acceptance in 1920 by staid organs like the British journals *The Spectator*, *The Morning Post* and *The Times*.

What made a radical difference in the case of Hitler was not so much the distinctiveness of his ideas, a populist rehash of contemporary currents, but the entire political complex in Weimar Germany that made it possible for the dictator to seize power in 1933 and to translate such a 'racial dystopia' into the horrific reality of a racial state. An older school of historical writing, particularly prevalent immediately after the Second World War, and recently revived by Daniel Goldhagen, ascribed the Holocaust to a peculiarly German 'ideology' of anti-Semitism that was so deep-rooted in the national character and traditions of the people that the vast majority of the population was prepared to tolerate or engage in genocide. As Goldhagen claims: 'Not economic hardship, not the coercive means of a totalitarian state, not social psychological pressure, not invariable psychological propensities, but ideas about Jews that were pervasive in Germany, and had been for decades, induced ordinary Germans to kill unarmed, defenceless Jewish men, women, and children by the thousands, systematically and without pity.'[15] Such an emphasis on the unique power of ideas cannot provide an adequate explanation for the Nazi phenomenon: if Hitler had not come to power in 1933, historians would today rank him alongside numerous other obscure and third-rate street agitators who promoted racial utopias. Significantly, political commentators and Jewish organizations in the period before the First World War were more apprehensive about the potential for state violence and repressive political anti-Semitism in France and Russia than in Germany.

Eugenics, Medical Science and the Nazi Racial State

However, this still leaves open the highly charged moral and political issue, one that continues to be central to the debate among historians, of the extent to which the dramatic shift after 1933 towards state-backed racism was supported, tolerated or opposed by the general population. Two aspects of this immensely complex and contentious issue will be briefly examined, the role of a growing body of experts in the construction of racial praxis (race institutions, research centres, legislation etc.) and the extent of popular anti-Semitism, as measured by government and opposition surveys of public opinion. As current research demonstrates, the grim road to Auschwitz was neither the sole responsibility of a Nazi élite that forced genocide on a terrorized and cowed nation, nor was it the work of an entire people who were actively complicit in mass killing. Rather the extent of racism in German society was a complex, frequently contradictory, phenomenon that cut across class and varied by region and religious affiliation.

A growing body of research has uncovered the close relationship between the Nazi implementation of a racial state and an expanding corps of race-scientists and technocrats who made medical murder and the technical machinery of mass killing possible. By the first decade of the twentieth century the German medical profession was already, through the development of 'racial hygiene' or eugenics, staking out a claim to determine government policy and to resolve major social problems, from crime to economic inefficiency. The huge loss of life during the First World War, and alarmist anxieties concerning imminent national and racial collapse, provided a further impulse to the status of eugenics and to the power of professionals that offered scientific solutions to a society in crisis. Under Weimar, medical race-science was already moving in a dangerous direction: most symptomatic of a growing body of professional thought was the idea that Christian or liberal traditions had made a pernicious dogma of the sanctity of human life. A powerful authoritarian current maintained that the life of the individual was subservient to that of the racial collective and that the state thus held the power of life and death over lower or 'worthless' forms of life, from 'aliens' to the hereditarily diseased, that weakened the *Volk*. Most disturbing was the spread of a dehumanizing, utilitarian discourse that treated human life in terms of 'materials' and cost-benefit analysis. The logic of euthanasia found a growing audience, as in the book by the lawyer Karl Binding and the psychiatrist Alfred Hoche, which in 1920 called for 'permission for the destruction of worthless life'.[16] During the Great Depression of 1929, which paved the way for the collapse of the Weimar Republic, the crisis shattered the economic base of a costly welfare state and provided further impetus for euthanasia programmes that would save the exchequer the 'high costs' of maintaining thousands of insane, mentally feeble and 'racial degenerates' in asylums and hospitals. However, while Weimar doctors did engage in some sterilization, in general the potential dangers of state racism and 'legalized' murder were kept in check by a Republic that remained true to the protection of individual rights. German eugenics was no more 'totalitarian' than the sterilization programmes that were legalized in the United States, Sweden, Norway, Denmark and elsewhere during the inter-war period.

The Nazi seizure of power in January 1933 led to the immediate implementation of 'race hygiene' legislation that introduced a vast programme of measures to eliminate the hereditary capacity of those designated as 'cretins', 'feeble-minded', 'criminals', 'homosexuals', 'gypsies', 'Jews' and 'mixed-race Negroes'. On 28 June 1933 the Minister of the Interior established the Committee of Experts for Population and Racial Policy, which included Nazi politicians like Himmler and Walther Darré, along with civil servants and academic experts like Professor Fritz Lenz. The *Law for the Prevention of Hereditarily Diseased Progeny* of 14 July 1933, the *Law against Dangerous Habitual Criminals* of 24 November 1933 and other measures opened the way for the compulsory sterilization or castration of over a third of a million children and adults. Later acts and decrees, in particular the *Law for the Protection of German Blood and Honour* (14 November 1935) facilitated the racial identification and registration of Jews and 'aliens' and forbade intermarriage or sexual relations with Aryan Germans. The euthanasia programme, authorized by Hitler on October 1939, led to the secret killing of over 5000 children and the medical and technical experts in charge of the gassing were later deployed to find a means to the 'Final Solution'. The programme for the total elimination of Jews (and other groups) presented a major bureaucratic, technical and medical problem that could only be resolved through the collaboration of many thousands of professionals, large teams of anthropologists, biologists, hygienists, economists, geographers and statisticians. Such experts were crucial to the legal constructions of 'race' (who was or was not a 'Jew'), to the complex card-index systems used to identify Jews, to the Hereditary Health Courts which adjudicated on sterilization, and to the overall invention, co-ordination and running of a mass killing apparatus. The pragmatics of racial genocide was thus very much a responsibility, not only of fanatical Nazi leaders, but also of professional élites.

There is an intense, ongoing debate about how it was possible for apparently civilized and highly educated people, lovers of Beethoven or Goethe, to engage in such horrific acts. On a material level the immense proliferation of professional posts, the establishment and extensive funding of race laboratories, research institutes, Health Courts and the overall structures of the racial state, provided a rich opportunity for academics, lawyers, civil servants and doctors to promote their careers and to achieve upward social mobility, high status and considerable wealth. Those race-scientists who were willing to engage with the Nazi agenda found opportunities for rapid promotion, while the lukewarm or resistant sank into obscurity. Such individuals, many of whom were apolitical and not fanatical in their anti-Semitism, had undoubtedly had their moral sensibility corrupted and blunted by a technocratic and scientific rationale which claimed that policy should be dictated by the unsentimental 'laws of nature', and which at the same time both depersonalized the victims and masked the brutal reality of murder through a veiled language. In the thesis of Zygmunt Bauman and others, genocide was a distinctive feature of modernity: for example, the extensive division of labour typical of capitalist society, a specialization of function that was reproduced in the killing apparatus of Nazi Germany, meant that a white-coated technician or researcher working in a laboratory dedicated to the physical properties of chemical gases could be quite distanced from the moral implications and dreadful reality of the 'end-use' of Zyklon B.[17] The process of desensitization, and the clinical or pathological dissociation between feelings or conscience and the reality of murder, was shown by the work of the medical assessors who, without ever seeing the patient, marked forms for disabled children with a '+' or '–' according to whether they were to die or not. One assessor, Dr Josef Schreck, was proud to have shown his dedication to efficient work by processing 15 000 forms 'very conscientiously' in nine months.

Anti-Semitic Repression and the German Public

The medical/biological level of the Nazi racist programme represents one small part of the governmental apparatus that persecuted the Jews, but it is typical of the way in which racist practice was implemented by élites working within the state apparatus. It remains to be seen how far such policies were made possible through the support of the general population. The intention here is not to examine the contested issue of how far the public was aware of the existence of the concentration camps: clearly such knowledge was quite extensive, but it has little to tell us about anti-Semitism. Far more revealing are the popular reactions to the much more visible manifestations of anti-Semitism between 1933 and 1939, prior to the 'Final Solution', such as Nazi racial propaganda, storm-trooper (SA) street-level violence (particularly the pogrom of November 1938) and discriminatory legislation. Fortunately, there exists in the security reports of the Nazi government, as well as in the intelligence reports by agents of the Socialist Party in exile, an extensive body of evidence on the mood of public opinion. Such material provides an excellent opportunity to explore the limits to the impact of racist propaganda, even under a dictatorial regime that could impose its will with the most extreme forms of violence.

Firstly, regional surveys of Nazi party mobilization show enormous variations in the extent to which anti-Semitism was a significant local issue. In some areas anti-Semitic *Gauleiters* could impose their ideas on local Nazi activists, as in Franconia and parts of Hesse, while other leaders were indifferent. In many rural areas attempts to remove Jews as cattle-dealers and middlemen met with resistance because they were seen to play an important economic function, and the Gestapo bemoaned 'the attitude of the peasants in which any sort of racial consciousness was missing'.[18] The most powerful core of opposition to

National Socialism came from the two working-class parties, the Social Democratic Party (SPD) and the Communist Party (KPD), along with the trade unions. However, within six months of seizing power the Nazi regime had not only banned all three, but also crushed the social base of the workers' movement in the housing estates, clubs and neighbourhood associations of the major cities. The growing reign of terror, the deployment of well-armed SA thugs, the mass incarceration of Socialists and Communists in concentration camps, and new legislation that made it a serious offence to marry, aid or even publicly sympathize with Jews, meant that acts of resistance required a considerable degree of courage. The impact of the totalitarian system was to destroy the organizational bases of protest, apart from the Catholic and Protestant Churches, and to drive individuals back into a private and isolated world. The overall position was well summed up by a Gestapo report from Münster: 'The true mood of the population is reflected in the passivity of great parts of the public towards the [Nazi] movement's activities. Only because of fear of reprisals has this attitude remained submerged.'[19]

In the summer of 1935 Nazi Party activists engaged in a wave of violent actions against the Jews, but secret reports show that this alienated the public, rather than winning approval. Many people ignored the boycott of Jewish shops and services, even though it meant defying intimidation by thugs. On the night of 9–10 November 1938 the Nazis co-ordinated a national pogrom of extreme violence, the so-called *Kristallnacht*, during which mobs smashed up or burned over 7500 Jewish shops and houses and 276 synagogues, and murdered 91 Jews. This was the one occasion during the Third Reich when the German public was directly and overtly confronted, on a national scale, with the full savagery of anti-Jewish violence. The overall response, far from one of support for this supposed expression of 'popular' feeling, was one of shame and disgust at the barbaric, orchestrated violence of Nazi fanatics. One witness wrote: 'No one to whom I spoke rejoiced in the shambles; on the contrary, those who were supposed to have been spontaneous about it stood around the newspaper kiosks registering puzzlement, perturbation, even disgust, or else they hurried past the hastily boarded-up windows on the Neuerwall with their gaze fixed firmly on their boots.'[20] Many people suspected that destruction of Jewish stores, far from being an expression of 'principled' ideological racism, was part of a campaign to destroy business competition. The National Socialist leadership was sufficiently chastened by the adverse public response to ensure later moves towards genocide were concealed. The secrecy which surrounded both the euthanasia programme as well as the 'Final Solution' shows all too clearly that the Nazi leadership knew that it could not rely on popular backing for its extermination policies.

From this it cannot be concluded that the German public was, in general, free from anti-Semitism: there was a deeply entrenched tradition of anti-Jewish prejudice that meant that the levels of resistance to the Nazi onslaught were weakened. Many Germans were not particularly opposed to 'decent' and 'proper' forms of legal discrimination against Jews, those measures that had the sanction of the state, but rather hostile to the unpleasant and 'unruly' forms of violence practised by SA thugs. But the tolerance of the initial legislation that inexorably chipped away at Jewish rights eventually opened the way to more insidious and murderous forms of repression. In general, the kind of anti-Semitism which was prevalent among the public was far removed from the ideological and exterminationist forms that were current among a small minority of Nazi leaders and activists. The government supported a vast propaganda apparatus to impose its racial *Weltanschauung* upon the 'national community', from cinema films and radio to school textbooks and exhibitions, but much of this had a limited impact. A Nazi party report commented: 'There is not a place without a *Stürmer* showcase, or other posters; every child learns about the Jewish menace; antisemitic propaganda is delivered in lectures everywhere; at every meeting, the party raises the Jewish question – and despite all this, the campaigns have not the slightest success.'[21] One of the reasons for this was that not even the most totalitarian of states could erase profoundly entrenched traditions and value systems, like that of the Catholic South and West of Germany, in which Jews were still fundamentally viewed as fellow human beings.

What the history of Nazi Germany confirms is a general feature of all forms of modern racism. The ideological elaboration of racism and its practical implementation through political programmes and governmental acts has been primarily the work of the middle class, of educated élites. The impetus to racism has in general been a top-down phenomenon in European societies rather than a consequence of popular initiatives and pressures from below. In particular, the detailed elaboration of racial legislation and decrees has invariably been the work of 'experts' operating within the state apparatus, particularly within ministries of the central government, with considerable degrees of autonomy from public opinion.

Anti-Semitism in Poland

When we turn to anti-Semitism in the rest of Europe during this period (1914–45), quite clearly the most dramatic shifts came with the Nazi conquest of Europe and the attempt to extend the 'Final Solution' to the whole Continent. The degree of collaboration with, or resistance to, Nazi Germany by occupied or satellite regimes, some 23 states in all, has been taken as a comparative measure of the depth of anti-Semitism across Continental Europe. Space does not allow an examination of all these countries, but the situation is analysed next in relation to Poland, Italy, France and Hungary, which provide a representative overview.

The situation in Poland was in many ways quite typical of many nations in Central and Eastern Europe, from Romania and Bulgaria to the Baltic states, in which anti-Semitism served as the cement for xenophobic right-wing movements of a conservative, Christian and traditionalist kind. This authoritarian and extremely nationalistic politics, located within traditional and predominantly agrarian or peasant economies, had little in common with fascism or with modern forms of scientific racism. Many of the new inter-war states of Central Europe faced the difficult task of nation-building after a long period of dependency on, or partition by, the Russian and Habsburg empires. All dreamed of establishing a coherent and unified order through ethnic homogeneity, but found their drive towards an integral nationalism frustrated by the presence of large minority groups. This was particularly true of Poland where, in addition to a Jewish population of 3 million (10 per cent of the total), there were German, Ukrainian and Byelorussian minorities.

At the end of the First World War the newly independent Polish government, against its wishes, was compelled to sign the Minorities Treaty (28 June 1919) which gave full rights to racial, religious or linguistic minorities, and full equality and state protection for Jews was ensconced in the 1921 Constitution. Many Poles felt resentment that such guarantees had been imposed on the new sovereign state by external, 'cosmopolitan' Jewish forces. Such feelings were especially strong in the National Democratic Party (the Endeks) founded in 1897, which under its leader Dmowski (1864–1939) engaged in political anti-Semitism that attempted to find a mass electoral base through whipping up hostility to the Jews.

The Polish Jews, as elsewhere in Central Europe, held a leading position in commerce, industry and the university-trained professions, and this fuelled economic anti-Semitism among the conservative middle classes, who were keen to remove them as competitors. But, above all, the Endeks thrived on a quasi-racist and exclusionary form of nationalism which refused to accept that Jews could become a part of a Polish nation that was defined in *volkish* terms as an organic community founded on Catholicism, language, culture and an essential identity of 'spirit'. Unlike the situation in Western Europe, Poland not only had a very large Jewish population, one-fifth of the world's total, but the majority were Orthodox, were quite distinctive in dress, culture and language (87 per cent Yiddish- or Hebrew-speaking) and clearly identifiable as a community which was separate from the Poles, for whom national identity was defined by Catholicism. Dmowski maintained that even assimilated or converted Jews could never become true members of the Polish nation, and that if such integration was attempted, it would radically undermine and even destroy the nation from within. Armed with a virulent and exclusionary nationalism, the Endeks organized a large-scale boycott against Jewish business in 1912, and in the inter-war years pushed for legislation which would severely restrict the political and economic rights of Jews and, ultimately, force their physical expulsion from the nation.

Although the Endeks were fully aware of the virulent forms of 'scientific' racism that were spreading in inter-war Germany, on the whole they appear to have avoided formulating their own anti-Semitism in biological terms. The Endeks were profoundly anti-German and concerned to block the historic drive of the Germans towards the east, and this may explain why Dmowski established much closer links with fascist Italy which he admired as a model of the authoritarian, anti-Bolshevik state. However, much more significant than this restriction on Nazi influence was the difficulty faced by a profoundly Catholic movement in formulating a biological and radical anti-Semitism, while not breaching the official and doctrinal condemnation of scientific racism by the Church. The central role of Catholicism in Polish integral nationalism explains why, unlike in secularized Western Europe, racism was not elaborated in a modern, biological form, but rather in terms of a much older tradition of anti-Semitism in which Jews were accused of ritual murder or being the collective killers of Christ. Cardinal Hlond, the Primate of Poland, in a pastoral letter that was read from the pulpit in parish churches, proclaimed: 'It is a fact that the Jews fight against the Catholic Church, they are free-thinkers, and constitute the vanguard of atheism, of the Bolshevik movement and of revolutionary activity... their publishers spread pornographic literature. It is true that the Jews are committing frauds, practising usury, and dealing in white slavery.' However, Hlond went on to qualify his vicious circular by warning against, 'the fundamental, unconditional anti-Jewish principle' imported from Nazi Germany since it was against Catholic ethics and 'not permissible to hate anyone. Not even Jews.'[22]

The leading anti-Semitic ideologue Boguslaw Miedzinski, who in 1938 called for the forced emigration of all Jews, made use of a biological language: the Jew 'is a foreign body, dispersed in our organism so that it produces a pathological deformation' requiring 'removal of the alien body'. However, he went on to reject racism and to support 'positive nationalism' and 'the position that the distinctiveness of a nation's culture is an immeasurably high value that must be defended and developed'.[23] Inter-war Poland demonstrates how the far right, within a nation undergoing a profound crisis of modernization, expressed anti-Semitism in 'archaic' forms, rather than through an elaborate anthropological or biological racism. However, through making cultural difference and group boundaries absolutely impermeable, such formulations of cultural racism could serve an identical function of exclusion as the 'modern' form and give rise to similar levels of repression and violence (see Chapter 7 on the 'New Racism').

There has been much debate as to whether Poland, the location of so many of the Nazi camps and mass killings, was taking an independent path towards genocide during the inter-war period. During the hardship of the Depression and after the death of the dictator Pilsudski in 1935, who had provided a bulwark against the fascist right, anti-Semitism assumed a much more extreme and violent form. During 1935–6 some 1289 Jews were wounded in attacks in over 150 locations. Nazi racism began to find a more receptive audience and in 1934 Goebbels lectured on the 'Jewish question' at Warsaw University. The Endeks formally broke with the anti-racist policy of the Catholic Church, and the ruling Sancja began to resort to anti-Semitism to retain its base of political support. However, this dangerous drift towards violence was restrained by a number of factors. The Polish government, right down to the outbreak of war with Germany, never broke with the liberal Constitution of 1921 nor implemented a single piece of anti-Semitic legislation, while various fascist organizations were banned in 1933. Secondly, the main class base of the Endeks and of ultra-nationalism was found among a small and fragile middle class, spear-headed by militant students, who felt inferior alongside the superior commercial and professional skills of the Jews. However, as in Germany, racial anti-Semitism found little support among either the peasantry or the working class that fell under Communist or Socialist leadership. It is not at all certain that had Poland retained its independence and avoided conquest by Nazi Germany, it would ever have implemented a genocidal programme, although there can be little doubt that the widespread diffusion of traditional anti-Semitism in Polish society did prepare the way for public indifference towards repression of the Jews and for a minority to become actively involved in collaboration and mass murder.

Anti-Semitism in Fascist Italy

Italy under Mussolini (1922–43), one of the most advanced industrial nations in Western Europe, provides an interesting contrast with both Poland and Hitler's Germany since it would indicate that an authoritarian fascist nationalism, that emphasized corporate unity in opposition to Marxism and class-conflict, was not necessarily built upon anti-Semitic racism. The Italian Jews constituted not only a minute percentage of the total population (0.1 per cent), but were highly integrated such that in 1938, 43.7 per cent of Jews were married to Gentiles and also held numerous positions within the Fascist Party. Anti-Jewish sentiment was so insignificant within Italian society that the opportunist Mussolini appears to have seen no political gain from espousing it during the period 1922–36. Mussolini, the 'elder statesman' of fascism until 1933, disliked the extreme ideological forms of racism that emerged on the German right, objected to the rise of Nazi violence, and denounced scientific racism as untenable and unacceptable within the Italian context. A first significant shift towards state racism took place in 1936–8, however, within the context of the Abyssinian War and arose mainly from colonial racism and an imperial hostility to miscegenation with black Africans. In a key document, the *Manifesto of the Race* (July 1938), Mussolini defined all races in purely biological terms, classified the Jews as separate from the Italian 'Aryans' and unassimilable and banned intermarriage.

It would appear that this shift in policy came about not because Mussolini was giving way to pressure from Nazi Germany (Hitler withheld from interference in Italian domestic politics), but as a sign of solidarity with his powerful ally. Sir Andrew Cadogan, in a memorandum of January 1939, remarked on the shallow roots of Italian racism: 'in spite of anti-Semitic policy and legislation, anti-Semitism outside a restricted Government circle is non-existent'.[24] In spite of Jewish internment from

June 1940, the conditions in the camps were relatively comfortable, and the fascists opposed the geographic extension of the 'Final Solution' and intervened against the massacre of Jews in Croatia and Greece. In November 1942 Italy, after it had occupied eight French departments east of the Rhone, banned the wearing of the yellow star imposed by the Vichy regime, stopped all deportations to the concentration camps, and created a temporary haven for Jews escaping from western France. It was only after the Germans had occupied Italy in 1943 that they were able to accelerate the brutal round-up of Jews and extend the 'Final Solution'.

Anti-Semitism in France

Racial anti-Semitism had far deeper roots in French culture than it did in that of Italy. After the defeat of the Dreyfusards, who had utilized anti-Semitism as a weapon with which to attack the core values of the secular Republic (see Chapter 3), the forces of the far right were reduced to an impotent and weakened minority. Significantly, *La Libre Parole*, the flagship of the anti-Semitic press, was forced to close down in 1924 for lack of subscribers. However, where France differed from most other European states during the inter-war period was in the formidable literary and intellectual skills of its anti-Semitic writers: Georges Bernanos, Charles Maurras, Maurice Barrès, Robert Brassillach, Drieu de La Rochelle, Louis-Ferdinand Céline, Léon Daudet and others. However, their diatribes – which reached unprecedented levels of verbal violence and pornographic insult – were influenced by the style of Drumont and differed little from the anti-Semitism of the late nineteenth century. The Jews were depicted, in the classic tradition, as eternal outsiders who could never become assimilated to the French 'blood', a vile race of parasites who were, through hereditary instinct, dedicated to the destruction of traditional France by means of cosmopolitan capital, prostitution, sexual perversion and disease. Typical of the vicious style of French anti-Semitism was Charles Castellani's denunciation of the 'Jew's Moloch' as 'the emblem of all foreign lewdness: filthy, sensual, patron of pederasts: a black and viscous reptile'.[25] But no matter how mordant or destructive was the expression of literary fascism, it can, taken on its own, tell us little about the degree of support for anti-Semitism generally among the French public.

During the 1930s conditions became ripe for the spread of xenophobia. The great economic depression, in conjunction with the arrival of many hundreds of thousands of immigrant workers and refugees, most notably one million Spanish Republican exiles in 1939, created a strong current of anti-foreigner sentiment. The growth of fascist leagues like the Parti Social Français and the Parti Populaire Français, and the tense climate of impending civil war that was ushered in by the Popular Front, marked a resurgence of right-wing activity. Léon Blum, as prime minister (1936–7), became the object of a sustained anti-Semitic campaign: Blum, wrote Jules Blacas, 'is the complete traitor who turns your skin into money and gambles on your failure or your blood in the cesspool of shit of the international banks . . . shake off all the Blums hooked to your shoulders, who are sucking your blood like a tick or a flea. He is not French! He stinks of the ghetto and he hates you.'[26] However, the growing wave of racism was firmly contained until the defeat by Germany in 1940. The Communist and Socialist Parties both strongly opposed fascism and racism, and the government in 1936 dissolved the Action Français, imprisoned its leader Maurras for incitement to violence and banned the paramilitary Camelots du Roi. The Marchandeau Decree (21 April 1939) banned press incitement to hatred on the basis of race or religion. France, unlike many other European states, also resisted the call for negative eugenics and a law on sterilization or premarital medical examination for hereditary fitness.

All this changed dramatically following the rapid defeat by Germany in June 1940 and the retreat of the collaborationist French government into the southern, unoccupied zone. The historians Marrus and Paxton have shown in close detail that the enormous range of anti-Jewish legislation introduced by Vichy, as well as the mass deportation to the concentration camps after July 1942, was not the consequence of a German diktat, but was to a considerable extent carried out voluntarily by French initiative. However, racial measures which destroyed Jewish rights, 'aryanized' their property, and facilitated internment, were largely the work of relatively small, but powerful, groups of anti-Semitic ideologues or dutiful functionaries, like Xavier Vallat and Darquier de Pellepoix, and not the consequence of popular anti-Semitic pressure. The reactions of the French public to deepening repression provides a good indication of the scale of anti-Jewish feeling and the limits or cut-off points beyond which violence or mistreatment became unacceptable. In general, the early Vichy legislation, which imposed economic and professional disabilities on Jews, such as a *numerus clausus* of 2 per cent for university students and the professions of medicine, law, pharmacy and architecture, seems to have received a significant degree of assent.

However, the imposition of a Yellow Star on 15 March 1942, the first clearly visible sign of persecution, produced widespread opposition among a public who felt it to be profoundly offensive and shameful. The German extension of the 'Final Solution' into France after July 1942 and the sight of Jews being arrested or herded into cattle-wagons caused an outcry, even among ordinary people who had been loyal to Marshal Pétain. The Bishop of Toulouse, Jules-Gérard Saliège, composed a pastoral letter that was read in all the parishes of his diocese on 23 August 1942: 'That children, that women, fathers and mothers be treated like cattle, that members of a family be separated from one another and dispatched to an unknown destination, it has been reserved for our own time to see such a sad spectacle . . . The Jews are real men and women . . . They are part of the human species. They are our brothers like so many others.' The bishop of Montauban, in another pastoral, also reaffirmed the church's doctrinal opposition to racism: 'all men, Aryans or non-Aryans, are brothers.'[27]

The underlying situation in the transition to state racism, the elaboration of an extremely complex and far-reaching body of anti-Semitic laws and practices, was similar in France post-1940 to Germany under the National Socialists after 1933. In both states the creation of legislation that removed civil rights from Jews was only possible under the exceptional conditions of dictatorship or war that destroyed the normal safeguards of liberal democracy. Such exceptional conditions enabled small minorities of racist ideologues to infiltrate or seize the machinery of state power, and to impose their obsessive and murderous fantasies of racial purity. Although both societies, prior to the collapse of Republican legality, had some of the most sophisticated racial ideologues in Europe and were also generally suffused with 'low-level' and traditional forms of anti-Semitism, there is no evidence that racist opinion in itself created a popular pressure for the anti-Jewish measures that were introduced by the Nazis or by Vichy France. However, a high level of propaganda and the dissemination of anti-Jewish sentiment appears to have created a climate of public indifference or apathy towards the fate of the Jews and made it possible for the first fatal steps to be taken towards repression without significant opposition. Many French people were quite willing to accept those first-phase measures that appeared to be executed according to 'due process of law', that superficially carried all the appearances of legitimate state acts, but this compliance began to disintegrate when overt acts of ritual humiliation and of violence began to indicate that the state itself had fallen into the hands of a brutal and inhuman clique. But it was in the very nature of dictatorship or a regime built on violence that by the time the public came to recognize the full reality of state terror, it was extremely difficult, or too late, to engage in political opposition.

However, for a small minority of racist ideologues, the collapse of liberal democracy created a window of opportunity. As racial states began to construct elaborate institutions and administrative machinery for the 'scientific' study, identification, census and legal destruction of Jews, so a whole new field of employment and promotion arose for previously obscure 'experts'. In France during the 1930s the Swiss-trained physician George Montandon wrote a number of works in which he claimed to have made new advances in the science of identifying Jews by physical characteristics, in reality a hotchpotch of techniques from what was already an outmoded physical anthropology (the measurement of an 'average nose', of feet shape, the lips etc.). Darquier de Pellepoix, the head of the Commissariat-General for Jewish Affairs, the main Vichy agency involved in the 'Final Solution', recruited racist thinkers to carry out research and lecture in a number of new centres, among them the Institute for the Study of Jewish and Ethno-Racial Questions headed by Montandon. Such race specialists as René Martial, Claude Vacher de Lapouge, Gérard Mauger, Charles Laville, would in the normal course of events have remained obscure and minor academics, even derided outsiders, but Vichy opened the way to rapid promotion and power. Most deadly of all, it made possible the transition from the purely theoretical plane towards the practical implementation of their 'science'. Montandon, for example, acted as a leading consultant and deployed his expertise to undertake racial examinations to determine whether an individual was a Jew, a procedure which was to decide the fate of many and whether they were to be sent to the concentration camp or not.

Anti-Semitism in Hungary

Such a transition in France towards genocide, and the rise to power of individuals keen to participate in the racial state, was only made politically possible, despite high levels of French collaboration, through Nazi conquest and domination. In general this remains true for the rest of Europe, as is shown most clearly by the case of Hungary. Although Hungary, like Poland and Romania, had a strong anti-Semitic tradition and an indigenous fascist movement (the Arrow Cross), the authoritarian regime of Admiral Miklós Horthy represented an old-style authoritarian government rather than a 'modern' totalitarian or fascist form of rule. In 1938 Horthy, like the leaders of other Central and East European states, had attacked the strong position of Jews as entrepreneurs and professionals within the traditional, agrarian society of Hungary, and imposed a quota of 20 per cent on Jews in sectors of private business and the professions. Such forms of economic anti-Semitism were not, however, driven by a logic of genocide and Hungary, although an ally of Nazi Germany, strenuously defended its Jewish nationals against all German pressures to implement the 'Final Solution' and to deport them to the extermination camps. However, this all changed quite dramatically when German troops occupied Hungary in March 1944 and, although facing inevitable defeat, the Nazi racial apparatus set about annihilating over 300 000 Jews in a last desperate attempt to wipe out the 'biological enemy'.

Anti-Semitism in the Soviet Union

Lastly, the Russian Revolution, and the survival of the Soviet Union after a phase of civil war, ensured that a large bloc of Continental Europe, with one of the biggest Jewish communities, would fall under a Communist regime with a radically different, anti-racist ideology. Prior to the First World War, Tzarist Russia, among all European states, had retained the most powerful and elaborate legal and political system for the segregation and oppression of the Jewish minority. Since, at a later stage, the Stalinist regime remained tainted with anti-Semitism, it is often overlooked how far the Russian Revolution marked, if not a liberating moment for Jews, at least a dramatic elimination of the Tzarist Pale and a modicum of protection against both pogroms and a descent into the forms of genocide that developed further to the West.

The Revolution and Civil War (1914–21) created a situation of chaos in which the anti-Bolshevik White Army, as well as anarchist forces under Nestor Makhno, were able to give vent to anti-Semitism, pillaging and murdering on a vast scale. Some 600 000 Jews were displaced or became refugees, 150 to 200 000 were killed or wounded, while 300 000 children were orphaned. The aristocratic and conservative officers of the White Army, confronted with the disintegration of the old order, were obsessed with the myth of a global Jewish conspiracy. As the English journalist John Hodgson noted, officers 'held that the whole cataclysm

had been engineered by some great and mysterious society of international Jews'.[28] The White Army would not recruit those who had a Jewish parent or grandparent, and an apocalyptic vision of disintegration
was described in a pathological anti-Semitic language ('it is necessary to
neutralize the microbe') that was comparable to later Nazi propaganda.
However, the wave of pogroms was firmly opposed by the Communists
who took a clear ideological position against racism. The Provisional
Government had, in a decree of 22 March 1917, annulled the great mass
of legal restrictions on Jews that had accumulated under the Empire,
and the Constitution of the Russian Soviet Republic (July 1918) granted
equal rights to all citizens irrespective of racial or national affiliation.

Marxist and Leninist theory, which formed the base of Communist
rule throughout the Soviet period, opposed Zionism and all forms of
Jewish nationalism. The Jews, it was thought, did not constitute a people
or nation, but a 'sect' that should be rapidly assimilated into Communist
society. The anti-religious and assimilationist drive to end Jewish identity
can be interpreted as an egalitarian and pseudo-universalizing doctrine,
like that of French secular Republicanism, that recognized equal rights
for all, as long as they abandoned cultural particularism. Communist
doctrine, although acting in a repressive way towards minority rights,
was fundamentally opposed to all forms of racist ideology. The Soviet
Union thus offered a profound break with the anti-Semitic traditions
of Tzarist Russia and the Red Army offered a haven to the thousands
of Jews who were threatened by the Whites during the Civil War. The
Bolsheviks undertook a large-scale propaganda campaign against anti-
Semitism within the armed forces and the work-place. However, it is
hardly surprising that such a dramatic change in direction, largely
imposed from above, could not readily eliminate centuries-old traditions
of anti-Semitism embedded within Russian popular culture. The prominent position of Jews in the Soviet government and in economic and
educational institutions revived the old hatreds and the claim that Jews
were taking over at the expense of the Russian people. During 1926 to 1929
there was a resurgence of anti-Semitism, of physical attacks, beatings
and even pogroms. This was met by a large-scale official campaign which
countered anti-Semitism through books, pamphlets, plays, films and
public meetings in work-places and elsewhere. In January 1931 Stalin
denounced 'Anti-Semitism as an extreme form of racial chauvinism, it is
the most dangerous vestige of cannibalism'.[29]

Stalin was himself ready to deploy anti-Semitic slurs in his attack on
opponents like Trotsky, Zinoviev and Kamenev, and as his paranoia

deepened so did his anti-Semitism towards 'foreign' or international agents, as during the Moscow Show Trials of the mid-1930s. However, in spite of a totalitarian and repressive regime that engaged in a vast abuse of human rights, neither Stalin nor the Soviet state as a whole engaged in official support for racist or anti-Semitic ideology. The underlying philosophy of Marxism, which placed a crucial emphasis upon sociological explanations of society rather than upon essential and unchanging elements such as national character and race, did not readily lend itself to a naturalization of difference or to a racial world-view. Thus, although the Soviet system was flawed by the deep-lying sediments of anti-Semitism that resurfaced from time to time, in general terms the powerful bloc of the USSR acted as a serious impediment to the racial doctrines and practices that swept across the rest of Europe between 1933 and 1945.

PART 3

1945–2000

The Second World War and the disclosure of the almost unimaginable atrocities of the Holocaust marked a major watershed in European racism. The universal acceptance of 'race' as a central tool in the understanding or interpretation of history was now powerfully challenged and genocide cast a deep shadow over all debate on racism. Post-1945 no discussion of race could retain the 'innocence' and widespread acceptance of the 'natural' and scientific veracity of the pre-War era. A major movement by scientists to discredit the idea of 'race', although initiated in the 1930s, began to make a major impact from the 1950s onwards. Post-war governments and the general public, from Germany to Russia, could not readily tolerate anti-Semitism, particularly as commemoration of the allied struggle was structured in terms of the heroic sacrifice of those who had given their lives to ensure the defeat of the hideous forces of racist Nazism and fascism.

However, the first post-war phase explored in Chapter 6 (1945–74) was also one of mass labour migration into Western Europe. This was partly encouraged by governments to resolve a problem of labour shortage during a period of sustained economic growth and partly triggered by the processes of decolonization. The crisis in colonialism, which was marked in many regions of the globe by extremely bloody wars and high costs in manpower and military expenditure, further stoked up European racism towards 'inferior' peoples and national liberation struggles that shook imperial self-confidence and white superiority to the roots. The concomitant arrival of some 15 to 16 million colonial immigrants inside Europe, of peoples that were physically and culturally distinct and highly visible, meant that popular racism began to target the new black minorities, while prejudice against the Jews became more muted or concealed. However, anti-Semitism did not disappear, but went underground and remained central to the far-right political movements that began to find electoral support by attacking immigration. Governments and political movements post-1945 were obliged to define their position in relation to both modalities of race, anti-black prejudice and anti-Semitism, unlike the pre-Second World War era when this was not necessary.

The first phase of mass labour immigration (1945–73), when European economies actively sought 'Third World' labour, gave way to a second phase of strict immigration control and frontier closure (Chapter 7). Although the 1973/4 watershed coincides neatly with the oil crisis, global recession and increasing unemployment, it will be argued that the deepening racism that affected mainstream parties and government had as much to do with pressures developed within the political system as it did with purely economic causes. The last two decades of the twentieth century were marked by a resurgence of extreme right-wing movements that operated outside democratic, electoral politics and engaged in systematic violence. But more threatening to the liberal order was the emergence of a new type of far-right party, of a populist and xenophobic nationalism, that did seek power through the electoral system and sought legitimacy by a propagandist distancing from the taint of Nazism. The French Front National served as a model for similar parties that began to make significant gains in Germany, Belgium, Italy, Switzerland and Austria. This strategic shift and transformation of the traditional far right was greatly assisted by the formulation of a so-called 'New Racism' that replaced scientific and biological racism with a discourse of cultural racism defending the right to 'difference', to protect national or European identity from the 'swamping' effect of alien, immigrant cultures. Traditional parties, both of the Social Democratic left or the conservative right, responded to this serious electoral challenge not by placing a *cordon sanitaire* around national-populism, but by themselves taking a 'firm' line on immigrants and refugees that further legitimated hostility towards minorities.

Finally, the Conclusion examines some of the general implications of this study, the usefulness or otherwise of theorizing about racisms in the plural, as well as some prognostications as to the development of contemporary racism as we move into the twenty-first century.

6

RACISM IN THE AGE OF LABOUR IMMIGRATION, 1945–1974

The Second World War, and the recognition of the appalling reality of the Holocaust, marked a major turning point in the history of racism. The biological theories of race that had been so widely shared in Europe for two centuries were exposed by mainstream science as lacking in validity. This revisionism went hand-in-hand with a post-Holocaust awareness that the 'myth' of race had led, and could continue to lead, to inter-group hatred, discrimination, and large-scale violence and systematic murder. After 1945 any debate on the issue of 'race' was informed, whether explicitly or implicitly, by the consciousness of the hideous reality of genocide, and this universal awareness meant that the kind of 'innocence' with which the validity of race-science had been taken for granted in the century before the Nazi phenomenon was no longer possible. The 1945 break in the paradigm of race-science functioned at various, mutually reinforcing levels. Firstly, the old science that was grounded in a belief in the concrete reality of absolutely distinct and separate races was fundamentally challenged by a majority consensus of anthropologists, sociologists and geneticists who demonstrated the radical flaws within earlier forms of race thinking. Secondly, there was a political break in that post-1945 European governments created a 'post-hoc' legitimation for the war against Nazism, on the grounds that it was necessary to defeat a regime capable of the horrors of the 'Final Solution'. Having recently sacrificed millions of lives in the war against fascism, a sacrifice of those who were only recently dead and who were mourned and commemorated on a large scale through new monuments, parades and

169

ritual, the post-war political order could not readily tolerate a resurgence of racism. Thirdly, there was a widespread moral revulsion
against genocide, the full horror of which was only gradually revealed to
the public through film and print, which meant that any attempts to
openly support racism immediately brought into play associations with
the gas ovens and triggered a powerful, hostile response.

The Attack on the Science of 'Race'

The attack on scientific racism had already begun to gather strength
during the inter-war period, particularly among British and American
scientists who set out to discredit Nazi racism. That 'race' was no longer
universally accepted as a self-evident fact, like the force of gravity, was
indicated by the first use in English during the 1930s of the neologism
'racism', the idea that belief in the reality of fixed races was itself a misguided
doctrine or 'myth'. The single most famous expression of this anti-racist
revisionism was a small book by Julian S. Huxley, A. C. Haddon and
A. M. Carr-Saunders *We Europeans* (1935), which explained modern genetic theory in layman terms to show that biological races did not exist.
Mendelian theory, it argued, demonstrated that human populations were
so intermixed by millennia of migration, and shared such a vast pool of
genetic material, that it was not possible to divide them up into 'pure
races'. Racism, including contemporary Nazi theories of Aryan or
Nordic supremacy, was based on an original ideal type, a myth of a pure
race that had never existed, and which could never be recovered in the
present through some kind of eugenic selection that would filter out the
'inferior' elements that had become 'mixed' into the 'blood'. Contemporary 'violent racialism', or Nazism, was interpreted as a symptom of
virulent nationalism which was seeking to provide itself with scientific
legitimacy and false explanations for problems that had deep economic,
political and social roots. The book recommended that the term 'race'
should be dropped from the vocabulary of science and be replaced by
the term 'ethnic group'.[1]

We Europeans was an important text since it clearly established the
central components of the anti-racist paradigm that became dominant
throughout the second half of the twentieth century. However, in spite
of the attempts by liberal scientists to counter Nazi racism through populist works before the outbreak of the Second War, in reality they were
able to change the attitudes of only a very tiny segment of the educated

public. A more significant shift had to wait until the more receptive political climate of post-Holocaust Europe. The most important initiative was undertaken by UNESCO (United Nations Educational, Scientific and Cultural Organization) which in December 1949 convened a Committee of Experts on Race in Paris, symbolically in the same building that had been five years earlier the German military headquarters. The Committee of international experts in anthropology, sociology, genetics and social psychology drew up a *Statement on Race* (18 July 1950) which was widely disseminated in the media and used world-wide as the key text in educational programmes. The *Statement* presented, in an abbreviated and clear form, ideas very similar to those of *We Europeans*: all mankind belonged to the same common stock and biology supported 'the ethic of universal brotherhood'. Since 'educability and plasticity' had been at a premium in man's mental evolution, cultural experience rather than 'race' had been crucial in the development of human groups. There was an 'essential similarity in mental characteristics among all human groups'. The concept of 'race' was so scientifically untenable, and had been the cause of so much barbarism, that it would be better to drop the term altogether and to speak of 'ethnic groups'.[2]

In the immediate post-war years UNESCO exemplified the official anti-racist position, which showed an overly optimistic faith in the power of education and enlightened rationalism to dispel racism by showing that it was built on unscientific and mythical ideas. However, the crusade against racism, while it did much to create a climate of opinion in which most politicians avoided public statements of prejudice, did not eradicate the deep historic roots of European racism. A number of factors contributed to a powerful continuity between pre- and post-war racism, although this was often concealed under an official discourse that excoriated the evils of Nazism and vowed that such barbarism should never be allowed to recur. Firstly, it was not easy for the new anti-racist science to demonstrate, and convince public opinion of, the rather difficult genetic and anthropological theories that would rationally dissolve the racial categories. Science was counter-intuitive and seemed to be denying the differences of 'black' and 'white' that were so real and objective to 'common-sense racism'. Instead of going into retreat, the unhyphenated term *race* continued to be used at all levels of society, including within legislative acts, thus reifying the very concept that some were seeking to dissolve. Secondly, anti-racist education could do very little, at least not in the short term, to change or uproot the racial stereotypes and opinions that had over many centuries become so powerfully woven into the very fabric of European culture. Pre-war generations, brought up, socialized and educated in a world saturated with racism, could not readily discard old ways of seeing and thinking. For the younger, post-war generation, popular culture continued to be steeped in negative racist images and messages, from school textbooks, boys' comics and Hollywood films, to advertising. It would take many decades for European sociologists and education theorists to begin to recognize the sheer complexity and root-edness, the subtle disguises and power of racism, embedded in language and constructions of individual and group identity. Thirdly, as was to become increasingly apparent towards the close of the century, as archives were opened and Europeans began to come to terms with their complicity in genocide, the post-war exposure and purging of Nazis and fascist collaborators involved in the 'Final Solution', from Switzerland to Hungary, was in reality applied only to a tiny fraction. Post-war Germany and France quietly and discreetly reintegrated racists into the structures of the state, from ministers and civil servants to academics, doctors, judges and police officers. There was a significant continuity between pre-war and post-war political élites, who carried with them the baggage of colonial racism and anti-Semitism. Although these élites trimmed and often adopted new credentials as democrats, liberal progressives or socialists, there is extensive evidence from private diaries and letters of ongoing, but concealed prejudice.

Post-War Labour Immigration and Racism

However, despite such continuities, the overall social, economic and political contexts within which this racism operated were profoundly transformed. During the period from 1945 to 1974, the age of mass labour immigration, European political racism switched its prime target from Jews to the 'black' minorities. As we have seen, during the period from c.1870 to 1945, although black minorities were the object of racial stereotyping, in general throughout Europe they never came to consti-tute a major concern of political racism. On the whole blacks were viewed as an external 'Other', and although boys' literature and film could portray the African savage with a *frisson* of horror as a cannibal and idol worshipper, blacks were located in an external and distant imaginary space that constituted no real threat to the Europeans' sense of internal security. Anti-Semitism, however, was far more potent a force, extended itself right across Continental Europe, and drew its strength from deeply felt anxieties and phobias that perceived the Jews as a dangerous and even deadly power entrenched within the heart of society. With the arrival of many hundreds of thousands of immigrant workers from Africa, Asia and the Caribbean, black people moved from the distant colonial sphere into the heart of metropolitan society, where they constituted a palpable presence and a perceived threat. Blacks thus became the main target of racism just at the moment when post-Holocaust anti-Semitism was in retreat or had gone underground.

A number of factors worked towards this inversion of racisms, so that anti-black racism began to take precedence over anti-Semitism. Although the UNESCO Statement opposed all forms of racism, in reality the barbarism of Nazism became associated for most Europeans almost uniquely with the extermination of six million Jews. The extermination of other minorities, including Gypsies, Slavs and homosexuals was also largely suppressed or neglected. This meant that a particular brand of racism (anti-Semitism) aroused the most powerful feelings of revulsion and horror, while the legitimacy of more 'benign' forms of anti-black and colonial-based racism was relatively unaffected. Negative racist stereotypes of the black continued to have wide currency in the media, while the traditional anti-Semitic stereotype (the thick-lipped, hooked-nose Jew, grasping bags of gold) was seen as politically unacceptable. The small and fragmented political movements of the extreme right found that espousal of anti-Semitism left them marginalized, while campaigning against the newly arrived immigrants found a ready, public response. For example, Oswald Mosley's Union Movement, the post-war successor to the British Union of Fascists, began from c.1951 to convert its public campaigning and propaganda from anti-Semitism to attacks on immigrants as criminals, carriers of disease and sexually promiscuous primitives, who would subvert the white race through miscegenation. This evolution was in later years followed by most far-right parties throughout Western Europe, from the French Front National (FN) to the German Republikaner and Austrian Freedom Party. As we shall see (Chapter 7), this does not mean that anti-Semitism disappeared, indeed for many fascist groups it remained the core doctrine of the militants, but it was concealed or overlaid for purposes of political campaigning by anti-immigrant racism.

The rest of this chapter will centre mainly on the phenomenon of immigration during the period 1945–74, and how this generated strong forms of anti-black racism. This extremely rapid and large-scale movement was, during this phase, largely confined to the more advanced industrial economies of North-West Europe: Britain, France, West Germany, Belgium, the Netherlands, Switzerland and Scandinavia, and it is with these states that we will be mainly concerned. The poorer nations of the South, with a large, traditional peasant sector, like southern Italy, Greece, Spain, Portugal and Yugoslavia, acted as reservoirs of migrant labour during this period, and only in the last quarter of the twentieth century, after modernization and industrialization, did they, in turn, become countries of immigration, receiving migrants from North and sub-Saharan Africa. Anti-immigrant racism in this southern zone only began to build up at a much later stage, during and after the 1990s, with, for example, violent anti-Moroccan riots in the Spanish town of El Ejido in February 2000. Behind the 'Iron Curtain' the Communist states (Poland, Hungary, the USSR, Czechoslovakia etc.) remained largely free of the forms of international migration that most commentators interpreted as specific to neo-colonial and capitalist states, although the Democratic Republic of Germany (GDR) had by the late 1980s developed a curiously similar pattern of cheap contract labour from Communist regimes in Vietnam (60 000 migrants), Mozambique (16 000 migrants), Cuba, Angola and elsewhere.

Anti-black racism needs to be understood within the general context of 'guest-worker' or labour immigration systems. The years 1945–74 witnessed an almost unprecedented phase of sustained economic growth and of low unemployment, an 'economic miracle' that, given the general shortage of labour in North-West Europe, could only be sustained by recourse to mass immigration. By c.1980 Western Europe contained a population of about 16 million foreign workers, of both European and non-European origin. The economic benefits of recruiting workers from North Africa (Algeria, Morocco, Tunisia), from sub-Saharan Africa (Senegal, Mali, Nigeria etc.), the Caribbean, Pakistan, India, Bangladesh, Indo-China, Turkey and elsewhere were considerable. Many of those recruited were young men, in the peak of physical strength, and without dependants: they constituted a 'reserve army' of mobile, flexible labour that could be put to work on the back-breaking and dangerous tasks that Europeans were refusing to take on (work in the great heat of foundries, in toxic chemical plant, in coal-mines, road sweeping, road construction) or that involved 'unsocial hours' and shift-work. These migrants, of mainly peasant origin, had no experience of industrial labour and trade unionism so that management could deploy them to break strikes, to undercut wages and to weaken class solidarity. Because first-wave migrants were mainly single, without children, wives or elderly parents, they involved very low social costs for the host state (schools, health care, family housing). Ideally, at a time of labour shortage, such immigration could be encouraged, but in times of recession and increasing unemployment migrants could be both the first to be made redundant, and also be repatriated to the country of origin, thus avoiding the high costs of unemployment benefits. Such a system of labour migration was remarkably close in structure to South African apartheid, under which natives were forced into 'homelands', in which the costs of reproduction, of raising and educating children to the age at which they could form a reserve of adult labour, was borne by the impoverished Bantustans. South African gold mines, industry and service sectors could then call on this labour at will, but the migrant force had no settlement or political rights within 'white' South Africa across the 'border' from their artificially created 'homeland'.

In reality, the advantages to be gained from such an ideal 'guest-worker model' of international migration began to break down or became eroded from an early stage, and most European states were seeking to close the doors on primary labour immigration by 1973/4. Governmental failure to regulate immigration, to control recruitment in an efficient way that would match numbers and skills to the requirements of the economy, remove foreign labour when contracts expired and prevent the build up of minority communities, in the long run created conditions that contributed significantly to the rise of a current of anti-immigrant racism. Although Britain, France and the Netherlands made some attempt to control labour recruitment through official state agencies, in reality these colonial powers were faced with an immediate post-war situation in which colonial peoples had full rights as subjects to free and unimpeded movement to the metropolis. Thus 'New Commonwealth' citizens migrated freely to the United Kingdom, until the Commonwealth Immigration Act of 1962; and the same applied to migration to France from Algeria, French West Africa, and the Caribbean dependencies; and to movement to the Netherlands by Surinamese, Moluccans and Antillians. European governments, as long as the demand for labour ran high, followed a *laissez-faire* practice and turned a blind eye to an uncontrolled entry which left millions of immigrants to their own devices, without any specialist support in the areas of housing, health, education or general welfare. This hands-off, free-market attitude saved governments from expenditure in the short run, but led to the accumulation of huge, long-term problems. The concentration of immigrants in slum 'ghettos', zones of mass exclusion and endemic poverty, created the conditions under which a 'poor white' racism began to grow and in which extremist parties were able to mobilize and build support.

By the end of the twentieth century, all EU nations had come to accept a similar negative and frequently racialized view of non-European economic migrants or of asylum seekers who were widely viewed as 'bogus' political refugees. The aim of this chapter is to examine the processes by which the question of immigration became equated with a 'race problem', to such an extent that the term 'immigrant' (and at a later stage 'refugee'), on its own, came to carry immediate associations of danger, of an 'alien' and 'primitive' presence that threatened European 'civilization', and 'white priority' in the area of housing, employment, education and welfare. While extreme right-wing political movements did play some part in this process, on the whole they had only a limited electoral impact prior to the 1980s: far more crucial to the racialization of European politics was the way in which mainstream parties and governments of the centre-right and left, 'respectable' defenders of liberal democracy and of 'human rights', became responsible for the spread of racist attitudes and discriminatory legislation. While much contemporary anti-racist activism has targeted extremist, neo-Nazi movements as the prime enemy, marching skinheads with swastika regalia, this has often obfuscated the fact that both governments and major parties have had a more significant impact on society through the reproduction of a less visibly dramatic, but far more generalized and 'legitimate' racism.

In general, throughout Western Europe during the post-war period, the racialization of politics, the process through which minorities of non-European origin became a central issue in domestic politics, was closely tied to the issue of labour immigration. Most, if not all, states passed through a transition from a first phase, during which primary labour immigration was encouraged by the state and was more or less tolerated by the general public, to a second stage in which governments moved to halt further immigration, a phase that was accompanied by a more negative discourse on migrants (described as a 'burden' on the welfare system, as 'parasites', 'criminals', 'unassimilable' etc.) both at the official and at the popular level. The timing of this transition varied significantly from one state to another. For example, the appearance of 'race' as a major political issue, tied into a rejection of labour immigration, occurred at a relatively early stage in Britain, from c.1958 to 1964. In the case of France, although Algerian migrants had been the target of racist hostility since the First World War, a hatred that was further deepened by the Algerian War (1954–62), in general immigration flows from outside Europe by *travailleurs immigrés*, a common term that emphasized the positive economic contribution of such 'workers', were seen as beneficial until the late 1960s. Immigration, perceived as a negative phenomenon, only became an issue central to French politics, to party agendas and electioneering, between *c*.1972 and *c*.1982. In the case of Italy, like Spain and Greece a country of late African immigration, the transition to a politics of 'race' came even later, from *c*. 1986 to 1990. The following sections look more closely at Britain and France to illustrate the 'racial transition', an evolution in policy and practice that had become generalized throughout the EU states by the late 1980s.

Immigration and Racial Politics in Britain

In November 1946 the British Cabinet Manpower Working Party calculated a national labour shortage of 1 346 000 workers, a shortage that government sought to resolve through the recruitment of white European workers (the Irish, Poles and European Voluntary Workers). Secret Cabinet and government papers (now released) show that both Labour and Conservative governments of the 1950s had a distinct racial preference for white migrant labour over the Caribbeans and Asians who had full rights of entry under the 1948 Nationality Act. A Royal Commission report (1949) noted that large-scale immigration, 'would only be welcomed without reserve if the immigrants were of good stock and were not prevented by their religion or race from intermarrying with the host population and becoming merged in it'.[3] Barely concealed beneath this discreet or coded language were the traditional colonial phobias about racial miscegenation. By 1950 a total of 5000 West Indian immigrants had arrived in the UK since the end of the war; yet this tiny number was already giving rise to high and exaggerated levels of anxiety among ministers that tells us more about pre-existing racial attitudes among political élites than about any social reality. During the decade 1955–65 both Labour and Conservative governments, in spite of their public condemnations of racism, moved towards a *de facto* support of the racist Commonwealth Immigration Act (1962) and the 1965 White Paper on Immigration.

An examination of the background to the 1962 Act, a crucial watershed in the growth of state racism, provides vital evidence of the underlying forces that led to a deepening of post-war institutional racism. Caribbean migrants, who were offered employment in the 'unwanted' tasks avoided by British workers, inevitably constituted the lowest paid strata in the working class and became concentrated in the most deprived slum areas of the inner city. Black migrants competed for housing in precisely those blighted zones of decaying properties, unemployment and multiple deprivation, where the 'poor whites' felt 'left behind' and were unable to move out to the new towns and council estates. The indigenous population, steeped in an imperialist culture that emphasized the superiority of the Englishman, his civilizing mission to the African savage in his mud-hut, experienced the physical presence of black neighbours as an ultimate symbol of their own degradation and marginalization in British society. The white population interpreted the black presence as an 'invasion', a threat to 'British culture', a taking over of 'our jobs', 'our housing' or 'our women'. Racism was a way of blaming immigrants for problems that were very real (poor housing, unemployment etc.) and provided simplistic explanations for complex phenomena or diverted attention away from government failure to tackle issues of urban decay, underinvestment and poverty. At the same time, racism was a psychological mechanism by which the most deprived and insecure could reconstitute a sense of 'worth', a sense of 'Britishness', that referred to a mythical and homogeneous community, to the 'good old days' before the black intruder arrived. Working-class racism during the 1950s was rarely expressed in the form of a coherent theory or ideology, but rather in the form of lapidary, 'common-sense' racist phrases – 'Coloureds have filthy habits', 'they molest our women', 'blacks come over here to take our jobs', 'they are lazy and sponge off the welfare', 'let them go back to the jungle', 'they attack and rob old ladies'. Within the inner-city areas of immigrant concentration, mainly in London and the Midlands, black people were increasingly subject to racial abuse, assault, exclusion from clubs and dance-halls, and full-scale mob actions or 'race riots' as in Liverpool (1948), Deptford (1949), Camden Town (1954), Nottingham and Notting Hill (1958). In the latter riot, which continued from 23 August to 2 September, white crowds of several hundred people carrying banners with the slogan 'Deport all Niggers' assaulted West Indians and besieged their homes and clubs.

However, popular 'grass-roots' racism was not the crucial pressure that led to anti-immigrant legislation. Racial tensions were far too scattered and sporadic to have had any inexorable impact on local, let alone central, government practice. In 1968 Enoch Powell noted that immigration affected only a 'minority' of towns, perhaps 60 out of 600 Parliamentary constituencies. Far more crucial than the strength of popular pressure was the extent to which racism 'of the people', no matter how weak, was used by political élites to legitimate anti-black measures. At local level what were claimed to be 'spontaneous' expressions of popular hostility turn out on closer inspection to have been channelled and stimulated by educated members of the middle class, whether activists from extreme right-wing movements, editors of local newspapers or members of pressure groups like the Birmingham Immigration Control Association (1960). But most crucial of all was the failure of political élites, of MPs and government ministers, to tackle racist movements, and a tendency to cave in to the slightest pressure from within their constituencies.

Backbench MPs from both parties began to press for black immigration controls after the 1958 riots, much in line with the thinking of the *Daily Sketch*, which called for an 'end to the tremendous influx of coloured people from the Commonwealth ... Overcrowding has fostered vice, drugs, prostitution and the use of knives. For years the white people have been tolerant. Now their tempers are up.'[4] Quite crucial to the entrenchment of racism was the way in which blacks/immigrants were perceived as the 'problem', rather than those indigenous people who subjected them to abuse, violence and discrimination in housing and employment. MPs, instead of seeking to tackle prejudice through education, firmly rejecting Teddy-boy rioters and bigots, or supporting programmes to reduce inner-city blight, blamed the immigrants for those conditions of which they were the principal victims. Already in the 1950s government carefully avoided social and economic programmes that would have helped newly arrived West Indians to adjust to life in Britain, and also reduced racial tensions, since it was feared that improved conditions would attract further immigration. In general politicians, in demanding controls, claimed to speak up for the 'legitimate fears' of the 'British people', thereby promoting the racism of small, scattered and unrepresentative groups into an expression of the national will.

However, both Conservative and Labour politicians, in the very moment of supporting immigration controls, were keen to assert their public opposition to any forms of prejudice on the grounds of 'race, colour or creed'. The term 'racist' in the 1950s and early 1960s carried a high degree of obloquy and moral condemnation, and no leading politician or mainstream party wished to be tarred with the accusation of racism. Cabinet papers, now released, reveal that a major dilemma facing both Conservative and Labour governments was how to impose strict controls on black or 'New Commonwealth' immigrants, but not on 'white' immigrants from the 'Old' Commonwealth or Ireland, while still claiming to be anti-racist. The solution was found by the Home Secretary Butler in the Commonwealth Immigration Act of 1962 which, through a voucher scheme that gave priority of entry to those who already had a job to come to or had qualifications that were in short supply, built in a bias against black immigrants, while leaving access open to migrants from Australia, Canada and South Africa. Butler in private noted: 'The great merit of this scheme is that it can be presented as making no distinction on grounds of race and colour . . . although the scheme purports to relate solely to employment and to be non-discriminatory, its aim is primarily social and its restrictive effect is intended to and would, in fact, operate on coloured people almost exclusively.'[5]

Although the Labour party in opposition, under the leadership of Hugh Gaitskell, had strongly opposed the 1962 Act as racist, the Labour government that came to power in 1964 under Harold Wilson introduced even more stringent controls in its White Paper on Immigration of 1965. In the 1964 general election the Conservative candidate for Smethwick, Peter Griffiths, ran a blatantly racist campaign in which the infamous slogan 'If you want a nigger neighbour, vote Labour' was deployed against Patrick Gordon Walker, a member of the shadow cabinet. Walker was defeated by a local swing to the Conservatives of 7.2 per cent, while the national swing to Labour was 3.5 per cent. From this humiliating defeat Labour drew the lesson that grass-roots, electoral mobilization against immigration presented a real danger, one that it would best counter by itself taking a hard anti-immigrant stance. The Labour government, in its drive to implement more draconian measures against non-European immigrants in the 1965 White Paper, was motivated by political and electoral considerations rather than any economic logic, since there was still a labour shortage. Richard Crossman, a Cabinet Minister, wrote in his diary at the time of the 1965 White Paper, which made the 1962 Act even tougher and more restrictive:

Ever since the Smethwick election it has been quite clear that immigration can be the greatest potential vote-loser for the Labour Party if we are seen to be permitting a flood of immigrants to come in and blight the central areas in all our cities . . . We have become illiberal and lowered the quotas at a time when we have an acute shortage of labour . . . We felt we had to out-trump the Tories by doing what they would have done and so transforming their policy into a bipartisan policy.[6]

Neo-Marxist or economistic theorists have argued that the ebb and flow of labour immigration into Western Europe was dictated by the needs of capitalism and that the imposition of controls, particularly after 1973, was primarily linked to economic recession, growing unemployment and a global restructuring of capital which, instead of bringing cheap labour into Europe, now placed its manufacturing investment in poor developing countries. The British case presents a problem for such an interpretation since the introduction of immigration controls preceded those of Continental Europe by a decade and, without any economic rationale, appears to have been inspired by political considerations and electoral opportunism. Britain was not as anomalous as it appears since the debate on immigration and refugee controls throughout Europe in the last quarter of the twentieth century, in spite of closer correlation with global recession, was similarly determined more by surges in polit-ical racism than by economic considerations.

Britain was in the 1960s a precursor, in another way, of a second phase that spread through Continental Europe during the last two decades of the twentieth century. This arose from a perception that even watertight controls on external frontiers could not prevent minority populations from settling permanently and, through their higher birth rates, demographically 'swamping' the indigenous people and their cul-ture. If the 'enemy' was now within, immigration controls alone would no longer suffice, and the 'logical' solution was repatriation. The 1962 Immigration Act, reinforced by the 1965 White Paper, brought a virtual halt to primary labour immigration from the 'New Commonwealth'. However, the Act led to a surge in immigration by those aiming to 'beat the ban': in 1961 some 136 400 New Commonwealth immigrants arrived, compared to 57 700 in 1960. But far more crucial in the long run was that migrants, predominantly males who had left their families at home and regarded their stay as temporary, decided to bring over wives and children, rather than risk being refused re-entry after a visit home. Immigration control thus had the opposite effect from that inten-ded and resulted in the acceleration of family reunification and the formation of permanent minority settlements. The near total ban on *labour* immigration could not bring a halt to the process of *family* reunifi-cation, which was protected in both national and international law, and this continued for many decades to fuel the racist debate, particularly as dependants seemed to increase the 'burden' on welfare and social costs (education, state housing, health). A first phase of racism, one targeted at 'temporary' labour migrants, thus gave way to a second phase which was fuelled by the recognition that black immigrants were 'here for good' and constituted a permanent presence within British society. This second phase was precipitated by Enoch Powell in his notorious speeches of 1968.

The core of Powell's message was constructed in two parts. Firstly, he claimed, black minorities could never assimilate into English society and their essential cultural and religious difference would always constitute an alien danger to indigenous identity. 'The West Indian or Asian does not, by being born in England become an Englishman. In law he becomes a United Kingdom citizen by birth; in fact, he is a West Indian or an Asian still.'[7] This was a secular equivalent of the old anti-Semitic tag that the converted Jew always remained a Jew, and at the same time pointed forward to the 'New Racism' which was grounded on cultural 'difference' (Chapter 7). Secondly, Powell estimated that even with a total halt to immigration the non-European rate of reproduction was so high that blacks would still, like a Trojan Horse, come to 'flood' the native English so that they were 'made strangers in their own country'. A constituent, one of the 'decent, ordinary, fellow-Englishmen' for whom Powell acted as tribune, claimed he would emigrate if he had the means: 'In this country in fifteen or twenty years time the black man will have the whip-hand over the white-man.'[8] This deliberate inversion of the historic association of blackness with the inferior position of the plantation slave, with the powerful white majority presented as the persecuted 'minority' or victim, was later to become a key device of European 'New Racism'. There could, argued Powell, be only one solution to the 'impending disaster', and that was to end family reunification and to remove non-European immigrants through a Ministry of Repatriation. Powell succeeded in providing a whole new impetus to British racism by shifting the focus from immigration control (a goal that had been largely achieved by cross-party consensus) to the permanence of the 'enemy within'. By 1968 Powell had developed all the key components of the anti-black racist discourse that remained essentially unchanged down to the present time. All later controversies over further immigration legislation, relating to the arrival of Ugandan, Kenyan, Hong Kong and other ex-colonial passport holders, as well as illegal immigrants, asylum seekers and 'bogus' refugees, continued to be formulated in identical terms.

Immigration and Racial Politics in France

The trajectory followed in the racialization of British politics between *c*.1958 and 1968 is informative of a pattern that was to be followed at a later stage by most EU states. Space does not allow a discussion for all these nations, but here an examination of the evolution in France is compared to Britain in order to illustrate a process that was general to Western Europe. In 1945 the French government calculated that economic reconstruction required the introduction of five million immigrants, about four times more than the British estimates for the UK economy in 1946. Although the French also favoured the selection of 'sound elements', those national or 'white' ethnic groups which would be most readily assimilable, in reality they were unable to halt the massive arrival of Algerians who had complete freedom of movement between 1946 and 1962. However, France was quite different from Britain in that throughout the period from 1945 to 1974, the long phase of dynamic post-war economic growth, the rationale of labour immigration never became an issue central to political debate, party campaigning and the electoral process. The question of immigration was regulated almost solely by civil servants and ministers, from a technocratic and economic perspective, through administrative decrees and circulars. Their prime concern was with estimations of labour supply within the parameters of the various Five Year Plans. Not a single act of legislation on immigration came before Parliament between 1945 and 1980. This is not to deny the high levels of hostility towards ethnic minorities that was fermenting at the grass-roots, within local French society. But this was generally inchoate and not channelled in such a way as to find strong political expression. Immigration was thus peripheral to mainstream French politics and before 1974 few challenged the idea that cheap and 'temporary' migrant labour was to be encouraged, especially since it maintained French competitiveness by exerting a strong downward pressure on wage inflation.

How and why did this neutral issue move to the centre of French politics and public debate between *c*.1972 and 1982? Firstly, although in principle the state recruited all foreign labour through the Office National d'Immigration (ONI), established in November 1945, in reality the majority arrived as clandestine workers (79 per cent in 1965). This unregulated *immigration sauvage* meant that enormous and largely ignored social problems were building up and it was with some sense of 'shock' that the Prime Minister, Chaban-Delmas, acknowledged in

1970 the existence of nearly 400 shanty-towns. Secondly, by the early 1970s immigrants were becoming increasingly organized and militant, and engaged in rent strikes in government hostels, factory occupations, and a series of bitter strikes on the theme, 'Equal pay for equal work'. Such involvement in trade-union activity threatened to undermine the whole logic of a 'guest-worker' system in which quiescent migrants represented a malleable productive force, a proletarian labour power devoid of social costs.

Thirdly, immigrant workers – particularly those from North Africa – became the target of a 'grass-roots' wave of racial violence and murders in the summer of 1973. Algerian migrants had, ever since the First World War, been the object of French racism, and were perceived as volatile and 'hot-blooded' primitives who endangered French women and children, spread disease and increased crime. French decolonization had been far more traumatic and bloody than in the British case, with the crushing defeat at Dien Bien Phu in 1954 and the Algerian War of 1954–62, and the sudden retreat from empire nourished deep-seated hatreds against 'inferior peoples' who were not only the victors, but who continued to 'invade' the metropolitan heartland as immigrants. During the Algerian War the National Liberation Front (FLN) had established a sophisticated organization in the émigré community, raised funds and opened a 'second front' against police and military targets, and the French state riposted with mass arrests, torture and exceptional counter-violence. On the night of 17 October 1961 the Paris police massacred dozens of Algerians peacefully demonstrating in favour of the FLN. The utilization in Paris of Algerian police brigades (the *harkis*) and of military intelligence officers, placed under the command of the Prefect of Police, Maurice Papon, a senior administrator renowned for his harsh counter-insurgency operations in Morocco and Algeria, represented the penetration of colonial forms of repression, violence and racism into the capital.

By the end of the war in 1962 some 2.3 million conscripts had seen service in Algeria, many returning to civilian life infected by colonial and barrack-room racism. A million *pieds noirs*, European refugees from Algeria, settled in France, many bringing with them deeply engrained colonialist attitudes of 'native' inferiority, which were now further accentuated by the bitterness of expulsion. However, while bloody processes of decolonization fuelled anti-immigrant racism, it is interesting to note that the *pieds noirs* presence made little impact on French racial politics until the watershed of 1973–4, a decade after their arrival. In other words racial mobilization was crucially dependent, not on grass-roots or localized prejudice, but on the national political context. Fascist activists in organizations like Ordre Nouveau and the Front National, which had a significant *pieds noirs* membership, only placed anti-immigration policies on the agenda in 1973 and late in that year they orchestrated a wave of anti-Arab killings and bombings in Marseilles. Although government officials were investigating and moving towards the idea of immigration controls from *c*.1968, the 1973 violence, not unlike the Notting Hill riots of 1958, constituted a significant watershed in the racialization of politics. President Georges Pompidou, like the judiciary and ministers in the British case, asserted an official condemnation of racism, noting that 'France is profoundly antiracist . . . There is no racism or at least there should not be any.' But he went on to utilize the violence of a tiny minority of racist agitators as an excuse for, 'the only solution, a general and effective control of immigration'.[9] Implicit in this, as in the British case, was a process by which immigrants became 'problematized'; instead of tackling racism at its source in the French population, solutions would be found by shutting out the 'alien'.

The process of post-war decolonization was to have a major impact on the racialization of politics in a number of West European states (Britain, France, Belgium, the Netherlands, Denmark, Italy and Portugal). Independence struggles were portrayed in the European media as the work of 'terrorists' and 'criminals' engaged in the savage butchery of white settlers. The gaining of independence and the process of decolonization, whether carried out through violent or peaceful means, led to the repatriation of many thousands of government officials and settlers who injected colonial racism into metropolitan society. While empires were intact imperial governments had an interest in restraining racism at home or keeping immigration open since this fostered good relations with native élites, restrained nationalist militancy and favoured economic relations with the metropolis. After independence many European politicians were prepared to jettison empire completely so as to remove all obligations to post-colonial governments and peoples. A paternalist imperialism, tempered by the need to care for backward black societies, was displaced by an insular nationalism which aimed to expunge from memory the enormous 'debt' owed to colonial societies that had for centuries been plundered and stripped of their wealth. Enoch Powell, an arch imperialist, was by the late 1950s moving to a 'little Englander' position, as he abandoned the Commonwealth as a liability, and called for a halt to the 'black invasion'.

All primary labour immigration to France was stopped by a circular of 19 July 1974. However, as with the Immigration Act of 1962 in Britain, far from marking a termination of anti-immigrant agitation it opened the way to a deepening racialization of politics. As in Britain, the virtual closing of the frontiers led to a realization that this alone was not going to resolve the issue of family reunification and the growth of permanent minority settlement. Strict immigration controls only served to terminate 'rotation', the tendency for male migrants to periodically return home to visit their families in North Africa, Turkey and West Africa, and accelerated family reunification in Europe. A particularly dramatic shift in racial politics occurred during the period 1980–4, with all mainstream parties, including the Socialist Party (PS) and the Communist Party (PCF), shifting over to a 'hard' anti-immigrant position.

Why this shift occurred when it did still requires closer investigation by historians, but, in general, it appears that political factors, especially electoral opportunism, played a more fundamental role than pure economic causes (a cost-benefit calculation of immigration in a context of recession). Although the Giscard d'Estaing Presidency (1974–81) introduced a series of harsh anti-immigrant measures, like the Fontanet circular, it has been widely argued that the PCF was the first major party to stir up anti-immigrant prejudice and to use it as a means to mobilize public opinion. Although the PCF prided itself on its traditions of solidarity with foreign workers, from the late 1960s onwards party leaders began to complain that conservative governments were systematically 'dumping' immigrant workers and their families in the 'Red suburbs', the Communist controlled communes in the industrial zones that encircled central Paris. The immigrants, who had large families, pressed hard on scarce resources of council housing, education and health in precisely those working-class municipalities that were suffering from inadequate state funding and had the most overstretched social services. Although there was some basis to the critique of a capitalist system and bourgeois government that failed to invest in the working-class and immigrant 'ghettos', the PCF campaign on this issue began to assume a racist colour. From 1978 onwards a number of Communist mayors blocked immigrant access to public housing within their communes and even placed a quota limit of 15 per cent on immigrant children going to the summer holiday camps for deprived children. Such measures were legitimated by the discriminatory concept of a 'threshold of tolerance', through which it was claimed that immigrants reaching a certain level of population in local housing or schooling would automatically trigger a 'natural' hostile and even violent response among the French inhabitants. The exclusionary strategy was officially endorsed by the central party, the Political Bureau, on 5 November 1980, and was soon followed by the infamous bulldozer wrecking of an immigrant worker hostel at Vitry by a Communist commando led by the mayor. In February 1981 the Communist Mayor of Montigny, Robert Hue, later to become leader of the PCF, co-ordinated a 'law and order' campaign in which a Moroccan family, accused of drug dealing, were made the target of street demonstrations. Throughout France, at a time of deepening recession, immigrants became those to blame for unemployment, the housing crisis, a decline in educational standards, rising crime rates and 'insecurity', drug dealing, a breakdown in morality, an overstretched health service and every other conceivable social ill.

Why did the PCF, which had an honourable tradition of anti-racism, become infected with racism at this particular juncture in 1978–81? Firstly, the anti-immigrant stance did not come about through an inexorable pressure from below, a popular agitation before which Communist leaders were forced to bow. There was some rank-and-file hostility towards immigrants, but the PCF leadership only decided to channel this, and to give it official blessing, in the intense campaigning that preceded the Presidential and parliamentary elections of 1981. The rupture of the electoral alliance with the Socialists, the Union of the Left, the erosion of the traditional working-class base of the Communists, as well as bitter internal splits and the expulsion of leading intellectuals, drove the PCF leadership into a desperate populist strategy and an appeal to the worst prejudices of its cadres within the 'Red Fortresses' of outer Paris. The PCF case, like that of the British Labour Party at a similar conjuncture in 1964–5, demonstrates that the racialization of mainstream politics was fundamentally the work of political élites, both at local and central levels, rather than a response to inexorable public pressure.

The PCF was not alone in this since a growing racist response to immigration swept across the political spectrum. In 1980–1 the Socialists attacked the Communists for engaging in a vile, and demagogic racist campaign, and yet numerous Socialist municipalities with a large immigrant presence were engaged in identical manoeuvres. The 'leftist' Socialist government that came to power in 1981 did introduce a liberal policy on immigration, legalizing the position of thousands of clandestine workers and injecting investment into the most deprived 'ghettos', but this progressive stance was rapidly eroded as the Socialist economic 'experiment' collapsed by 1983 and the PS swung to the right. The Front

National, which had been a marginal force in French politics, made a dramatic breakthrough in 1983–4. In the small town of Dreux the FN, playing a crude racist and anti-immigrant campaign in the 1983 municipal elections, entered into an electoral pact with the Gaullists and came to share power in the town hall. Such an alliance indicated how far centre-right parties were willing to go in accepting populist racism in order to make electoral gains, but at the same time such actions legitimated Le Pen's movement. In the European elections of 1984 the FN won over 11 per cent of the national vote. All the major political parties took fright at this dramatic surge, but instead of trying to contain this danger through a coherent anti-racist position, they took on a 'hard' anti-immigrant stance to outflank the FN on the right, a move that only served to further legitimate and reinforce racist attitudes in French society.

In many ways France presents a more typical example of the growth of anti-immigrant politics in Europe than the British case. The French government closed its borders to labour immigration by a circular of 19 July 1974; West Germany and Denmark had already followed a similar line in November 1973 and were soon imitated by Norway, Belgium, the Netherlands, Sweden and Austria in 1974. The synchronicity of frontier closure would suggest that national governments were responding to the same fundamental causes, and the most plausible explanation is that which links immigration controls to the onset of the oil crisis and global recession of 1973–4. The economic crisis led to an increase in unemployment and simultaneously undermined the ability of European states to raise taxation and to sustain the post-war liberal consensus built upon Keynesianism, and state welfare systems that included well-funded public housing, education and health – the very resources, now under attack from Thatcherite policies, that immigrants appeared to be in competition for. However, the introduction of immigration controls, far from following a purely economic logic, may have been determined primarily by political considerations and economic recession served more as an excuse for illiberal measures rather than as a prime cause.

Immigration controls across Europe were fundamentally racist in a number of ways: firstly, they were not 'colour-blind', but quite selective, allowing preferred 'white' migrants continuing access. At a purely 'cost-benefit' level of analysis immigrants in many states continued to contribute far more to the national wealth than they took from it in social costs. But, most crucially, governments and political leaders of most major parties quietly concurred with a shared discourse that presented immigrants as the cause of deteriorating conditions in 'inner-city' slums, growing crime, educational failure, social and cultural dislocation, and threatening racial tensions and violence. Ethnic minorities constituted the 'problem', not indigenous racism or the failure of government policy. The political drive behind anti-immigrant measures was also shown by the fact that whenever legislation was introduced to impose tight and often repressive controls, agitation inevitably continued for further prohibitions and police regulation to stem 'floods' and 'invasions', even when immigration had been reduced to a trickle and the numbers were so low that they were almost totally insignificant in relation to total population size. In such campaigns that continued to exercise tabloid editors, xenophobic pundits and politicians of all political persuasions, what was most crucially at stake was the assertion of a national identity and sovereignty that was perceived to be at risk from barbaric hordes pressing, in teeming numbers, against the fragile external walls of Europe (Chapter 7).

7

THE 'NEW RACISM' AND NATIONAL-POPULISM

In the immediate post-war era the official rhetoric of anti-fascist victory, both in Western and Eastern Europe, combined with the powerful challenge to scientific, biological racism, created optimism among contemporaries that the evil of racism was definitively in retreat and would eventually be eliminated through education, enlightened progress or socialism. In general, the period 1945–74, one of unprecedented economic growth, low unemployment and solid welfare-state provision, was not conducive to fascist or racist movements, which remained miniscule, fragmented and underground. In spite of the fact that unregulated immigration was generating deep-seated problems that would erupt later into extensive racism, explicitly racist and fascist movements remained weak and politically marginalized during the third quarter of the twentieth century. Typically, the vote for extreme right-wing racist parties, like the German National Democratic Party (NPD), the Italian Social Movement (MSI), the British National Front (NF) or the French Front National (FN) rarely reached 5 per cent in local, regional or national elections. However, the last quarter-century, 1975–2000, witnessed a strong resurgence of racism.

The media and public opinion became concerned with a rising tide of extreme violence (street-level murders and fire-bombings), especially by fascist youth gangs, para-military organizations or skinheads, aimed at immigrants or ethnic minorities. By the 1990s police forces in Britain, France, Germany and elsewhere were beginning to investigate more thoroughly racist incidents that had been previously neglected or under-recorded and began to collect more systematic data. Although the upward curve in racist incidents in part reflected a more effective procedure, it also indicated a real increase in violence, while exposing a level of everyday terror that had been previously swept under the carpet by many police forces. In Britain the Home Office reported an increase in racially motivated incidents from 4383 in 1988 to 7793 in 1992; in Germany racist crimes rocketed dramatically from an average of about 250 per year between 1987 and 1990 to 2427 in 1991, and then reached a peak of 6721 in 1993. This was accompanied by an alarming tendency towards more lethal forms of violence, of bombings, arson, and the use of guns and knives. In Germany the organized attacks on refugee hostels at Hoyerswerda (1991) and Rostock (1992), and the burning to death of immigrants in Mölln (1992) and Solingen (1993) created widespread concern that Nazism had not been laid to rest, but was now resurfacing.

Whether there was a real revival of fascism, or any degree of continuity with inter-war Nazism, is open to debate. Certainly, many of the most violent, anti-democratic, and often illegal, para-military organizations, as well as skinhead and football hooligan gangs, consciously referred to the symbols of a Nazi or fascist past, from the display of swastikas to fascist salutes. For the majority of the young males who became involved in such networks, pre-war fascism did not provide a set of ideas or coherent political traditions, an ideology, but emblems of revolt, badges that helped to assert an aggressive youth sub-culture that could readily shock a 'respectable' bourgeois order. The apparent continuity between extreme right-wing movements and Nazism was further reinforced by journalists and anti-racist organizations, like the British Anti-Nazi League, which sought to undermine the legitimacy of violent racists by depicting them, in an over-simplistic way, as the direct descendants of Mosley, Hitler, Goebbels and Mussolini. While the wave of vicious beatings and murders that descended on Europe is in no way to be trivialized, I would argue that any attempt to analyse contemporary racism solely in terms of neo-Nazi organisations or the cult of violence among youth gangs runs the risk of obscuring the deeper and more significant roots of racism. The high-profile nature of hooligan violence in the media, a violence that has made for sensational 'good copy', has often diverted attention from the analysis of the way racism has been more powerfully reproduced in 'normal' society, including by the selfsame journals that condemn skinhead knife attacks. There is no contradiction between the fact that the *Daily Mail*, which ran a front-page campaign to expose the hooligan killers of Stephen Lawrence, had also for many years run the most vociferous and disturbing of anti-asylum seeker campaigns. An over-preoccupation with 'Nazi' movements, and a widespread belief that the defeat of such organizations will represent a definitive victory over the forces of darkness, not only lends itself to a misreading of the nature of racism, but, more seriously, can drive anti-racist action in the wrong direction.

Social-psychological studies of violent racists show that the majority were young males, often from a deprived background of family breakdown and educational failure, who used anti-immigrant scapegoating as a means to assert their own self-esteem and priority as 'Germans' or 'English', over and against 'parasitic' outsiders. Violent attacks were invariably not planned or premeditated and were the work of individuals who were not members of neo-Nazi organizations or had little sense of a political agenda. Violence was frequently expressive, a central means by which youth sub-cultures (often skinheads) countered a diffuse sense of anxiety, marginalization and failure by asserting a sense of group solidarity, bravery and the testing of masculinity – tests of violence that could also be directed towards women or homosexuals and changing gender roles that were also perceived to be threatening to a 'natural order' of male dominance. Racist violence did not represent a continuity with inter-war fascism, a revival of the same animal, but can be better analysed and understood within the entirely different context of late twentieth-century, 'post-industrial' society.

Although the surge of youth violence, the horrific killing and maiming of blacks and Jews, must not be understated, it is important that such manifestations are not misread as the key indicator of society as a whole (the great majority of Europeans abhor such acts) nor that the danger that they presented to the political system, a kind of 'Weimar syndrome', be exaggerated. Far more significant in late twentieth-century racism than revived swastikas has been the growth of three inter-related phenomena: the skilful elaboration and diffusion of a 'New Racism' that offered a powerful ideological revision of traditional biological racism; the concurrent emergence and electoral challenge of xenophobic, 'National-Populist' parties that made use of the new current of thinking on cultural racism and national identity; and lastly, the tendency of 'New Right' conservative parties, as well as socialist and all mainstream parties, to play to the same gallery, particularly through the construction of a 'Fortress Europe' and the scapegoating of refugees. These three levels are next analysed in more detail.

The 'New Racism'

The so-called 'New Racism' derived from a consciously elaborated, and highly effective strategy, to recast the ideological expression of racism so that it assumed a new 'cultural' form that would enter into common usage and influence the way people viewed the world, a racism in disguise. The problem with building a politics based on 'race', meaning specifically the biological racism derived from the pre-1945 era, was that scientific racism was widely discredited both as a pseudo-science as well as for its association with Nazism. As Alain de Benoist, the guru of the French 'New Right', remarked: 'It is evident that the word "race" scares people, because of its affective charge. So, one doesn't use it any more.'[1] The fascist intellectual Maurice Bardèche claimed in 1979 that the 'substitution of the idea of culture for the idea of heredity is the pivot at the centre of the whole renewal of the right proposed by the GRECE'.[2] It might be argued that there was nothing really new about this: as I have shown in the Introduction, the scientific racism that developed during the Enlightenment and throughout the nineteenth and early twentieth centuries was fundamentally an expression of cultural attitudes that were re-coded through the methodologies and discourse of 'objective' and empirical research, the measurement of skulls, miscroscopic investigation of blood and tissues, linguistic analysis. In this sense all racism is cultural. The 'New Racism' may not be so new, but it did mark an important strategic shift in the way in which not only fascists and overt racists, but many other groups, from conservatives to liberals, have sought to legitimate exclusionary forms of difference or identity.

In France the strategy of what has been called 'differentialist' racism was formulated primarily through an attack on, and subversion or inversion of, multiculturalism. During the later 1970s anti-racist movements in France, faced with the assimilationist traditions of Republicanism, laid claim to the *'droit à la différence'*, the right of immigrant ethnic minorities to retain their own language, religion and cultural identity. The 'New Right' subtly transformed this into the 'right to differ' of majority European national cultures which were under 'threat' from the intrusion of alien, non-European peoples and their traditions. The French, along with any other European nation, had as much right to prevent the decline and erosion of their ethnicity as did primitive tribal peoples of the Amazon jungles faced with extinction. The universalism and egalitarianism of the Enlightenment or of the Judaeo-Christian tradition which lay at the core of Republicanism, would lead to a levelling, a uniform and standardized culture that would eradicate the rich diversity of global languages, customs and traditions. The 'New Right' revived a highly conservative or *volkish* discourse that endowed a people (i.e. race) with a mythic unity that was rooted in untold ages, thousands of years of shared language, customs and kinship. Just as pre-war racism had shown an abhorrence of intermarriage between races, a mixing of 'blood' that would lead to an inevitable biological degeneration, so the 'New Right' deplored the mixing of cultures since this would lead to irreparable damage to the cultural integrity and identity of both autochthonous and minority groups. The Front National programme stated: 'A people that loses its identity, that no longer knows who it is or where it comes from, or what values it embodies, is a people condemned to death...No people can assimilate and integrate a large number of foreigners belonging to civilizations totally different from its own.'[3] Logically, it followed from this that peoples (races) with radically different cultures should not intermingle, but be spatially segregated and follow a separate development, as in the apartheid system of South Africa. The 'New Right' and the FN used such arguments to justify policies of exclusion and repatriation: Arab Muslims, Afro-Caribbeans, Asians and others should be sent 'home', both to protect French culture from being 'swamped' (a basic right to difference), as well as to enable immigrants, whose cultural identity was also damaged through contact with European society, to recover their own traditions.

A number of advantages followed from the 'New Racist' discourse. Politicians and ideologues of the far right could strenuously deny that they were racists, since they did not argue that one group was superior to any other. Enoch Powell, challenged in a 1969 television interview as to whether he was a 'racialist', replied: 'If by being a racialist, you mean a man who despises a human being because he belongs to another race, or a man who believes that one race is inherently superior to another in civilization or capability of civilization, then the answer is emphatically no.'[4] Le Pen has used the same tactic: when challenged on his virulent hostility to minorities of North African descent in France, he replies that he has nothing but admiration for 'Arab' civilization, but Muslims can best enjoy their own culture in an unspoilt form at 'home', just as white Christian Europeans should be allowed to protect their cultural heritage. 'I am not xenophobic, nor does the fact that I like the French and France best mean that I hate foreigners or hate other countries.'[5] However, in this discourse 'culture' is synonymous with 'race', identical in meaning and in political import to the older tradition of biological racism. This is revealed by the way in which cultural boundaries are made absolute or are founded on the 'natural' order: national (racial) identities are so rooted in the language and culture of the organic community that no outsider can ever become assimilated into the people. Again as Powell, a precursor of the 'New Right', stated in 1968: 'The West Indian or Indian does not, by being born in England, become an Englishman. In law he becomes a United Kingdom citizen by birth; in fact he is a West Indian or Asian still.'[6] The 'New Right' underpinned its arguments by reference to sociobiology; if nations/peoples best functioned as homogeneous units this was because genetic evolution had ensured that kin groups operated most effectively as an organic whole. Sally Shreir was typical of those who deployed a naturalizing discourse suffused with socio-biological meanings: 'human beings live in nations with the same certainty as certain species of fish live in shoals, and certain species of dogs live in packs'. 'Nationalism', she claimed, ' is . . . a ubiquitous attitude stamped on the human species by nature', or again 'national identity is founded on natural emotions and natural allegiances'.[7] In this circular reasoning, certain ways of doing are right because they are natural, and if they are natural they must be true. Underlying the discourse of the 'New Right' is a message of cultural racism, difference and exclusion that rejects the presence of immigrants within European society. Even if minorities try to assimilate into the host society, they can never succeed in becoming one of 'us', separated as they are by cultural or 'natural' boundaries as absolute as those of inter-war scientific racism which argued that the converted Jew always remained a Jew. In this discourse the distinction between the terms 'nation', 'race' and 'culture' was deliberately blurred, enabling Le Pen, for example, to make a powerful emotional appeal to a populist French nationalism founded on the symbolism of a mythical and idealized past: 'The homeland is the land of our fathers . . . a country fashioned by its countryside, its cities, its language, history and enriched by efforts, fertilized by their sweat and blood . . . All living things are assigned by *nature* to those areas conforming to their dispositions or affinities. It is the same thing for men and peoples.'[8]

The 'New Racist' discourse also provided a powerful weapon in the fight against anti-racism by confusing critics who continued to see racism within traditional biological terms as an unaltered Nazism and by neatly side-stepping any challenge formulated in this way. It also inverted the logic of racism in which minorities were the target by presenting the majority white society as the 'victim' of multicultural bigots or of a 'race relations industry' bent on disrupting indigenous society through the imposition of foreign religions, customs, and language. In 1984–5 Ray Honeyford, the right-wing head of a Bradford school in which 90 per cent of the pupils were Asian, was forced to resign over his public attack on multiculturalism. Honeyford was immediately supported by senior Conservative politicians and the tabloid press as a 'victim' of intolerant left-wing groups determined to destroy 'English' national identity. Tensions within society, it was argued, did not therefore arise from white racism, but rather from an 'anti-British racism' intent on destroying the previously harmonious indigenous community. Similarly, the FN presented itself as the victim of 'anti-French racism' or defined racism as a 'doctrine denying the right of people to be themselves. The French are today the principal victims of it in their own country.'[9] The attack on anti-racism was one strand in a much wider authoritarian nationalism, of Thatcherism and its Continental equivalents, which presented a picture of a 'healthy' society undermined by moral decay, the disintegration of the family, a breakdown of law and order, and the promotion of feminism and homosexual rights. Anti-racism was frequently attacked in tabloid cartoons by associating it with 'loony left' fanatics, a subversive grouping of lesbians, pot-smoking hippies, Marxists, feminists, radical teachers, and other demons of the populist-right imagination, intent on the destruction of religion, morals, the family and the traditional order.

The strategy of the 'New Right', drawing upon the theory of the Italian Marxist philosopher Antonio Gramsci, was based on the perception that state power depended not solely on material force and economic relations, but also on cultural hegemony, the ability to control the way people perceived the world through the formation of ideas, language and discourse, the basic building blocks of meaning. The attempt to invert and subvert the multiculturalist meaning of '*droit à la différence*', providing a defence of segregation and apartheid, or the displacement of 'race' by 'culture', thus denying any racist intent, was typical of this hegemonic strategy. How successful was the 'New Right' in achieving its goal? Firstly, the hegemonic project was elaborated with considerable sophistication by intellectuals who operated within far-right think tanks or circles; in Britain the Monday Club, Tory Action, the Salisbury Group (founded 1976) and its journal the *Salisbury Review*; in France the Group for Research and Study of European Civilization (GRECE, founded in 1968) and the Club de l'Horloge; in Germany by those grouped around the review *Neue Anthropologie*, and similar organizations in Italy, Belgium, Russia, the USA and South Africa. If the elaboration of a new racist discourse had remained confined to small élitist circles, it would have remained of quite limited significance, but the 'New Right' was highly successful in finding a bridge over and into mainstream politics and the formation of public opinion. The think tanks of the 'New Right' belonged to an international network, of shared publications, conferences and other fora, in which the central concepts were refined and disseminated: GRECE, for example, had a membership that extended to Italy, Germany, Britain, Belgium, Sweden, Spain, Austria, the Netherlands and Czechoslovakia.

One way in which the 'New Right' consciously planned its hegemonic strategy was by establishing a foothold in the mass media, where its ideas and the deployment of a new vocabulary could be recast in a more populist and 'common-sense' form. Members of the French GRECE had direct links to press magnates Raymond Bourgine and Robert Hersant, who facilitated their access to key positions or as regular columnists or journalists. Louis Pauwels, editor of *Figaro* Magazine, disseminated right-wing ideas through this weekly. Ideologues of the new racism had regular columns in the *Sunday Telegraph* (Peregrine Worsthorne), the *Daily Telegraph* (T. Utley, member of the editorial board of the *Salisbury Review*), *The Times* (Sir Alfred Sherman, speech writer for Mrs Thatcher; philosopher Roger Scruton, editor of the *Salisbury Review*), the *Mail* (Andrew Alexander), the *Sun* (Professor John Vincent), the *Express* (George Gale) and the *Star* (Robert McNeill). Right-wing intellectuals and élitists, who in the past had avoided low-brow tabloids like the *Sun*, now revelled in skilfully adapting the cultural racism of the 'New Right' circles into a populist format.

Thatcherism was extremely successful in translating an authoritarian and xenophobic nationalism into the form of a 'common-sense' racism. Central to all the columnists lay the message that it was a natural instinct to bond with one's own kind, with 'kith and kin', and that this also 'naturally' should determine the priority of British or English culture and identity over that of 'aliens'. Such exclusionary messages were readily couched in the platitudes and 'obvious' truths of everyday discourse: that 'blood is thicker than water' and 'charity begins at home'. Moreover, those, like Honeyford, who utilized such common-sense categories, were presented as those who 'dared to speak their mind', to utter what most of the 'ordinary' people thought, in defiance of the 'intolerance' of the politically correct, the gang of socialists, lesbians, pacifists and anti-racists who would like to destroy the 'freedom of speech'. In a similar way, Le Pen projected an image of himself as the rough diamond, the man of the people, who stood up for the rights of the indigenous French (*les Français d'abord*) and who bravely said what everybody was secretly thinking. Again such a hierarchy of 'racial' preference was grounded in the common-sense 'truth' of a *natural* order: 'I love more my daughters than my cousins, my cousins more than my neighbours, my neighbours more than those I don't know, those that I don't know more than my enemies.'[10] The success of the 'New Right' hegemonic strategy can be shown by the extent to which its racist vocabulary and arguments became generalized, appropriated by a wider public and 'made its own': for example, supporters of the pro fox-hunting Countryside Alliance, leaning against the doors of their Range Rovers, have presented themselves as a disempowered and endangered minority. Ultimately, it is this 'everyday racism', almost universally diffused within society, sustained by millions of daily speech acts, that constitutes the bedrock of prejudice and violence.

The Rise of National-Populism

The strategies of the 'New Racist' ideologues made a significant contribution to the growth of a new kind of national-populist party, of which the French FN acted as the leader and exemplar for the radical right in Europe. Typical of this realignment of the far right are the German Republikaner Party, the Schweizerische Volkspartei (SVP) or Swiss People's Party, the Austrian Freedom Party (FPO) of Jörg Heider, the Flemish Bloc (VB), the Danish People's Party (DPP), the Northern League (NL) of Umberto Bossi, the Norwegian Progress Party and the Italian National Alliance (the former Italian Social Movement or MSI). The new populists tend to share a number of features. Although leaders like Le Pen and Haider have in the past made anti-Semitic, pro-Nazi or Holocaust denial statements, on the whole they have tended to play this down, to dissociate themselves from the old neo-Nazi tradition and anti-parliamentary violence, and opted instead for political legitimacy and a quest for power within the democratic electoral system. In an ambiguous way, while playing within the rules of parliamentary politics, these parties have generally been against the system, tapping into popular discontent with long-ruling parties of both right and left which are portrayed as corrupt and bloated with rich pickings, out of touch with the 'ordinary' man, and too élitist to sense the anxieties and problems of the 'little people' when faced with rising crime, parasitic immigrants, high taxes, the decline in moral standards and loss of national pride. For these parties, generally neo-liberal in their economic policies, the state is regarded as over-extended and liberty is defined in highly individualistic terms. Most national-populist parties are dependent upon a charismatic leadership, men like Le Pen, Haider, Anders Lange, Franz Schönhuber, Umberto Bossi, Christoph Blocher, who claim to speak up for the 'ordinary' people, whose dreams and sorrows they comprehend. But, invariably, at the core of national-populism is a crudely enunciated xenophobia, a scapegoating of ethnic minorities and refugees, as the principal source of those ills associated with the disintegration of the post-war settlement (full employment and the welfare state), and with perceptions of rising crime and insecurity.

The 'respectable' leaders and militants of the new parties lay claim to an insidious legitimacy, the 'acceptable face of racism', men who, in the words of Paul Taggart, 'are more likely to be wearing bespoke suits than military fatigues'.[11] Unlike their old neo-Nazi forebears, the national-populists have shown an ability to break the mould of the old party stranglehold and to make significant electoral gains. They also succeeded in breaking out from the ghetto of skinhead violence and parading to gain electoral support from all social classes, including middle-class and professional groups. Crucial to the process of legitimation was the skilful use of the 'New Racist' discourse to jettison overt forms of biological racism, and to claim merely a reasonable right to protect national identity and culture. The FN showed the way with its gain of 11 per cent of the national vote in the 1984 European election, rising to 14.9 per cent in the 1997 general election. Although the FN was later to disintegrate under the impact of an internal split and the breakaway of Bruno Mégret in January 1999, other parties have continued to show dynamic growth. The Flemish Bloc scored 9.9 per cent in the general election of 1999, the Italian National Alliance 15.7 per cent in 1996, the Norwegian Progress Party 15.3 per cent in 1997, the Northern League 10.1 per cent in 1996 and, most threatening of all, the Austrian Freedom Party won 27.7 per cent in October 1999, enabling it to enter government in alliance with the People's Party. In the same month the Swiss People's Party, led by millionaire Christoph Blocher, came from nowhere to take the largest share of the vote (25 per cent) and to challenge the two-party *status quo* held since the nineteenth century by the Christian Democrats and the Liberals. Blocher played to two basic fears, dislike of immigrants and refugees, and anxiety about the EU, particularly the projected enlargement to the East. Austria and Switzerland are two of the wealthiest nations in Europe, an indication of the fact that xenophobia and racism has not necessarily been an expression of economic hardship, but just as much linked to high levels of insecurity about national identity and a sense of impending doom.

Racism: The Ambiguities of Mainstream Parties

Although national-populism played an important role in the overt expression of racist attitudes and policies, it could be argued that the most crucial factor in the reproduction of racism has been the role of mainstream political parties and governments. Wherever racist movements have begun to make significant electoral inroads, traditional parties, instead of placing a *cordon sanitaire* around the extremists and trying to deny them legitimacy within the democratic political system, have invariably themselves tried to occupy the same terrain by moving to the right and taking a 'hard' anti-immigrant position. In France both the conservatives of the RPR and UDF, as well as the Socialists, drifted in this direction after Le Pen's FN gained 11 per cent of the national vote in the European elections of 1984, and in some cases began to imitate the language of the FN. Giscard d'Estaing stressed the dangers of an immigrant 'invasion' and proposed that France 'return to the traditional conception of the acquisition of nationality, that based on the right of blood'. Charles Pasqua, Minister of the Interior in 1986–8 and 1993, remarked: 'Yes, there are a few extremists in the National Front, but basically, the National Front has the same preoccupations, the same values as the majority. It merely expresses them in a more brutal and noisy way.'[12] Conservative leaders at local or regional level on numerous occasions showed a willingness to enter into electoral alliance with the FN where it was perceived that they held the balance of power, a practice that added to the legitimacy of Le Pen's movement. In France, as elsewhere, the national-populists often had a major impact on the political system even when their total vote was too low to gain entrance to government. The strategies of the 'New Racist' or 'New Right' ideologues impacted not only on the populists, but also on classic conservative or mainstream parties. In Britain Mrs Thatcher dramatically ended the electoral rise of the National Front by acknowledging the legitimacy of the 'problems' raised by it and being 'prepared to deal with it', a goal that was achieved by the adoption of a 'New Right' discourse.[13] While denying that she was a racist, Mrs Thatcher went on to spell out the dangers of four million New Commonwealth immigrants: 'Now that is an awful lot and I think it means that people are really rather afraid that this country might be swamped by people with a different culture.'[14] Members of the Salisbury Group, like Ray Honeyford, Jonathan Aitken, Rhodes Boyson, Julian Amery and Enoch Powell, played a key role in the formation of Tory ideology or had a direct entrée to Downing Street.

At the heart of European liberal democracy, at the beginning of the twenty-first century, lies a contradictory and Janus-faced attitude towards racism. David Goldberg has argued that the irony of liberal modernity, committed to idealized principles of equality, is that it has failed to take racism seriously, to recognize how far it is woven into the history and the very fabric and institutions of Western societies.[15] In a post-Holocaust universe, Western liberal democracies share a dominant discourse that asserts the fundamental values of freedom, equality and the protection of individual or minority rights, regardless of 'race', religion or ethnic affiliation. Post-war governments have set out to demonstrate their anti-racist credentials through passing legislation that outlaws racial discrimination and through acceptance, to a lesser or greater extent, of multicultural policies. All member states have signed the EU declaration which commits them to combat racism. Leading politicians, prime ministers and top officials constantly defer to a universal 'moral order' in which racism, fascism and the denial of basic human rights will not be tolerated. However, such formal declarations of high principle and good intent are often largely symbolic and have acted as a smoke-screen to hide the fact that anti-racist measures, invariably weakly enforced, have gone hand-in-hand with anti-immigrant acts that have undermined ethnic minorities and reinforced highly negative stereo-types. This has been shown most clearly in the debate on asylum seekers and refugees.

Official rhetoric constantly presents immigrants, refugees and asylum seekers as 'illegal', 'bogus' and potentially 'criminal'. The attempt to con-struct a 'Fortress Europe', a powerfully policed border around the EU, has been reinforced by an official discourse that presents an image of European civilization besieged by a terrifying and monstrous Third World. Across Europe the right-wing populist press has whipped up a 'moral panic' about 'bogus refugees' that has reproduced all the worse stereotypes of anti-black racism. Typical of the constant barrage of anti-refugee articles was a 1998 article in the *Sun* by the columnist Littlejohn. He described a scene at Heathrow Airport in which the 'gravy train [*sic*] now arriving at Terminal One' was carrying bogus asylum seekers, who were made most welcome and 'invited to form a queue at the nearest

DSS office and apply for political asylum . . . Staff are ready and willing to pander to your every need. Terrorists, rapists and muggers are especially welcome. The British taxpayer will be delighted to pick up the bill.'[16] The daily circulation of the *Sun* at 3.5 million copies is greater than that of all the 'quality' press combined (*The Daily Telegraph*, *Financial Times*, *The Guardian*, *The Independent* and *The Times*).

Both the Conservative and Labour leadership, during the later part of 1999 and early 2000, far from seeking to criticize or dampen such inflammatory press campaigns, sought to outvie each other in how tough and repressive they could be in relation to asylum seekers. The Home Secretary, Jack Straw, brought in a new Immigration and Asylum Act (1999), the main function of which was to deter further immigration by making conditions so harsh and unpleasant for asylum seekers, that none would seek to reach British shores. Deterrence included income support set at 70 per cent of the minimum, the opening of detention centres, the use of food vouchers and forced dispersal. In spite of increasingly draconian measures, the Shadow Home Secretary, Anne Widdecombe, accused the government of 'phenomenal complacency' and creating a situation where 'Britain is now a soft touch'.[17]

In April the United Nations High Commissioner for Refugees (UNHCR) accused both Labour and Conservatives of breaking an all-party commitment not to stir up prejudice; and similar complaints were made by the Liberal Democrats and the Commission for Racial Equality that the 'race card' was being played leading into the May local elections. The black trade-union leader Bill Morris accused ministers of creating a 'climate of fear' through their inflammatory language. The tabloids responded with a classic 'New Racism' line; criticism of William Hague's manifesto promise to tackle 'bogus' refugees was an 'exercise in moral McCarthyism' orchestrated by the 'race relations industry' (The *Daily Telegraph*) or, for the *Daily Mail*, a 'kind of liberal fascism that stifles any debate'.[18] On 18 April Hague upped the stakes by revealing Tory plans for the incarceration of all asylum seekers in some 20 new secure detention centres, and stated that he would not be gagged by 'attitudes of political correctness'.[19] The cynical electoral deployment of xenophobia was made clear by a spokesman in the Tory Central Office: 'What can the [Labour] government do? They can't go to the right of us on asylum, but they can't stay left either.'[20] Finally, a further UN Report of August 2000 which monitored British government policy on tackling racism condemned the contradiction between progress in some fields of race relations and the failure to respond to a vicious anti-asylum-seeker press campaign, as well as the introduction of dispersal policies that led to their social exclusion. As Anne Owers noted, the UN committee were right to conclude 'that racism is indivisible; there cannot be a trade-off between fair treatment of minority groups already here and those that newly arrive'.[21]

The contradictions at the heart of the Labour government's self-declared dedication to anti-racism and to uphold the principles of justice and equality was brought home by the widespread debate in February 2000 on the impact of the Macpherson Report one year on. The official inquiry into the 1993 murder of Stephen Lawrence was supported by the Home Office, and resulted in a major realignment of official thinking that racism was largely a matter of individual prejudice to an acceptance of the need to tackle institutional racism, especially within the police. While Jack Straw, in a progress report, claimed that half of Macpherson's recommendations had been implemented by February 2000, this provided an exaggerated sense of progress. The number of ethnic minority officers had actually fallen in nine of the 43 forces, while a third had failed to hire a single extra black or Asian officer. The overall picture was described by one leading QC as 'a grim one, littered with broken promises, inaction and reticence'.[22] Most crucial of all, it was at this very time that government, Conservative and media attacks on 'bogus' asylum seekers generated a climate of racial prejudice and xenophobic intolerance that entirely undermined the impact of the Macpherson Report and led to a dramatic increase in racial violence. In the 12 months to April 2000 the number of race-hate crimes in London doubled to reach a total of 23 346 offences, a pattern that was repeated across Britain. The alarming rise in attacks, many of which achieved unprecedented levels of brutality (burning to death with petrol; the beating to death of a father before his 14-year-old daughter), was fuelled by the rhetoric of politicians on asylum seekers and by harsh government policies.

Although the analysis here has been made mainly in relation to the British situation, an identical development could be found in most European states. In Greece, for example, police sweeps against illegal immigrants and the tabling of a harsh new immigration bill led to an anxiety among civil rights groups that racism was being used as a key issue in the run-up to the parliamentary elections of 9 April 2000. Leading politicians were accused of deploying a language that was close to that of Le Pen and Jörg Heider. The drive by EU member states to impose sanctions on Austria because of the entry of Heider's Freedom Party into a government coalition was riddled with contradictions. Many of the governments that engaged in this ethical policy had themselves a long track record of making anti-refugee statements that were similar to those of the Freedom Party. Secondly, moves to contain Heider could be interpreted as a strategy by traditional ruling parties to block the advance of a national-populist current which was regarded as a threat to their own electoral position. In general, it can be argued that European governments, through their overt or tacit support of racial rhetoric, the introduction of ever more restrictive and oppressive legislation and policing measures, and through their failure to combat institutional racism, have played a greater part in the reproduction of racism and discriminatory practices in Europe than have the violent and overtly racist political movements of the extreme right.

To what extent was the shift towards a 'New Racism' in the last quarter of the twentieth century elaborated in terms of the traditional modalities, of anti-black and anti-Semitic racism, that have been our main point of reference? Firstly, with the generalization of immigration controls across Western Europe after 1973, the term 'immigrant' began to take on a highly negative connotation so that it became synonymous with 'non-European'. Speeches by Le Pen, Chirac, or Giscard d'Estaing referring to *les immigrés* were universally understood to signify 'Arabs', all those who originated from North Africa. Within the EU in general, the terms 'immigrant' or 'refugee' began to refer, in the public imagination, to an increasingly diverse range of stereotyped 'aliens', a diversity that reflected the complexity of global migrant flows into Western Europe: of Turks, Somalis, Kurds, Roma and Sinti of the Balkans, Pakistani and Bangladeshi Muslims, Maghrebians, Afghans, Sri Lankans and so on. The term 'black', in the sense of African or Afro-Caribbean, did not readily catch this diversity, whereas the term 'immigrant' or 'refugee' could, while still carrying almost identical negative meanings – the 'Other' as racially inferior, criminal, lazy and parasitical, dirty and diseased. In particular, the 1980s and 1990s saw the revival of two ancient forms of racism that this study has had to neglect, of intolerance towards Gypsies and Muslims. Islamophobia, rooted in the age-old stereotypes of Orientalism, assumed a particular force as European society took fright at the perception of an external 'fundamentalist' threat (from Saddam Hussein and Gaddafi to Bin Laden) or of an internal Muslim danger to European culture and identity symbolized by mosque construction, veiled women and Muslim schools. While the diversity of stereotypical racisms thus widened in EU states at the turn of the century, the ascent of the 'New Right' was also marked by the unexpected revival of anti-Semitism.

Before examining this in the Conclusion, we take a look at how a similar phenomenon accompanied the rise of the extreme right and virulent forms of xenophobic nationalism in post-Communist Central and Eastern Europe.

Racism in Post-Communist Eastern Europe

Within the USSR, and the Communist bloc states that fell within its sphere of influence, the predominant form of racism after 1945 was anti-Semitism. As has been noted, this partly reflects the relative absence of a maritime colonial tradition and of a significant black presence. Conversely, Eastern Europe (especially Poland, the Ukraine and Russia) had until 1939 contained the historic and demographic core of world Judaism, as well as a tradition of anti-Semitism that was profoundly rooted in popular culture. After the Great Patriotic War (1941–5), Soviet ideology still officially upheld the principles of international socialism and denied that any Jewish 'problem' existed since there had been, it was claimed, a total and successful assimilation. In reality Jews continued to be persecuted under Stalin. As the Soviet Union turned against Israel after 1948, a wave of traditional anti-Semitic persecution took place under the disguise of 'anti-Zionism'. Purges and show trials swept through the Soviet satellite regimes in 1949–53, leading to the execution of Slansky, a Jew and General-Secretary of the Czechoslovakian Communist Party, along with ten other 'conspirators' in December 1952. Purges also occurred in Hungary, Poland, Romania and Russia, where a paranoid Stalin – following on a so-called Jewish 'Doctor's Plot' to murder senior officials – laid plans for the removal of the entire Jewish population to Siberia. Czech Jews, falsely accused of spying on behalf of Israeli and Western intelligence agencies and the capitalist enemy, were attacked in a thinly disguised, traditional anti-Semitism that saw the Jews as the eternal enemy within and the agents of a conspiracy to achieve global domination. As the Slovak *Pravda* claimed during the Slansky trial: 'It is in the service of the class enemy that the Zionists have wormed their way into the Communist parties in order to disrupt and undermine them from within. Certain members of our party, too, have come under the influence of Zionism. They have succumbed to the ideology of cosmopolitanism.'[23] In Poland the liberation of the concentration camps, far from leading to the end of genocide, was soon followed by the Kielce pogrom of 1946 and, by mid-1947, the murder of some 1500 Jews. In

1945 there were still 200 000 Jews in Poland, but as a result of persecution and traditional anti-Semitism, also sustained throughout the Communist era by the Catholic church, a mass exodus had almost entirely obliterated the Jewish community by the late 1970s and reduced numbers to a mere 6000.

The accelerating collapse of the old Soviet empire in the last decade of the twentieth century produced conditions that favoured the rise of virulent forms of nationalism and populist anti-Semitism. The official, but disguised, anti-Semitism of the Communist Parties in Eastern Europe had, in a rather contradictory way, ensured that it remained 'controlled' by government: the single-party state did not provide a political space for opposition movements to make significant use of the issue. However, the extension of *glasnost* from 1986 onwards, the collapse of the USSR in December 1991, and the first free elections in Poland in the same year, opened the way to the proliferation of new political parties, many of which cultivated a dangerous form of national-populism that appealed, at a time of considerable turmoil and economic dislocation, to an inexperienced electorate. Polish parties like the National Front, the National Front 'Fatherland' Party, National Democracy, and the National-Democratic Front sought potent symbols of national strength in the pre-Communist, inter-war leadership of Roman Dmowski and Marshal Pilsudski, the first epitomizing anti-Semitic nationalism, the second the strong, authoritarian leader. The inevitable turmoil that accompanied the chaotic transition to a free market and to parliamentary democracy provided an opportunity for populist anti-Semites to attack the Jews as the source of economic disorder, cultural and ideological disarray, and the 'cosmopolitan' force behind foreign capitalism, consumerism, moral decay and the destruction of Polish identity. The fascist Polish Nationalist Union, under its leader Boleslaw Tejkowski, now saw the hated years of Communist rule as the work of Jewish agents, and recruited among unemployed and alienated skinhead youths who began to attack Jewish targets, as well as African students, Gypsies and Romanian asylum seekers. However, by the late 1990s the relatively successful economic transition in Poland and the stabilization of the political system was a cause of growing optimism, and opinion polls showed an underlying decline in anti-Semitism. In 1975 some 41 per cent of Poles had a negative view of Jews; by 1990 this had declined to 20 per cent. Curiously enough, by 1991 hostility was much higher towards Gypsies, Arabs and blacks than towards Jews in Poland, Czechoslovakia and Hungary, suggesting a shift in these modernizing countries towards the pattern of prejudice to be found in Western Europe. The situation in Russia was, however, much more unstable and potentially dangerous as the Federation was threatened with total collapse in 1991–3. In 1992 the 'shock therapy' of privatization and deregulation was accompanied by massive economic dislocation, growing unemployment, inflation of over 1000 per cent, and a fall in production of 20 per cent. Seventy-three per cent of the population was living in acute distress. Such a crisis, accompanied by the humiliating disintegration of the Soviet Union, the withdrawal of troops to Russia, the growth of inter-ethnic conflict and violent crime, political instability and the loss of the ideological framework supplied by Marxism and Communism, even if it had been contested, provided ideal conditions for the proliferation of extreme nationalist movements. *Pamiat*, led by Dmitri Vasiliev, sought to reassert a sense of national pride by idealizing a great pre-Communist Russia that had been destroyed by the global conspiracy of the Jews, an evil 'cosmopolitan' force that operated both through capitalism, symbolized by the detested United States, as well as through the imposition of the 'alien' ideology of Marxism. An early 1986 'Appeal' of *Pamiat* claimed: 'Global imperialism, nurtured by Zionism and its mercenary Masonic lackeys, is trying to drag the world into the spiral of a new planetwide catastrophe.'[24]

The murky and paranoid anti-Semitism of the Black Hundreds and the *Protocols of the Elders of Zion* resurfaced with a vengeance. In the Presidential elections of December 1993 the virulent anti-Semite and 'clown', Zhirinovsky, who promised a heady populist mix of Great Russian expansion, 'strong-man' dictatorship and cheap vodka, gained an astonishing six million votes. In 1999 bombs were planted in three out of the five synagogues in Moscow, while the Jewish leader Leopold Kaimonovsky was stabbed by a neo-Nazi youth. Political commentators claimed that the openly fascist antics of the 'Führer' Alexander Barkashov and his Russian National Unity movement posed no serious threat; far more worrying was the spread of anti-Semitism into the mainstream political parties. The Communist Party leader Gennady Zyuganov claimed that there was a 'Zionist' conspiracy to wreck the economy: 'Our people . . . cannot fail to see that the spread of Zionism in the government is one of the reasons for the current catastrophic conditions of the country, the mass impoverishment and the process of extinction of its people.' Zyuganov refused in the Duma to censor the Communist leader and populist demagogue, General Albert Makashov, who threatened to kill the 'Yids'.

As Russia moved into the twenty-first century, it appeared destined to be wracked by a profound and dangerous political, economic and social crisis, and by a potential for the growth of virulent anti-Semitism and/or by the authoritarian forms of nationalism represented by the new President, Vladimir Putin.

In many ways the crude and open anti-Semitism of Eastern Europe appears readily explicable in that its roots lie in conditions of economic and political dislocation that were not dissimilar to those of inter-war Europe. However, the revival of anti-Semitism within the ambit of the 'New Right' in Western Europe, an extreme right that was seeking legitimacy within parliamentary democracy, seems at first to be far more puzzling. The following Conclusion goes on to examine the continuing roots of anti-Semitism in Western Europe, as well as to provide some overall comparison of the two key modalities of racism, anti-black and anti-Semitic prejudice, which have been a major concern of this study.

CONCLUSION: BLACK AND JEW

The Two Racisms

Throughout this study we have tended to examine anti-black and anti-Semitic racism as if they constituted two quite discrete strands, which might suggest that individuals or groups located in one time and place would focus their prejudice almost uniquely on Jews (with little concern for blacks), and in other instances primarily on blacks (with little place for anti-Semitism). Historically, it can be argued that such a crude division makes some sense as shown in the European map of racisms, in the division between maritime colonial or ex-colonial states of the West, and the landlocked nations of Central and Eastern Europe that contained the demographic core of the Jewish people. However, such a perspective overlooks the complex and crucial interrelationship between racisms at the individual level, the fact that each person will be socialized into a world which may offer not one, but a whole range of potential 'outsiders' or minorities as objects of dislike. Social psychologists have demonstrated that individuals (as well as the group to which they belong) tend to maintain a hierarchy of 'race', in which, for example, black Africans may be placed on the bottom rung, perceived in terms of the most negative characteristics, followed in a sequence by other groups that are positioned ever further up the ladder as they approach the most perfect human type represented by the white European subject or 'in-group'. If the individual is usually prejudiced towards a range of 'Others', what are the factors which generate greater hostility towards some groups rather than others?

If racisms are historically located, determined by specific contexts, then it is to be expected that they will alter through time and that the 'hierarchy of race', the ranking order, will also undergo change. It might, for example, be predicted that an inter-war hierarchy in which hatred of Jews predominated over the relative lack of concern over blacks, would be reversed post-1945 as large-scale colonial immigration took off. Or that political conflict in the Middle East, the perceived rise of an Islamic threat, and a growing Muslim presence inside Europe, would generate a more recent 'anti-Arab' racism. Racial stereotypes do not, at the level of the individual psyche, exist as separate or discrete strands, but interrelate within a field. How and why individuals or groups focus their animus at a given moment against one minority rather than another, and how this can also be switched, provides an insight into the dynamics of racism.

An excellent opportunity to investigate the interrelationship between racisms is provided by the role of anti-black and anti-Semitic racism in contemporary extreme right-wing movements.[1] As has been noted (Chapter 7), the last quarter of the twentieth century saw the growth of far-right political parties in Western Europe that sought power through establishing a mass electoral base, a strategy that could only be effective if they dissociated themselves from the old Nazi or fascist traditions or acts of overt violence. Some parties, like the French Front National, have indeed achieved widespread legitimacy and electoral success through, for example, a shift to cultural racism. It may seem to be contradictory to such purposes, and rather surprising, that the FN, as well as other parties like the British National Front, should retain a core ideology of traditional anti-Semitism. Such 'respectable' racist parties operate at two levels: at the 'open' surface level the entire message, directed at potential voters, sympathizers and ordinary members is aimed against blacks and 'immigrants'; at a concealed level aimed at an inner core of militants or party activists, the key message is based on anti-Semitism. Party leaders therefore consciously manipulate a field of prejudice in which a dynamic relationship exists between the two racisms.

Why the allegiance to anti-Semitism in a political context in which it might seem to be counterproductive, alienating rather than winning over voters? Part of the answer can be found in the fact that the generation of far-right leaders that pioneered the shift after 1970 towards national-populism and an anti-immigrant politics, men like Le Pen, John Tyndall, Franz Schönhuber and Jörg Heider, had received their political education and ideological formation after 1945 within the ranks of overtly Nazi and anti-Semitic movements. Anti-black racism presented a case of electoral opportunism that did not fundamentally displace the core anti-Semitic values. Secondly, such leaders have constructed a 'New Racist' discourse that enables coded anti-Semitic messages to be conveyed to the initiated, the party 'hard-line' militants, while remaining opaque to a wider public who might otherwise be alienated. For example, the British NF in the 1970s claimed not to be anti-Semitic but 'anti-Zionist', while the FN through the use of coded terms, like 'cosmopolitanism', '*mondialiste*', 'rootless' or 'nomadic' people, 'usury', 'international finance' and so on, was able to construct anti-Semitic messages without once referring specifically to Jews. Such coding has served as a public signal, from the leadership to militants and an inner coterie of 'old-guard' neo-Nazis, who frequently showed opposition to the electoral strategy and the apparent ditching of traditional ideology, that the core values did indeed remain intact. Coding and ambiguity sometimes appears to have 'gone wrong' and to have backfired, as when Le Pen caused widespread scandal through his hinted support for the Holocaust denial (the genocide, he said, was a mere 'detail' of the Second World War) or his punning reference to the Jewish minister Durafour in terms of 'Durafour-*crématoire*', *four* meaning 'oven' in French, hence *four crématoire* for the Nazi gas ovens. But such 'gaffes' may also have been quite deliberate, part of a wider revisionist strategy to reintroduce or normalize anti-Semitism, which would at the same time appease hard-liners, and to create a legit-imate and acceptable image of Nazism and of Hitler through ridiculing the Holocaust or persuading the public that it never took place.

However, none of this explains why contemporary racists have remained so doggedly attached to anti-Semitism: such durability and resilience derives from the powerful ideological structures and political benefits of the stereotype, in particular as a brand of conspiracy theory. The racial stereotype of the black, deriving both from colonial conquest and slavery, is of a 'race' far inferior to the white European in innate intelligence, incapable of invention or rising to 'civilized standards' without assistance, lazy, dirty, driven more by animal instincts (violence and uncontrolled sexuality) than by reason, and prone to revert to a primitive state characterized by paganism, the 'jungle', the 'mud-hut' and cannibalism. The problem with a post-war politics grounded on the threat of black immigration was how to explain the fact that such an inherently inferior 'race', an inferiority that it would be beyond any educational programme or social improvement to alter, could offer any kind of challenge to white supremacy. The contradiction was resolved through anti-Semitism: the black, stupid and inferior did not present a fundamental threat, this came far more from the Jew, who represented intelligence and a high level of organization.

Frequently, racism has been defined as a system of belief that invariably assumes the genetic or cultural inferiority of the oppressed group: however, anti-Semitism is far more ambiguous in that it credits the Jews with superior qualities such as cleverness, strict moral standards, powerful group solidarity, energy, strong will and high levels of achievement. For Hitler, who recognized the Jew as 'the mightiest counterpart to the Aryan' with 'an infinitely tough will to live and preserve the species', the greater the diabolic cunning and power of the enemy, the deeper the level of anxiety and paranoia, and the sense of a desperate and final struggle for German survival.[2] Since the gravest of all threats to the Aryans stemmed from racial mixing with lower types and from degeneration, it was the Jews (who upheld their own racial purity and strength through strict racial endogamy) who procured this end through the deliberate introduction of blacks and 'interbreeding'. The inferior blacks were thus an instrument of a malevolent Jewish conspiracy. At the same time, Jews were portrayed by the Nazis as effeminate and physically degenerate. A 1935 Nazi sports manual by Kurt Münch noted: 'Among the inferior races the Jews have done nothing in the athletic sphere. They are surpassed even by the lowest of the negro tribes.' In the same year the racist propagandist Julius Streicher, incensed by the repeated victories of the black wrestler, Jim Wango, over white German contestants, interceded to halt a match in Nuremberg. The humiliation of defeat by a racial primitive was countered through the notion of Jewish subversion, a sequence of matches organized by the Jewish promoter Zurth: 'What we oppose is the linking of sport with dirty business interests and sales gimmicks. It is a sales gimmick, an appeal to inferior people, to subhumans, to put a negro on view and let him compete with white people. It is not in the spirit of the inhabitants of Nuremberg to let white men be subdued by a black man.'[3]

This type of thinking or formulation, the Jews as an evil manipulator of a race war, can be found quite consistently in contemporary anti-Semitism. In 1990 an FN leader, Georges-Paul Wagner, denounced the 'perils of *mondialisme* and cosmopolitanism' (i.e. the Jews), which favoured lowering barriers to immigration so as to undermine and weaken the French people from within. The 1993 FN election programme *300 Steps for the Rebirth of France* denounced the *mondialiste* doctrine which 'usually dressed up as the rights of man, preaches the destruction of nations, the abolition of frontiers, mixing of races, cultures and peoples'.[4] Similarly, the British NF journal *Spearhead* accused Jewish conspirators of promoting multiculturalism in order to achieve 'universal genocide by race-mixing', a strategy for eventual world domination that would be achieved by retaining Jewish racial purity. 'It must be recognized that immigration into this country is not simply some economically determined accident, but consciously permitted as a calculated act of genocide against the British people.'[5] A favourite metaphor or image in European far-right propaganda, especially in cartoons, is that of Jews as puppeteers, concealed from the audience, pulling the strings of black dolls. In a typical FN cartoon one black puppet, in a line of similar faces, complains, 'But I don't want to vote', while behind him a hook-nosed man with thick lips says, 'You'll do what I tell you to do'.[6] The British NF *Spearhead* frequently claimed that Jews fomented race wars in the USA or Britain, destructive conflicts that undermined states: 'The real enemy meanwhile smilingly sits upstairs, pulls all the strings and calls the tune to which both parties dance.' Such a logic determined the racial hierarchy and the real political agenda concealed from the wider electorate: 'if Britain were to become Jew-clean she would have no nigger neighbours to worry about.'[7]

The idea of racial manipulation of naive blacks by cunning Jews is just one small part of a much wider structure of anti-Semitic ideology founded on a conspiracy theory and what Richard Hofstadter has called the 'paranoid style' of politics.[8] Anti-Semitic conspiracy theory, although it may appear bizarre and irrational to the uninitiated, provides a very powerful and seductive framework for understanding and interpreting the world. Typically, important events and the huge, complex forces that underlie them (the Cold War, capitalism, Communism, economic crisis, international conflict, growing crime, 'moral decline' and so on) can be reduced to a simple cause. Supporters or members of extreme-right political movements, who suffer from high levels of insecurity and anxiety, are provided with a framework for understanding a chaotic and fast-changing world that seems at times overwhelming and out of control. At times of economic, social and political crisis and disorientation, like that facing contemporary Russia, conspiracy theory and populist, xenophobic nationalism offer a strong appeal to ordinary people. The demagogue and propagandist, from Le Pen to Zhirinovsky, offers simple solutions to complex issues. For ordinary Russians, the penetration of capitalism, of market relations and foreign multinationals has been, in part, a real cause of growing mass unemployment, hyper-inflation and extreme poverty: such insidious processes are readily presented in terms of American finance, and behind that, the evil machinations of rich and powerful 'cosmopolitans'. A further attraction of conspiracy theory is that it provides a 'fail-safe' mechanism to resolve any contradictions and to provide 'proof' in the absence of evidence. For example, a lack of public or demonstrable evidence about Jewish conspiratorial activities can be ascribed to the diabolic cunning with which they operate. The very absence of an exposure of Jewish conspiratorial power by the press, cinema and television is itself taken as proof of the extent to which Jews own or control the media and suppress the truth. Finally, the prevalence of a conspiracy theory helps explain why it is that powerful currents of anti-Semitism can exist even in regions or states where there is an almost total absence of Jews. A 1992 survey found that 10 per cent of Poles thought there were 4 to 7 million Jews in the country; 25 per cent put the number at 750 000 to 3.5 million, while the true number was 6000, so few that most Poles would have no contact whatsoever with Jews. However, even if the numbers are shown to be objectively small, this is of no consequence to the anti-Semite since for them Jews wield such immense individual power as financiers, government ministers or press barons that numbers are immaterial to the threat they pose.

Contemporary 'New Right' movements and 'respectable' racist parties appear to break the links to an older tradition of fascism and to swing over to an anti-immigrant politics, but in reality the rupture often takes place only at the surface. The failure to jettison anti-Semitism stems in part from the considerable explanatory power of the racial ideology. No attempt appears to have been made by the extreme right to 'modernize' racial doctrine by developing a theory in which blacks, Asians or any other group take on a similar function to the Jews, apart from a recent tendency to portray oil-rich Arabs and Islamic 'fundamentalists' in terms of powerful and global conspiratorial forces. When black immigration is presented as a danger, it is not in terms of a threatening, intelligent competitor, but rather of crude numbers, a primitive 'breeding-power' that will simply 'swamp' and displace the 'white-man' in his 'own country'.

It might be objected that such ideological constructions of anti-black and anti-Semitic racism, while demonstrating how two modalities might interrelate or be placed in a hierarchy, remains quite untypical, confined to an inner core of activists. This is indeed the case, and the anomaly of extreme-right parties is that, through their overt anti-immigrant stance, they have had a much bigger impact on generating a popular anti-black racism than anti-Semitism. However, it can be argued that racial conspiracy theory has historic roots in contrasting anti-black and anti-Semitic traditions and stereotypes that can be found almost universally within European culture. Although there has been a relative lack of contemporary research into hierarchies of race at the individual level, there does exist an interesting body of investigation by American social psychologists carried out immediately after the Second World War, in particular by

Adorno, Horkheimer, Bettelheim and Allport. Bruno Bettelheim and Morris Janowitz, through in-depth interviews of 150 ex-servicemen from Chicago, set out to establish the relationship between anti-Semitic and 'anti-Negro' prejudice.[9] In general this, and similar investigations, found that the two kinds of stereotype were made up of quite different, almost reciprocal sets of characteristics presenting a more or less integrated pattern. Jews were perceived to have the following traits:

- Controlling everything through the power of money, shrewd, mercenary, industrious, grasping, intelligent, ambitious, sly and clannish (refusal to intermarry, a closed-in group).

Blacks were perceived quite differently as:

- Of low intelligence, ignorant, lazy and slackers at work, dirty, carriers of disease, sexually promiscuous, immoral, emotionally unstable, given to crimes of violence with razors and knives, fondness for gambling, inability to save, superstitious, flashy in dress.[10]

Whether we accept the basically psychoanalytic approach of this American school or not, the research demonstrated that anti-black and anti-Semitic stereotypes, each one of them consisting of an interlocking pattern of characteristics, were universally present within US society at the individual level. In Bettelheim's sample almost all the ex-servicemen were in varying degrees prejudiced towards both groups. Only nine out of 150 were tolerant towards both Jews and blacks, and as the measure of the intensity of individual intolerance increased in scale towards Jews, so it also increased towards blacks. The more extreme the individual racist, the greater the hatred directed towards *all* minorities. Within any given historic context, any particular European society at a particular moment in time, one minority group may have been much more intensely disliked than another, to which a lesser degree of antipathy attached. What is of considerable interest to the history of racisms would be to track, through a long period of time, the processes that might lead a dominant prejudice to weaken and be superseded or displaced by a minor. One way of viewing this is to regard each individual as entertaining a whole complex of racial stereotypes, usually placed in a hierarchy, and that these modalities constitute a latent resource, a kind of wardrobe or kit of racial types, that can be called upon or activated within a specific historical context or conjuncture of events.

During the period under review (1870–2000) the image of the money-grasping, cunning, intelligent and conspiratorial Jew, as opposed to the sexually libidinous, lazy, primitive and unintelligent black, was diffused not only among an educated middle class, but among all Europeans. The origin of these powerful racial stereotypes was rooted in two distinct developments, one in the history of European expansion, the conquest of Africa, the slave system and colonialism, the other in an even older millennial tradition of Christian persecution of a 'deicide' minority. Until the end of the Second World War, anti-Semitism tended, throughout Western and Eastern Europe, to carry a greater psychic intensity, or level of anxiety and fear, since the Jew was both an intelligence, as well as lodged *inside*. The black, apart from the crucial experience within the terrain of white colonial societies, was for most Europeans a far more exotic, distant and *external* primitive that offered no real threat until he, too, migrated and in turn became an insider. This is not to say that the stereotypes were somehow the 'cause' of racism, or that they remained fossilized or unchanging in form. Rather, the stereotypes may be seen as latent, diffuse and generalized within European culture, a dangerous 'resource' that could be called upon or mobilized according to the specific social and political moment. For the peasantry of inter-war Central and Eastern Europe, the patterns of prejudice towards Jews were highly activated, but the same individuals would also have carried negative anti-black stereotypes that were diffused within popular culture through nursery rhymes, mission sermons and Hollywood films. The rapidity with which an anti-black 'moral panic' was generated in the 1920s in response to the presence of black French troops in the Rhineland is a testament to the latent power of stereotypes, even within a society in which the great majority had never seen a black person.

During the period from 1870 to 2000 we have also seen that the ideological formulations of the underlying patterns of prejudice can alter dramatically through time. From 1870 to *c*.1945 the rise of biological racism was a reflection of an age in which scientific explanation of difference carried enormous prestige and legitimating authority. After 1945 the educated public came to see the roots of difference in terms of social and cultural formations, an anti-racist perspective to which the 'New Racism' riposted by making cultural barriers absolute. Groups were 'naturally' and inexorably locked into separate compartments, different age-old cultures, that multiculturalism could only devastate. 'Mixaphobia', whether of intermarriage and degeneration or of cultural 'bastardization' and hybridization, showed an underlying continuity across the twentieth century.

In conclusion, what prognostications can be made about the likely trends in European racism as we move into the twenty-first century? This is a complex and controversial area of debate, but here attention is draw to three areas: developments within the European Union, the problem of institutional racism and, lastly, the impact of genetic science.

'Fortress Europe' and Racism

The disintegration of the old Soviet bloc has removed the firm controlling hand that suppressed and contained latent nationalism, while the descent into political anarchy, economic crisis and cultural/ ideological dislocation has produced conditions ripe for the proliferation of virulent forces of extremist nationalism both within and on the borders of Europe. This has been accompanied by the rise of anti-Semitism and of racialized ethnicity, in the sense that national hatreds are constructed in terms of minorities or opposing nations (Serbs towards Kosovans, Russians towards Chechens and so on) that are viewed in terms of unbridgeable difference, whether of a quasi-biological or cultural-racial kind. Countervailing such processes of disintegration is the fact that the EU constitutes a stable political bloc, dedicated officially to the protection of human rights and the outlawing of racism, and which acts as a moderating influence on those states like Poland, Hungary and Turkey that wish to join the 'club'.

However, wherever the boundaries of an enlarged EU may finally settle, such a Europe is still potentially exposed to racism from a number of directions. Firstly, the ever-powerful assertion of a 'Fortress Europe', backed up by an integrated system of laws and computerized frontier policing, seems likely to deepen perceptions of 'us' and 'them', of a higher 'civilized' European order situated like an island within a threatening sea of starving, brutalized, but determined-because-desperate inferior peoples. Exclusion of such a threatening 'invasion' is difficult to square with official multiculturalism that claims to extend political, cultural and civic rights to minorities now permanently located inside Europe. The simultaneous global expansion of migration flows, accompanied by cheaper and rapid air transport, means that the range of ethnic groups arriving in Europe as refugees has greatly expanded. The resultant heterogeneity (Sri Lankans, Kurds, Bangladeshi, Somalis, Chinese and so on) has either transferred anti-black stereotyping on to the catch-all racialized categories of 'immigrant' and 'refugee' (also seen as lazy, parasitic, dirty, violent, criminal, diseased or libidinous) or it has reinvigorated older stereotypes that had lain dormant, like anti-Gypsy prejudice or Islamophobia.

A United Nations report, published in March 2000, estimated that the natality rate in most EU states was now so low, on average 1.4 children per woman, that the Union would have to open its doors to some 159 million immigrant workers by 2025 in order to keep the economy going and have sufficient numbers in work to maintain the growing percentage of elderly pensioners. Some commentators have used such projections to argue that migrants, far from offering an economic burden, are vital to the European economy and that a liberal policy of controlled immigration should be encouraged. However, the danger implicit in the construction of a 'Fortress Europe' is that repressive border controls and policing could provide the precondition for the institution of a massive *Gastarbeiter* system in which migrants, on short-term contracts, could be exploited as a source of cheap labour, but denied basic legal, political and citizenship rights. EU states, having learned from their 'mistakes' in allowing an earlier phase of family reunification and permanent settlement, are likely to ensure that such a pattern is not repeated.

Institutional Racism

Moving on from EU policy, a second aspect of contemporary racism is that official eradication of prejudice is proving much more difficult that many had thought in the immediate post-war years. The issues here are extremely complex, but attention can be drawn to two elements. Common-sense forms of racism, powerfully reinforced and reproduced by socialization and the mass media, are not readily dissolved through academic or educational programmes that seek to demonstrate the irrationality of prejudice or the unscientific basis of racial categorization. Nor are governments always determined enough to implement legislation and policies that are effective in tackling institutional racism, itself crucially based on the everyday racism of police canteens, football terraces and employment panels. Secondly, the decline of socialist and trade-union movements, and the general shift of all mainstream political parties and governments towards the right and towards the market, privatization, the deregulation of capital, cuts in state expenditure and erosion of the welfare state has deepened the divide between rich and poor. Immigrants and ethnic minorities, concentrated within the lower ranks of the working class, have suffered disproportionately from such policies and become locked into zones of social exclusion, ghetto-like areas of poor housing, educational disadvantage, high crime, unemployment and multiple deprivation. This in turn helps reinforce racial stereotypes that associate minorities with inherent inferiority, low intelligence, dirt and criminality. The gap between official anti-racist discourse and policy statements and the reality of governmental actions remains ever wide.

Genetics and Cloning: The Revival of Race-Science?

As we enter the new millennium, there are growing signs of a revival in 'scientific racism' that is threatening to replay the pre-war eugenic debate, but this time backed up with the far more powerful tools of modern DNA analysis and genetic engineering. In 1969 the American educational psychologist Arthur Jensen published a long article in the *Harvard Educational Review*, 'How can we boost IQ and scholastic achievement?', in which he argued that educational programmes had failed to improve achievement and that genetic factors, not just social and economic environments, explained differences between blacks and whites on test scores. Since then this approach, the search for the so-called 'g' factor, or a claimed general intelligence factor that differed by racial group, has been adopted by a number of psychologists, including Richard Lynn of the University of Ulster, Hans Eysenck, J. Philippe Rushton of the University of Western Ontario, Christopher Brand of Edinburgh University, and Richard Herrnstein and Charles Murray, joint authors of *The Bell Curve* (1994).

While the work of such 'experts' has provided ammunition to extreme right-wing movements, and also received undue attention in the media because of their controversial claims, in general they have received little support from other scientists or sociologists who have had little difficulty in locating the statistical flaws and biases in the IQ approach. As the biologist Steven Rose has noted, this kind of work represents 'the last gasp of a pre-Copernican science, like the belief the sun goes round the earth'.[11] Nor have such race-scientists received any wider legitimacy: the publishers John Wiley rejected books by both Jensen and Brand in 1996–7, while Brand was sacked by Edinburgh University in August 1997. Similarly, the libel action brought by the right-wing historian David Irving against Deborah Lipstadt's book, *Denying the Holocaust: The Growing Assault on Truth and Memory* (1993), ended in the London high court in April 2000 with a devastating judgement that showed how he had twisted historical evidence to support his anti-Semitic and pro-Nazi views. In general the small band of academics promoting historical, sociological or 'scientific' racist theories, while attracting much media attention precisely to the extent that their maverick ideas have clashed with current liberal values, have gained little scholarly or public respectability.

However, much more scientifically valid and ethically complex issues have been raised by rapid advances in the field of human genetic engineering, including the cloning of Dolly the sheep by a team of Edinburgh scientists in February 1997, and the first-stage completion in June 2000 of the race to decipher the genome, the three-billion letter DNA alphabet that provides the blueprint for each individual. The rapid development of a range of new techniques – the ability of doctors to carry out artificial insemination; the processes of egg and sperm donation; the screening of foetuses and preventive abortion for a range of inherited diseases; the growing ability to isolate genes that cause cystic fibrosis, Huntington's chorea, diabetes, haemophilia, cancers, and possibly obesity; and processes of engineering that can purify genes of life-crippling flaws – such techniques undoubtedly have a huge future potential for the relief of suffering and the enhancement of life. At the same time such advances mean that biological science is rapidly achieving the technical means to realize the objectives that pre-war eugenics and Nazi scientists mistakenly thought they had cracked, the science of being able to control the births of some kinds of people rather than others.

The idea of engineering or cloning a standardized human being has long been a theme in twentieth-century science fiction. Aldous Huxley in *Brave New World* (1932) provided an alarming picture of technology producing artificial, assembly-line babies. In Ira Levin's *The Boys from Brazil* (1976) the Nazi scientist, Dr Mengele, after escaping to Brazil at the end of the war, secretly found the means to clone 94 children from tissue taken from Adolf Hitler's body. While such fiction appears to be entirely mythical or fanciful, the most recent discoveries in genetics are close to making such technologies entirely feasible, even if the political contexts for the realization of such eugenic dystopias are not. In January 1998 members of the European Parliament felt sufficiently concerned by the Dolly experiment to pass a resolution against cloning of human beings, since it represented 'a serious violation of fundamental human rights, and is contrary to the principle of equality of human beings as it permits a eugenic and racist selection of the human race'.[12] Many scientists have opposed such precipitate controls as ill-informed and also damaging to the enormous potential of genetic engineering for the prevention of major diseases.

Much of the debate on the ethical issues that arise from genetics relates to matters that are not specifically to do with 'race': for example, if genetic screening can, from an early age, detect the probability of an individual contracting in later life a particular degenerative disease or cancer, then insurance companies will undoubtedly refuse to provide medical or life insurance policies. Here, I am concerned solely with the issues that relate to race. Jonathan Glover, Director of the Centre for Medical Law and Ethics at Kings College London, has argued that genetic engineering is consistent with human rights as long as decisions about the kinds of children to be born are not taken by the state (the Nazi or eugenic scenario), but may be taken, with certain safeguards, by parents.[13] However, even within the realm of parental choice, the rapidly growing technical means to opt for 'designer babies' does carry with it a racial potential. American women already offer to sell their eggs commercially for IVF through advertising on the Internet and, in doing so, not only list their age and religion, but also their physical features (colour of hair, complexion, eye colour), state of health ('Teeth: excellent'), and 'race' (Caucasian, Japanese ...).[14] In Italy a black woman gave birth to a white baby after being implanted with an egg from a white donor, fertilized *in vitro* by her white husband. The woman felt that a white child would have better chances in life and not suffer from racial discrimination. There is a potential danger that such individual or parental choices, even if not coerced by the state, could, if multiplied many thousands of times and over a long time scale, lead to a 'racial drift', the dominance of some phenotypes and the elimination of others. However, such an elimination of biological diversity would not be primarily caused by genetic engineering, since this provides only the means, but rather by the depth of racist values within society.

A far more worrying potential for the abusive and racial deployment of genetics lies in the realm of the state. Those scientists and politicians who favour the largely unfettered advance of genetic engineering argue the impossibility of a 'Hitler scenario' and the breeding of a 'super-race' on a number of grounds. Firstly, responsible, democratic governments can ensure that proper national and international safeguards, laws and treaties can be put in place to prevent the globalization of 'dangerous science', just as was achieved with nuclear weapons. Secondly, the medical community, which dedicates itself to the relief of human suffering, can be trusted to police itself and to follow an ethical code. In reply it can be noted that, at the global level, the existence of political regimes that have in recent decades engaged in 'ethnic cleansing' and genocide should give strong grounds of concern about a future 'state eugenics'. In March 1999 prior to the murder trial of Dr Wouter Basson, former head of South Africa's chemical and biological warfare programme, it was revealed that he had once plotted a mass sterilization of blacks and sought to develop a drug to reduce fertility. While, within the present context of European politics, such a nightmare scenario seems impossible, there does remain a worrying potential for the future growth of authoritarian and highly xenophobic regimes that might reinforce a cultural racism of closed boundaries and *volkish* purity. Far more of a threat within Europe could come from a 'eugenic drift' within liberal democracies. There has, in the past, been a tendency to equate the worst excesses of eugenic practice with Nazi Germany: however, historians have in recent years shown not only that 'normal' doctors played a key role in the elaboration of Nazi genocide, but that wide-scale programmes of enforced sterilization took place in the United States from as early as 1907, and spread during the 1930s into European states with the most impeccable liberal or progressive credentials, including Norway, Denmark, Sweden and France. It only came to light in the 1990s that the Swedish sterilization of 60 000 women to remove 'inferior' racial and degenerate types, started in 1935, continued to the end of 1976. Similar practices survived in the USA until the early 1970s, while in September 1997 the French government launched an urgent inquiry after a report revealed that 15 000 women in psychiatric institutions had been sterilized without permission. The slippery slope to the eugenic abuse of human rights began (Chapter 1) from the 'reasonable' utilitarian and cost-benefit forms of welfare analysis that estimated the enormous costs to society and to the economy of feeding and caring for mentally and physically handicapped 'defectives'.

Lastly, even if legal and political controls are sufficiently rigorous to ensure that genetic engineering does not lead to a racial eugenics, the advances in biology may still serve to reinforce popular racism. The work of sociobiologists has reinforced the notion that 'nature' is more determinant than nurture, while journalists and other popularizers of the new genetics have promoted bogus ideas about the detection of 'genes' for criminality, homosexuality, violence and other 'deviancies', as did the old eugenics. However, the potential for genetic decoding to change social engineering and the arguments for biological determinism should not be exaggerated. What is unique to *Homo sapiens* is the ability to transform the world within which the species is located, to construct cities, to invent steam engines, cars, computers and aircraft. Each infant is born into an already existing universe of social customs, language and technologies, and although each individual necessarily brings with them a particular genetic framework, how their potentialities and knowledge develops depends most crucially on the vast body of culture, learned knowledge and behaviour that is transmitted across generations. The growing media attention to the genome project and genetics, frequently dished out in a spurious and sensational form, runs the risk of obscuring from sight that how we engage in a progressive politics, in educational reform, and the wider goals of attaining a society based on equality, is more crucial than any hereditary component. A biological essentialism that rests on a claim to the 'truth' of the gene and its all-powerful and determinant function reinforces the hand of extreme right-wing movements keen to revive a 'race-science' as well as conservative governments eager to place the irrevocably criminal in detention and to cut back on redistributive taxation, universally available health care and equal opportunity in education. Governments and educators have a major responsibility to ensure that no window of opportunity be provided for the reconstruction or resurgence of a dynamic, if mythical, race-science.

NOTES

Endnotes are used throughout the book to refer only to the source of direct quotations or to authors named within the body of the text. A supplementary brief guide to reading can be found at the end of the book.

Introduction: The Roots of Modern Racism

1. Douglas A. Lorimer, 'Race, science and culture: historical continuities and discontinuities, 1850–1914', in Shearer West (ed.), *The Victorians and Race* (Aldershot: Scolar Press, 1996), p. 18.
2. Paul Weindling, *Health, Race and German Politics between National Unification and Nazism, 1870–1945* (Cambridge: Cambridge University Press, 1989), p. 59.
3. George L. Mosse, *Towards the Final Solution* (London: Dent, 1978), pp. 56, 70.
4. Avtar Brah, 'Time, Place, and Others: Discourses of Race, Nation, and Ethnicity', *Sociology*, vol. 28, no. 3 (August 1994), p. 805.
5. Etienne Balibar and Immanuel Wallerstein, *Race, Nation, Class: Ambiguous Identities* (London: Verso, 1991), p. 100.
6. Tzvetan Todorov, *On Human Diversity: Nationalism, Racism and Exoticism in French Thought* (Cambridge, MA: Harvard University Press, 1993), pp. 90–5.
7. Teun A. van Dijk, 'Elite discourse and racism', in Iris M. Zavala et al. (eds), *Approaches to Discourse, Poetics and Psychiatry* (Amsterdam: John Bejamins, 1987), pp. 81–122.
8. Anne McClintock, *Imperial Leather: Race, Gender and Sexuality in the Colonial Contest* (London: Routledge, 1995), p. 209.
9. Nancy Leys Stepan, 'Race and gender: The Analogy of Science', Chapter 3 in David. T. Goldberg (ed.), *Anatomy of Racism* (Minneapolis: University of Minnesota Press, 1994), p. 39.
10. Quoted in James Hunt, *On the Negro's Place in Nature*, in *Memoirs of the Anthropological Society of London*, vol. 1, 1863–4, p. 46.
11. Thomas Bendyshe, *The History of Anthropology*, Anthropological Society of London. Memoirs, vol. I (1863–4), pp. 421–3.
12. Thomas Bendyshe (ed.), *The Anthropological Treatises of Johann Friedrich Blumenbach* (London: Longman, Green, 1865), p. 264.
13. Ibid., p. 307.
14. Robert Knox, *The Races of Men: A Fragment* (Miami: Mnemosyne edn, 1969), p. 191.
15. Ibid., pp. 7, 10.

16. Ibid., p. 158.
17. Ibid., p. 25.
18. Quoted in Jacob Katz, *From Prejudice to Destruction: Anti-Semitism, 1700–1933* (Cambridge, MA: Harvard University Press, 1980), p. 213.
19. Peter Pulzer, *The Rise of Political Anti-Semitism in Germany and Austria* (London: Halban rev. edn, 1988), p. 49.
20. Bendyshe, *Anthropological Treatises*, p. 266.
21. William B. Cohen, *The French Encounter with Africans: White Response to Blacks, 1530–1880* (Bloomington: Indiana University Press, 1980), p. 93.
22. Quoted in Douglas Lorimer, 'Theoretical Racism in Late-Victorian Anthropology, 1870–1900' in *Victorian Studies* (Spring 1988), p. 426.
23. Fritz Stern, *The Politics of Cultural Despair: A Study in the Rise of the Germanic Ideology* (New York: Anchor Books edn, 1965).
24. Benedict Anderson, *Imagined Communities: Reflections on the Origin and Spread of Nationalism* (London: Verso, 1983), p. 136.
25. Stella Cottrell, 'The Devil on two sticks: franco-phobia in 1803', in Raphael Samuel (ed.), *Patriotism: The Making and Unmaking of British National Identity. Vol. 1. History and Politics* (London: Routledge, 1989), pp. 263–4.
26. William B. Cohen, *French Encounter*, p. 275.
27. Ann Laurer Stoler, *Race and the Education of Desire: Foucault's History of Sexuality and the Colonial Order of Things* (Durham, NC, and London: Duke University Press, 1995), pp. 15, 75.

PART 1 1870–1914

1 The White Race: Degeneration and Eugenics

1. Richard Dyer, *White* (London: Routledge, 1997), p. 1.
2. Robin Cohen, *Frontiers of Identity: The British and the Others* (London: Longman, 1994), p.1.
3. W. H. Schneider, *Quality and Quantity: The Quest for Biological Regeneration in Twentieth Century France* (Cambridge: Cambridge University Press, 1990), p. 237.
4. William B. Cohen, *The French Encounter*, p. 51.
5. Daniel Pick, *Faces of Degeneration: A European Disorder, c.1848–c.1918* (Cambridge: Cambridge University Press, 1993), p. 24.
6. Quoted in Geoffrey R. Searle, *Eugenics and Politics in Britain, 1900–1914* (Leyden: Noordhoff International Publishing, 1976), p. 36.
7. Gareth Stedman Jones, *Outcast London: A Study in the Relationship between Classes in Victorian Society* (Harmondsworth: Penguin Edition, 1976), pp. 224–5.
8. Louis Chevalier, *Labouring Classes and Dangerous Classes in Paris During the First Half of the Nineteenth Century* (London: Routledge and Kegan Paul, 1973).
9. Daniel Pick, *Faces of Degeneration*, p. 71.
10. Ibid., p. 122.
11. Nancy Leys Stepan, 'Race and Gender: The Role of Analogy in Science' , pp. 38–57.
12. Daniel Pick, *Faces of Degeneration*, p. 41.

13. Gareth Stedman Jones, *Outcast London*, p. 287.
14. Daniel Gasman, *The Scientific Origins of National Socialism: Social Darwinism in Ernst Haeckel and the German Monist League* (London: Macdonald, 1971), p. 40.
15. Ibid., p. 41.
16. Ibid., p. 40.
17. Bernard Semmel, *Imperialism and Social Reform: English Social-Imperial Thought 1895–1914* (New York: Anchor Books, 1968), p. 41.
18. Geoffrey R. Searle, *Eugenics*, p. 36.
19. Ibid., p. 35.
20. Daniel Gasman, *Scientific Origins*, pp. 130, 136.
21. Ibid., pp. 91, 95–6.
22. Paul Weindling, *Health, Race*, p. 169.
23. Anna Davin, 'Imperialism and Motherhood', in *History Workshop*, vol. 5 (1978), p. 20.
24. William H. Schneider, *Quantity and Quality*, p. 179.
25. Anna Davin, 'Imperialism and Motherhood', p. 21.
26. Ibid., pp. 29, 53.
27. Thomas F. Glick (ed.), *The Comparative Reception of Darwinism* (Austin: University of Texas Press, 1974), p. 337.
28. Michel Foucault, *The History of Sexuality.Volume One. An Introduction* (London: Penguin Edition 1990), see, especially, Part 5.
29. Ibid., p. 147.
30. Clive Ponting, *Churchill* (London: Sinclair Stevens, 1994), pp. 100–4.
31. Geoffrey R. Searle, *Eugenics*, p. 93.
32. Daniel Kevles, *In the Name of Eugenics: Genetics and the Uses of Human Heredity* (Berkeley: University of California Press, 1985), p. 57.
33. Ibid., p. 48.
34. Enrique Ucelay Da Cal, 'The Influence of Animal Breeding on Political Racism', in *History of European Ideas*, vol. 15. nos 4–6 (1992), pp. 717–5.
35. Daniel Kevles, *In the Name of Eugenics*, p. 111.
36. Mike Hawkins, *Social Darwinism in European and American Thought, 1860–1945: Nature as Model and Nature as Threat* (Cambridge: Cambridge University Press, 1997), p. 199.
37. Ibid., p. 192.

2 Blackness Without Blacks

1. This chapter title is borrowed from the book by Sander L. Gilman, *On Blackness Without Blacks: Essays on the Image of the Black in Western Popular Culture* (Boston: G. K. Hall, 1982).
2. Douglas A. Lorimer, *Colour, Class and the Victorians: English Attitudes to the Negro in the Mid-Nineteenth Century* (Leicester: Leicester University Press, 1978), p. 11.
3. On stereotypes see, in particular, Sander L. Gilman, 'Introduction' to *Difference and Pathology: Stereotypes of Sexuality, Race and Madness* (Ithaca, NY: Cornell University Press, 1985), pp. 15–35.
4. Jan Nederveen Pieterse, *White on Black: Images of Africa and Blacks in Western Popular Culture* (New Haven: Yale University Press, 1992), p. 42.

5. Winthrop D. Jordan, *White Over Black: American Attitudes Toward the Negro, 1550–1812* (Williamsburg: University of North Carolina Press, 1968), p. 24.
6. Robin Blackburn, *The Overthrow of Colonial Slavery, 1776–1848* (London: Verso, 1988).
7. Sander L. Gilman, *On Blackness*, p. 31.
8. Peter Fryer, *Staying Power: The History of Black People in Britain* (London: Pluto Press, 1987), p. 158.
9. Moshe Zimmerman, *Wilhelm Marr: The Patriarch of Anti-Semitism* (Oxford: Oxford University Press, 1986), pp. 35, 49.
10. James Hunt, 'On the Negro's Place in Nature', *Memoirs of the Anthropological Society of London*, vol. 1 (1863–4), pp. 1–63.
11. Ibid., pp. 54–5.
12. Douglas A. Lorimer, *Colour, Class and the Victorians*, p. 173.
13. Thomas C. Holt, *The Problem of Freedom. Race, Labor, and Politics in Jamaica and Britain, 1832–1938* (Baltimore: Johns Hopkins University Press, 1992).
14. Ibid., p. 167.
15. Ibid., p. 315.
16. Douglas A. Lorimer, *Colour, Class and the Victorians*, p. 195.
17. Sander L. Gilman, *On Blackness*, p. 16.
18. Peter Fryer, *Staying Power*, p. 152.
19. A. B. C. Merriman-Labor, *Britons Through Negro Spectacles or A Negro on Britons* (London: The Imperial and Foreign Company, 1909), pp. 172–7.
20. Peter Fryer, *Staying Power*, p. 229.
21. Ben Shephard, 'Showbiz Imperialism: The Case of Peter Lobegula', in John M. Mackenzie (ed.), *Imperialism and Popular Culture* (Manchester: Manchester University Press, 1986), p. 107.
22. Annie E. Coombes, *Reinventing Africa: Museums, Material Culture and Popular Imagination* (New Haven: Yale University Press, 1994), p. 197.
23. William H. Schneider, *An Empire for the Masses: The French Popular Image of Africa, 1870–1900* (Westport, CT: Greenwood Press, 1987), p. 185.
24. Paul Greenhalgh, *Ephemeral Vistas: The Expositions Universelles, Great Exhibitions and World Fairs, 1851–1939* (Manchester: Manchester University Press, 1988), pp. 94–5.
25. Ibid., p. 86.
26. Ben Shephard, 'Showbiz Imperialism', p. 97.
27. Annie E. Coombes, *Reinventing Africa*, p. 102.
28. William H. Schneider, *An Empire for the Masses*, pp. 119–34.
29. John M. Mackenzie, *Propaganda and Empire: The Manipulation of British Public Opinion, 1880–1960* (Manchester: Manchester University Press, 1984).
30. Robert Roberts, *The Classic Slum: Salford Life in the First Quarter of the Century* (Harmondsworth: Penguin Books, 1974), pp. 142–4, 161.
31. Guido Convents, 'Des images non occidentales au coeur de l'Europe avant la Première Guerre mondiale: en Belgique, par example', in Roland Cosandey and François Albera (eds), *Cinéma sans frontières, 1896–1918: Images Across Borders* (Lausanne: Editions Payot, 1995), p. 50.
32. Yuri Tsivian, 'Russians in Russian Cinema: Construction and Reception of Nationality in Early Film Culture', in Cosandey and Albera (eds), *Cinéma*, pp. 128–9.

33. *The Guardian*, 20 January 1998. The article includes a photograph of a 'Darkie Day' revel in *c*.1900.
34. Susanne Zantop, *Colonial Fantasies: Conquest, Family, and Nation in Precolonial Germany, 1770–1870* (London: Duke University Press, 1997).
35. Jan Nederveen Pieterse, *White on Black*, p. 70.
36. Hans-Ulrich Wehler, 'Bismarck and Imperialism, 1862–1890', *Past and Present*, no. 48 (1970), p. 148.

3 The Rise of Political Anti-Semitism

1. Stephen Wilson, *Ideology and Experience: Anti-Semitism in France at the Time of the Dreyfus Affair* (London: Associated University Press, 1982), p. 738.
2. Michel Winock, *Nationalism, Anti-Semitism, and Fascism in France* (Stanford, CA: Stanford University Press, 1998), pp. 82–3.
3. Ibid., pp. 83–4.
4. Stephen Wilson, *Ideology*, p. 543.
5. Quoted from the *Labor Leader*, 19 December 1891, in Christopher Holmes, *Anti-Semitism in British Society, 1876–1939* (London: Edward Arnold, 1979), pp. 83–4.
6. Stephen Wilson, *Ideology*, p. 457.
7. Ibid., p. 460.
8. Juliet Steyn, 'Charles Dickens' *Oliver Twist*: Fagin as a Sign', in Linda Nochlin and Tamar Garb (eds), *The Jew in the Text: Modernity and the Construction of Identity* (London: Thames and Hudson, 1995), p. 51.
9. Geoffrey G. Field, *Evangelist of Race: The Germanic Vision of Houston Stewart Chamberlain* (New York: Columbia University Press, 1981), p. 193.
10. Jacob Katz, *From Prejudice to Destruction: Anti-Semitism, 1700–1933* (Cambridge, MA: Harvard University Press, 1980), pp. 143–4.
11. Jack Zipes, 'Oscar Panizza: The Operated German as Operated Jew', with a translation of Oscar Panizza, 'The Operated Jew', *New German Critique*, no. 21 (Fall, 1980), pp. 45–79.
12. Steven E. Aschheim, *Brothers and Strangers: The East European Jews in German and German Jewish Consciousness, 1800–1923* (Wisconsin: University of Wisconsin Press, 1982), p. 59.
13. Donald L. Niewyk, 'Solving the "Jewish Problem": Continuity and Change in German Antisemitism, 1871–1945', in *Leo Baeck Institute: Yearbook*, 1990, p. 354.
14. Ibid., p. 349.
15. Peter Pulzer, *The Rise of Political Anti-Semitism in Germany and Austria* (London: Peter Halban, 1988 edition), p. 192.
16. Wladylaw T. Bartoszewski, *Ethnocentrism: Beliefs and Stereotypes. A Study of Polish-Jewish Relations in the Early 20th Century*, Ph.D. dissertation, University of Cambridge, 1984, pp. 232–8.
17. Leon Poliakov, *The History of Anti-Semitism*, vol. 3 (London: Elek, 1966), p. 87.
18. Hans Rogger, *Jewish Policies and Right-Wing Politics in Imperial Russia* (Berkeley: University of California Press, 1986), p. 37.
19. John D. Klier and Shlomo Lambroza (eds), *Pogroms: Anti-Jewish Violence in Modern Russian History* (Cambridge: Cambridge University Press, 1992), p. 235.

20. Bernard Garrard, *The English and Immigration, 1880–1910* (London: Oxford University Press, 1971), p. 62.
21. W. D. Rubinstein, *A History of the Jews in the English-Speaking World: Great Britain* (London: St Martins Press, 1996), pp. 111–3.
22. Bernard Garrard, *The English and Immigration*, p. 80.
23. Nancy L. Stepan, *The Idea of Race*, pp. 125, 148.
24. Stephen Wilson, *Ideology*, p. 482.
25. Leon Poliakov, *History of Anti-Semitism*, pp. 43–4.
26. Zeev Sternhell, *Neither Right nor Left: Fascist Ideology in France* (Berkeley: University of California Press, c.1986).

PART 2 1914–1945

Anti-Black Racism in an Age of Total War

1. B. P. Willan, 'The South African Native Labour Contingent, 1916–1918', *Journal of African History*, vol. 19, no. 1 (1978), p. 82.
2. Ibid., pp. 63–4.
3. Arthur E. Barbeau and Florette Henri, *The Unknown Soldiers: Black American Troops in World War 1* (Philadelphia: Temple University Press, 1974), p. 177.
4. Ibid., p. 154.
5. Tyler Stovall, 'The Color Line behind the Lines: Racial Violence in France during the Great War', *American Historical Review*, June 1998, p. 766.
6. Peter Fryer, *Staying Power*, p. 297.
7. Jacqueline Jenkinson, 'The Glasgow Race Disturbances of 1919', in K. Lunn (ed.), *Race and Labour in Twentieth Century Britain* (London: Frank Cass, 1985), p. 63.
8. Peter Fryer, *Staying Power*, p. 310.
9. Neil MacMaster, *Colonial Migrants and Racism: Algerians in France, 1900–62* (Basingstoke: Macmillan – now Palgrave, 1997), p. 160.
10. Ibid.; Laura Tabili, *'We Ask for British Justice': Workers and Racial Difference in Late Imperial Britain* (Ithaca, NY: Cornell University Press, 1994).
11. Ben Shepherd, 'Showbiz Imperialism', pp. 99–102.
12. Peter Fryer, *Staying Power*, p. 311.
13. Paul Rich, *Race and Empire in British Politics* (Cambridge: Cambridge University Press, 1986), ch. 6.
14. Neil MacMaster, *Colonial Migrants*, p. 127.
15. Helmut Walser Smith, 'The Talk of Genocide, the Rhetoric of Miscegenation: Notes on Debates in the German Reichstag Concerning Southwest Africa, 1904–14', in Sara Friedrichsmeyer, Sara Lennox and Susanne Zantop (eds), *The Imperialist Imagination: German Colonialism and Its Legacy* (Ann Arbor: University of Michigan Press, 1998), pp. 112–13.
16. Ibid., p. 121.
17. May Opitz, Katharina Oguntoye and Dagmar Schultz (eds), *Showing our Colors: Afro-German Women Speak Out* (Amherst: University of Massachusetts Press, 1992), p. 42.

18. Ernst Haeckel, *Eternity: World-War Thoughts on Life and Death, Religion, and the Theory of Evolution* (New York: The Truth Seeker Company, 1916), pp. 36, 42, 106–7.
19. Tina Campt, Pascal Grosse and Yara-Colette Lemke-Muniz de Faria, 'Blacks, Germans, and the Politics of Imperial Imagination, 1920–60', in Sara Friedrichsmeyer et al. (eds), *The Imperialist Imagination*, p. 211.
20. E. D. Morel, *The Horror on the Rhine* (London: Union of Democratic Control, 2nd edn, August 1920), pp. 10, 13. Italics as in the original text.
21. Francesco Nitti, *The Decadence of Europe: The Paths of Reconstruction* (London: T. Fisher Unwin, 1923), pp. 123–8.
22. Claude McKay, *A Long Way From Home* (London: Pluto Press, 1985 edition) p. 239.
23. Adolf Hitler, *Mein Kampf* (trans. by Ralph Manheim, London: Pimlico edition, 1996), pp. 286, 295.
24. John Newsinger, 'Lord Greystoke and Darkest Africa: The Politics of the Tarzan Stories', *Race and Class*, vol. 28, no. 2 (1986), pp. 61, 69.
25. Earl R. Beck, 'German Views of Negro Life in the United States, 1919–1933', *Journal of Negro History*, vol. 48 (1963), p. 31.
26. Karen C. C. Dalton and Henry Louis Gates, Jr, 'Josephine Baker and Paul Colin: African American Dance Seen through Parisian Eyes', *Critical Inquiry*, no. 24 (Summer 1998), p. 916.
27. Phyllis Rose, *Jazz Cleopatra: Josephine Baker in Her Time* (London: Chatto and Windus, 1989), pp. 134–45.
28. Horst J. P. Bergmeier and Rainer E. Lotz, *Hitler's Airwaves: The Inside Story of Nazi Radio Broadcasting and Propaganda Swing* (New Haven: Yale University Press, 1997), pp. 137–8.
29. Tyler Stovall, *Paris Noir: African Americans in the City of Light* (Boston, MA: Houghton Mifflin, 1996), p. 71.
30. Frederick S. Starr, *Red and Hot: The Fate of Jazz in the Soviet Union* (Oxford: Oxford University Press, 1983), p. 90.
31. R. Vasey, 'Foreign Parts: Hollywood's Global Distribution and the Representation of Ethnicity', *American Quarterly*, vol. 44, no. 4 (December 1992), p. 628.
32. Neil MacMaster, *Colonial Migrants*, p. 122.

5 Anti-Semitisim in the Nazi Era

1. Michael Burleigh and Wolfgang Wippermann, *The Racial State: Germany 1933–1945* (Cambridge: Cambridge University Press, 1991).
2. Daniel J. Goldhagen, *Hitler's Willing Executioners: Ordinary Germans and the Holocaust* (London: Little, Brown and Company, 1996).
3. Adolf Hitler, *Mein Kampf*, p. 308.
4. Ibid., p. 568.
5. Ibid., p. 347.
6. Ibid., p. 194.
7. Ibid., p. 297.
8. Ibid., pp. 224–5, 277.
9. Ibid., p. 258.
10. Ibid., pp. 226, 259, 297.

11. Ibid., p. 286.
12. Ibid., pp. 366–71.
13. M. Burleigh and W. Wippermann, *The Racial State*, p. 107.
14. Mark Neocleous, *Fascism* (Buckingham: Open University Press, 1997), p. 15.
15. Daniel J. Goldhagen, *Hitler's Willing Executioners*, p. 9.
16. M. Burleigh and W. Wippermann, *The Racial State*, p. 141.
17. Zygmunt Bauman, *Modernity and the Holocaust* (Cambridge: Polity Press, 1989).
18. Ian Kershaw, 'The Persecution of the Jews and German Popular Opinion in the Third Reich', *Leo Baeck Institute: Yearbook*, vol. 26 (1981), p. 267.
19. David Bankier, *The Germans and the Final Solution: Public Opinion under Nazism* (Oxford: Blackwell, 1996), p. 15.
20. Lawrence D. Stokes, 'The German People and the Destruction of the European Jews', *Central European History*, vol. 6 (1973), p. 175.
21. David Bankier, *Public Opinion*, p. 96.
22. Celia S. Heller, *On the Edge of Destruction: Jews of Poland Between the Two World Wars* (New York: Columbia University Press, 1977), p. 113.
23. Edward D. Wynot, '"A Necessary Cruelty": The Emergence of Official Anti-Semitism in Poland, 1936–39', *American Historical Review*, vol. 74, no. 4 (1971), p. 1051.
24. Meir Michaelis, *Mussolini and the Jews: German–Italian Relations and the Jewish Question, 1922–1945* (Oxford: Oxford University Press, 1978), p. 205.
25. Pierre Birnbaum, *Anti-Semitism in France: A Political History from Léon Blum to the Present* (Oxford: Blackwell, 1992), p. 62.
26. Ibid., p. 206.
27. M. R. Marrus and R. O. Paxton, *Vichy France and the Jews* (Cambridge: Cambridge University Press, 1995), pp. 271–2.
28. John. D. Klier and Shlomo Lambroza (eds), *Pogroms: Anti-Jewish Violence in Modern Russian History* (Cambridge: Cambridge University Press, 1992), p. 305.
29. Benjamin Pinkus, *The Jews of the Soviet Union: The History of a National Minority* (Cambridge: Cambridge University Press, 1988), p. 87.

PART 3   1945–2000

6 Racism in the Age of Labour Immigration, 1945–1974

1. J. S. Huxley, A. C. Haddon and A. M. Carr-Saunders, *We Europeans: A Survey of 'Racial' Problems* (London: Jonathan Cape, 1935), pp. 107–8.
2. Ashley Montagu (ed.), *Statement on Race: An Annotated Elaboration and Exposition of the Four Statements on Race Issued by UNESCO* (London: Oxford University Press, 3rd edn 1972), pp. 7–13.
3. Robert Miles and Annie Phizacklea, *White Man's Country: Racism in British Politics* (London: Pluto Press, 1984), p. 24.
4. Ibid., p. 36.
5. Dennis Dean, 'The Conservative government and the 1961 Commonwealth Immigration Act: the inside story', *Race and Class*, vol. 35, no. 2 (1993), p. 68.

6. Anthony Howard (ed.), *The Crossman Diaries: Selections from the Diaries of a Cabinet Minister 1964–1970* (London: Methuen, 1979), pp. 73, 132.
7. Bill Smithies and Peter Fiddick, *Enoch Powell on Immigration* (London: Sphere Books, 1969), p. 77.
8. Ibid., p. 36.
9. Catherine Wihtol de Wenden, *Les Immigrés et la politique* (Paris: Presses de la FNSP, 1988), p. 162.

7 The 'New Racism' and National-Populism

1. Alain de Benoist, *Les idées à l'endroit* (Paris: Editions Libres-Hallier, 1979), p. 145.
2. Anne-Marie Duranton-Crabol, *Visages de la Nouvelle Droite: le GRECE et son histoire* (Paris: Presses de la fondation nationale des sciences politiques, 1988), p. 58.
3. Harvey G. Simmons, *The French National Front: The Extremist Challenge to Democracy* (Boulder, CO: Westview Press, 1996), pp. 163–4.
4. Gill Seidel, 'The White Discursive Order: The British New Right's Discourse on Cultural Racism with Particular Reference to the *Salisbury Review*', in Iris M. Zavala (ed.), *Approaches to Discourse, Poetics and Psychiatry* (Amsterdam: John Benjamin, 1987), p. 42.
5. Harvey G. Simmons, *French National Front*, p. 207.
6. Bill Smithies and Peter Fiddick, *Enoch Powell*, pp. 63–77.
7. Gill Seidel, 'White Discursive Order', pp. 43–4.
8. Harvey G. Simmons, *French National Front*, p. 162. My italics, NM.
9. Ibid., p. 224.
10. Franklin Hugh Adler, 'Racism, *différence* and the Right in France', *Modern and Contemporary France*, vol. 3, no. 4 (1995) p. 445.
11. Paul Taggart, 'New Populist Parties in Western Europe', *West European Politics*, vol. 18, no. 1 (January 1995), p. 36.
12. Harvey G. Simmons, *French National Front*, p. 91
13. Stan Taylor, 'The Radical Right in Britain', Chapter 7 in Peter H. Merkl and Leonard Weinberg (eds), *Encounters with the Contemporary Radical Right* (Boulder, CO: Westview Press, 1993), p. 179–80.
14. Robert Miles and Annie Phizacklea, *White Man's Country*, p. 5.
15. David Theo Goldberg, *Racist Culture: Philosophy and the Politics of Meaning* (Oxford: Blackwell, 1993), pp. 6–8.
16. The *Sun*, 1 September 1998.
17. The *Guardian*, 23 August 1999.
18. Ibid., 14 April 2000.
19. Ibid., 19 April, 1 May 2000.
20. Ibid., 29 April 2000.
21. Anne Owers, 'Straw's Race Strategy is Racist', The *Guardian*, 25 August 2000.
22. Ibid., 17 February 2000: Michael Mansfield, President of the National Civil Rights Movement.

23. Bernard Wasserstein, *Vanishing Diaspora: The Jews in Europe since 1945* (London: Hamish Hamilton, 1996), p. 54.
24. Vladislav Krasnov, 'Pamiat: Russian Right-Wing Radicalism', Chapter 5 in Peter H. Merkl and Leonard Weinberg (eds), *Encounters*, p. 116.

Conclusion: Black and Jew

1. I have examined the history of this interrelationship in more detail in Neil MacMaster, '"Black Jew: White Negro": Antisemitism and the Construction of Cross-Racial Stereotypes', *Nationalism and Ethnic Politics*, vol. 6, no. 4 (Winter 2000), pp. 65–82.
2. Adolf Hitler, *Mein Kampf*, p. 272.
3. Duff Hart-Davis, *Hitler's Games: The 1936 Olympics* (London: Century Hutchinson, 1986), pp. 71, 73.
4. Harvey G. Simmons, *The French National Front*, p. 129.
5. Michael Billig, *Fascists: A Social Psychological View of the National Front* (London: Harcourt Brace Jovanovich, 1978), pp. 182, 186.
6. Harvey G. Simmons, *The French National Front*, p. 22.
7. Michael Billig, *Fascists*, pp. 154, 128.
8. Richard Hofstadter, *The Paranoid Style in American Politics* (London: Jonathan Cape, 1966).
9. Bruno Bettelheim and Morris Janowitz, *Dynamics of Prejudice* (1950), reprinted in *Social Change and Prejudice* (New York: Free Press of Glencoe, 1964).
10. G. W. Allport, *The Nature of Prejudice* (New York, 1954), pp. 192–9.
11. Quoted by Tim Cornwell, 'Too Dangerous for Words', *The Times Higher Educational Supplement*, 13 September 1996, p. 19.
12. Justine Burley (ed.), *The Genetic Revolution and Human Rights: The Oxford Amnesty Lectures 1998* (Oxford: Oxford University Press, 1999), p. 65.
13. Ibid., p. 116.
14. Nicole Veash, 'Internet Donors offer Perfect Babies to Order', *The Sunday Observer*, 15 August 1999.

A SHORT GUIDE TO FURTHER READING

The total volume of publications on the history of racism in Europe is vast and any short guide is bound to be highly selective. The works listed below provide some direction for anyone wishing to pursue in more detail any aspect of the broad field covered in this study. The reading has been divided into seven sub-categories. There are a number of journals that specialize on issues of racism and ethnicity in which the reader can find up-to-date articles and reviews: the most useful is the *Journal of Ethnic and Racial Studies* (prior to 1998, *New Community*), *Race and Class*, *Patterns of Prejudice*, *International Migration*, *Nationalism and Ethnic Politics*, *Diaspora*, *European Race Bulletin* (Institute of Race Relations), *Migration News Sheet*. For those who read French, *Migrations Société*, *Revue Européenne des Migrations Internationales*, and *Homme et Migrations*.

Theories of Race and Racism

Anthias, Floya, and Nira Yuval-Davis, *Racialized Boundaries: Race, Nation, Gender, Colour and Class and the Anti-Racist Struggle* (London: Routledge, 1993).

Back, Les, and John Solomos (eds), *Theories of Race and Racism: A Reader* (London: Routledge, 2000).

Balibar, Etienne, and Immanuel Wallerstein, *Race, Nation, Class: Ambiguous Identities* (London: Verso, 1991).

Banton, Michael, *Ethnic and Racial Consciousness* (London: Longman, 2nd edn 1997).

Goldberg, David T. (ed.), *Anatomy of Racism* (Minneapolis: University of Minnesota Press, 1994).

Guillaumin, Collette, *Racism, Sexism, Power and Ideology* (London: Routledge, 1995).

Holt, Thomas C., 'Marking: Race, Race-Making and the Writing of History', *American Historical Review*, vol. 100 (February 1995), pp. 1–20.

Malik, Kenan, *The Meaning of Race: Race, History and Culture in Western Society* (Basingstoke: Macmillan – now Palgrave, 1996).

Miles, Robert, *Racism and Migrant Labour* (London: Routledge and Kegan Paul, 1982).

Racism (London: Routledge, 1989).

Racism after 'Race Relations' (London: Routledge, 1993).

Rattansi, Ali, and Sallie Westwood (eds), *Racism, Modernity and Identity: On the Western Front* (Cambridge: Polity Press, 1994).

Rex, John, *Race and Ethnicity* (Milton Keynes: Open University Press, 1986).

Rex, John, and David Mason (eds), *Theories of Race and Ethnic Relations* (Cambridge: Cambridge University Press, 1986).

Solomos, John, and Les Back (eds), *Racism and Society* (Basingstoke: Macmillan – now Palgrave, 1996).

Wieviorka, Michel, *The Arena of Racism* (London: Sage Publications, 1995).

Zubaida, Sami (ed.), *Race and Racialism* (London: Tavistock, 1970).

The History of the Idea of 'Race': Scientific Racism and Eugenics

Banton, Michael, *The Idea of Race* (London: Tavistock, 1977).

Barkan, Elazar, *The Retreat of Scientific Racism: Changing Concepts of Race in Britain and the United States between the World Wars* (Cambridge: Cambridge University Press, 1992).

Biddiss, Michael, *Father of Racist Ideology: The Social and Political Thought of Count Gobineau* (London: Weidenfeld and Nicholson, 1970).

Bolt, Christine, *Victorian Attitudes to Race* (London: Routledge and Kegan Paul, 1971).

Breman, Jan (ed.), *Imperial Monkey Business: Racial Supremacy in Social Darwinist Theory and Colonial Practice* (Amsterdam: VU University Press, 1990).

Broberg, Gunnar, and Nils Roll-Hansen (eds), *Eugenics and the Welfare State: Sterilization Policy in Denmark, Sweden, Norway and Finland* (East Lansing: Michigan State University Press, c.1996).

Clark, Linda L., *Social Darwinism in France* (Alabama: University of Alabama Press, 1984).

Dikötter, Frank, 'Race Culture: Recent Perspectives on the History of Eugenics', *American Historical Review*, vol. 103 (April 1998), pp. 467–78.

Efron, John M., *Defenders of the Race: Jewish Doctors and Race Science in fin-de-siècle Europe* (New Haven: Yale University Press, 1994).

Gould, Stephen Jay, *The Mismeasure of Man* (Harmondsworth: Penguin Books, 1992).

Jahoda, Gustav, *Images of Savages: Ancient Roots of Modern Prejudice in Western Culture* (London: Routledge, 1999).

Kohn, Marek, *The Race Gallery: The Return of Racial Science* (London: Vintage, 1996).

Montagu, Ashley, *Man's Most Dangerous Myth: The Fallacy of Race* (London: Sage, 6th edn 1997).

Poliakov, Leon, *The Aryan Myth: A History of Racist and Nationalist Ideas in Europe* (London: Chatto and Windus, 1974).

Rose, Paul Lawrence, *Wagner: Race and Revolution* (London: Faber and Faber, 1996).

Rose, Stephen, Richard C. Lewontin and Leon J. Kamin, *Not in Our Genes: Biology, Ideology and Human Nature* (Harmondsworth: Penguin Books, 1990).

Todorov, Tzvetan, *On Human Diversity: Nationalism, Racism and Exoticism in French Thought* (Cambridge, MA: Harvard University Press. 1993).

Anti-Semitism

Abramsky, Chimen, Maciej Jachimczyk and Antony Polansky (eds), *The Jews in Poland* (Oxford: Blackwell, 1986).

Almog, Shmuel, *Nationalism and Antisemitism in Modern Europe, 1815–1945* (London: Pergamon Press, 1990).

Burleigh, Michael (ed.), *Confronting the Nazi Past: New Debates on Modern German History* (London: Collins and Brown, 1996).

Cohn, Norman, *Warrant for Genocide: The Myth of the Jewish World Conspiracy and the Protocols of the Elders of Zion* (London: Serif, 1996).

Felsenstein, Frank, *Anti-Semitic Stereotypes: A Paradigm of Otherness in English Popular Culture, 1660–1830* (Baltimore: Johns Hopkins University Press, 1995).

Fischer, Klaus P., *The History of an Obsession: German Judeophobia and the Holocaust* (New York: Continuum, 1998).

Graml, Herman, *Antisemitism in the Third Reich* (Oxford: Blackwell, 1992).

Hagen, William W., 'Before the "Final Solution": Toward a Comparative Analysis of Political Anti-Semitism in Interwar Germany and Poland', *Journal of Modern History*, vol. 68, no. 2 (June 1996), pp. 351–81.

Kershaw, Ian, *The Nazi Dictatorship: Problems and Perspectives of Interpretation* (London: Arnold, 3rd edn 1996).

Klier, John D., *Imperial Russia's Jewish Question* (New York: Cambridge University Press, 1995).

Lindemann, Albert S., *The Jew Accused: Three Anti-Semitic Affairs (Dreyfus, Beilis, Frank) 1894–1915* (Cambridge: Cambridge University Press, 1991).

Esau's Tears: Modern Anti-Semitism and the Rise of the Jews (Cambridge: Cambridge University Press, 1997).

Malino, Frances, and Bernard Wasserstein (eds), *The Jews in Modern France* (Hanover, NH: University Press of New England, 1985).

Marrus, Michael R., *The Holocaust in History* (Hanover, NH: University of New England, 1987).

Mendelsohn, Ezra, *The Jews of East Central Europe Between the Two World Wars* (Bloomington: Indiana University Press, 1983).

Oxaal, Ivar, Michael Pollack and Gerhard Botz (eds), *Jews, Anti-Semitism and Culture in Vienna* (London: Routledge and Kegan Paul, 1987).

Peukert, Detlev J. K., *Inside Nazi Germany: Conformity, Opposition and Racism in Everyday Life* (Harmondsworth: Penguin Books, 1993).

Steiman, Lionel B., *Paths to Genocide: Anti-Semitism in Western History* (New York: St. Martin's Press – now Palgrave, 1998).

Tal, Uri, *Christians and Jews in Germany: Religion, Politics, and Ideology in the Second Reich* (Ithaca: Cornell University Press, 1975).

Volkov, Shulamit, 'Antisemitism as a Cultural Code: Reflections on the History and Historiography of Antisemitism in Imperial Germany', *Leo Baeck Year Book*, vol. 23 (1978), pp. 25–46.

Wynot, Edward D., '"A Necessary Cruelty": The Emergence of Official Anti-Semitism in Poland, 1936–39', *American Historical Review*, vol. 76, no. 4 (1971), pp. 1035–58.

Anti-Black and Colonial Racism

Brock, Colin (ed.), *The Caribbean in Europe: Aspects of the West Indian Experience in Britain, France and the Netherlands* (London: Cass, 1986).

Cross, Malcolm, and Hans Entzinger (eds), *Lost Illusions: Caribbean Minorities in Britain and the Netherlands* (London: Routledge, 1988).

Gates, Henry Louis, Jr (ed.), *'Race', Writing, and Difference* (Chicago: University of Chicago Press, 1986).

Gilroy, Paul, et al. (eds), *The Empire Strikes Back: Race and Racism in 70s Britain* (London: Century Hutchinson, 1986).

Gilroy, Paul, *There Ain't No Black in the Union Jack: The Cultural Politics of Race and Nation* (London: Hutchinson, 1987).

The Black Atlantic: Modernity and Double Consciousness (London: Verso, 1996).

James, Winston, *Inside Babylon: Caribbean Diaspora in Britain* (London: Verso, 1993).

Kiernan, Victor G., *The Lords of Human Kind: Black Man, Yellow Man, and White Man in an Age of Empire* (London: Century Hutchinson, 1988).

Mangan James A. (ed.), *The Imperial Curriculum: Racial Images and Education in the British Colonial Experience* (London: Routledge, 1993).

Owusu, Kwesi, *Black British Culture and Society: A Text Reader* (London: Routledge, 2000).

Rich, Paul, *Race and Empire in British Politics* (Cambridge: Cambridge University Press, 1986).

Small, Stephen, *Racialised Barriers: The Black Experience in the United States and England in the 80s* (London: Routledge, 1994).

Stoler, Ann L., 'Sexual Affronts and Racial Frontiers: European Identities and the Cultural Politics of Exclusion in Colonial Southeast Asia', *Comparative Studies in Society and History*, vol. 34 (1992), pp. 514–55.

'Carnal Knowledge and Imperial Power: Gender, Race and Morality in Colonial Asia', in Michaela di Leonardo (ed.), *Crossroads of Knowledge: Feminist Anthropology in the Postmodern Era* (Berkeley: University of California Press, 1991), pp. 51–101.

Young, Robert J. C., *Colonial Desire: Hybridity in Theory, Culture and Race* (London: Routledge, 1995).

Immigration, Refugees, 'Race' and Government Policy

Brubaker, Roger, *Citizenship and Nationhood in France and Germany* (Cambridge, MA: Harvard University Press, 1992).

Castles, Stephen, and Mark J. Miller, *The Age of Migration: International Population Movements in the Modern World* (Basingstoke: Macmillan – now Palgrave, 1998).

Cesarani, David, and Mary Fulbrook (eds), *Citizenship, Nationality and Migration in Europe* (London: Routledge, 1996).

Cohen, Robin, *Frontiers of Identity: The British and the Others* (London: Longman, 1994).

Collinson, Sarah, *Beyond Borders: West European Migration Policy Towards the 21st Century* (London: Royal Institute of International Affairs, 1993).

Freeman, Gary P., *Immigrant Labor and Racial Conflict in Industrial Societies: The French and British Experience, 1944–1975* (Princeton: Princeton University Press, 1979).

Hargreaves, Alec G., *Immigration, 'Race' and Ethnicity in Contemporary France* (London: Routledge, 1995).

Hargreaves, Alec G., and Jeremy Leaman (eds), *Racism, Ethnicity and Politics in Contemporary Europe* (Aldershot: Edward Elgar, 1995).

Joppke, Christian, *Immigration and the Nation-State: The United States, Germany and Britain* (Oxford: Oxford University Press, 1999).

Kubat, Daniel (ed.), *The Politics of Migration Policies: Settlement and Integration: The First World into the 1990s* (New York: Center for Migration Studies, 2nd edn 1993).

Layton-Henry, Zig, and Paul B. Rich (eds), *Race, Government and Politics in Britain* (Basingstoke: Macmillan – now Palgrave, 1989).

Layton-Henry, Zig, *The Politics of Immigration* (Oxford: Blackwell, 1992).

Paul, Kathleen, *Whitewashing Britain: Race and Citizenship in the Post-War Era* (New York: Cornell University Press, 1997).

Piper, Nicola, *Racism, Nationalism and Citizenship: Ethnic Minorities in Britain and Germany* (Aldershot: Ashgate, 1998).

Silverman, Max (ed.), *'Race', Discourse and Power in France* (Aldershot: Avebury, 1991).

Deconstructing the Nation: Immigration, Racism and Citizenship in Modern France (London: Routledge, 1992).

Sivanandan, Ambalavaner, *A Different Hunger: Writings on Black Resistance* (London: Pluto, 1982).

Solomos, John, *Race and Racism in Contemporary Britain* (Basingstoke: Macmillan – now Palgrave, 2nd edn 1993).

Spencer, Ian, *British Immigration Policy since 1939: The Making of Multi-Racial Britain* (London: Routledge, 1997).

Thranhardt, Dietrich (ed.), *Europe: A New Immigrant Continent* (Münster: LIT, 1996).

Wrench, John, and John Solomos (eds), *Racism and Migration in Western Europe* (Oxford: Berg, 1993).

Post-War Extreme-Right Movements

Betz, Hans-Georg, *Radical Right-Wing Populism in Western Europe* (Basingstoke: Macmillan – now Palgrave, 1994).

Betz, Hans-Georg, and S. Immerfall (eds), *The New Politics of the Right: Neo-Populist Parties and Movements in Established Democracies* (Basingstoke: Macmillan – now Palgrave, 1998).

Bjorgo, Tore, and Rob Witte (eds), *Racist Violence in Europe* (Basingstoke: Macmillan – now Palgrave, 1994).

Bjorgo, Tore (ed.), *Terror from the Extreme Right* (London: Frank Cass, 1995).

Braun, Aurel, and Stephen Scheinberg (eds), *The Extreme Right: Freedom and Security at Risk* (Boulder, CO: Westview Press, 1997).

Cheles, Luciano, et al. (eds), *The Far Right in Western and Eastern Europe* (Harlow: Longman, 2nd edn 1995).

Fyshe, Peter, and Jim Wolfreys, *The Politics of Racism in France* (Basingstoke: Macmillan – now Palgrave, 1998).

Hainsworth, Paul (ed.), *The Extreme Right in Europe and the USA* (London: Pinter, 1992).

(ed.), *The Politics of the Extreme Right: From the Margins to the Mainstream* (London: Pinter, 2000).

Harris, Geoffrey, *The Dark Side of Europe: The Extreme Right Today* (Edinburgh: Edinburgh University Press, 1990).

Hockenos, Paul, *Free to Hate: The Rise of the Right in Post-Communist Eastern Europe* (London: Routledge, 1993).

Husbands, Christopher T., *Racial Exclusionism and the City: The Urban Support of the National Front* (London: Allen and Unwin, 1983).

Kitschelt, Herbert, *The Radical Right in Western Europe: A Comparative Analysis* (Ann Arbor: University of Michigan Press, 1995).

Laqueur, Walter, *Black Hundred: The Rise of the Extreme Right in Russia* (New York: HarperCollins, 1994).

Lipstadt, Deborah, *Denying the Holocaust: The Growing Assault on Truth and Memory* (Harmondsworth: Penguin, 1994).

Marcus, Jonathan, *The National Front and French Politics: The Resistable Rise of Jean-Marie Le Pen* (Basingstoke: Macmillan – now Palgrave, 1995)

Merkl, Peter H., and Leonard Weinberg (eds), *Encounters with the Contemporary Radical Right* (Boulder, CO: Westview Press, 1993).

Merkl, Peter H., and Leonard Weinberg (eds), *The Revival of Right Wing Extremism in the Nineties* (London: Frank Cass, 1997).

Gill Seidel, *The Holocaust Denial. Antisemitism, Racism and the New Right* (Leeds: Beyond the Pale Collective, 1986).

Representations of Race in Literature, Culture and the Media

Brantlinger, Patrick, *Rule of Darkness: British Literature and Imperialism, 1830–1914* (Ithaca NY: Cornell University Press, 1988).

Cheyette, Bryan, *Construction of 'the Jew' in English Literature and Society: Racial Representations, 1875–1945* (Cambridge: Cambridge University Press, 1996).

(ed.), *Between 'Race' and Culture: Representations of 'the Jew' in English and American Literature* (Stanford, CA: Stanford University Press, 1997).

Cohen, W. B., 'Literature and Race: Nineteenth Century French Fiction, Blacks and Africa 1800–1880', *Race and Class*, vol. 16 (1974), pp. 181–205.

Donald, James, and Ali Rattansi (eds), *'Race', Culture and Difference* (London: Sage, 1992).

Ferguson, Robert, *Representing 'Race': Ideology, Identity and the Media* (London: Arnold, 1998).

Gabriel, John, *Whitewash: Racialized Politics and the Media* (London: Routledge, 1998).

Gilman, Sander L., *The Jew's Body* (New York: Routledge, 1991).

Hall, Stuart (ed.), *Representation. Cultural Representations and Signifying Practices* (London: Sage, 1997).

Hargreaves, Alec G., and Mark McKinney (eds), *Post-Colonial Cultures in France* (London: Routledge, 1997).

McClintock, Anne, *Imperial Leather: Race, Gender and Sexuality in the Colonial Contest* (London: Routledge, 1995).

Nochlin, Linda, and Tamar Garb (eds), *The Jew in the Text: Modernity and the Construction of Identity* (London: Thames and Hudson, 1995).

Pieterse, Jan Nederven, and Bhiku Parekh (eds), *The Decolonization of Imagination: Culture, Knowledge and Power* (London: Zed Books, 1995).

Said, Edward W., *Culture and Imperialism* (London: Vintage, 1994).

Searle, Chris, 'Your daily dose: racism and the *Sun*', *Race and Class*, vol. 29, no. 1 (Summer 1987), pp. 55–71.

Shoat, Ella, and Robert Stam, *Unthinking Eurocentrism: Multiculturalism and the Media* (London: Routledge, 1994).

Slavin, David H., 'French Colonial Film before and after "Itto": From Berber Myth to Race War', *French Historical Studies*, vol. 21, no. 1 (Winter 1998), pp. 125–55.

Van Dijk, Teun A., *Racism and the Press* (London: Routledge, 1991).

'Analyzing Racism Through Discourse Analysis', in John H. Stanfield (ed.), *Ethnicity in Research Methods* (London: Sage, 1993).

West, Shearer (ed.), *The Victorians and Race* (Aldershot: Scolar Press, 1996).

INDEX

Abel, Dr W., 134
African Races Association, 122
Action Français, 160
Africa
  early European contact with, 60–1
  German colonialism in, 84
  'New Imperialism' and partition of, 24, 41, 66–9
  violence and repression in, 67–8
  see also under blacks
Aksakov, Ivan, 107
Aldridge, Ira, 70–1, 72, 73
Algerian National Liberation Front (FLN), 184
Algerians
  Paris massacre of 1961, 184
  post-1945 immigration to France, 176–7, 183, 184
  racism towards in France, 127–8
  soldiers from, 117, 120, 123, 132
Algerian War (1954–62), 176, 184
Alien's Bill (1905), 110
Alsace-Lorraine, 40, 111
Amsterdam, 72
animal breeding and race theory, 54–5
Anthropological Society of London, 63
Anti-Semitism
  and degeneration, 92
  and the 'blood libel', 88, 91, 104, 156
  as a science of race, 94–7
  as an ideology, 87–9, 214
  Christianity and, 15
  compared to anti-black racism, 209–17
  during the Nazi era, 140–65
  economic form, 89–90, 99–100, 105
  Hitler and, 143–8
  in Britain, 109–11
  in France, 111–14, 159–62
  in Germany and Austria, 98–103
  in Hungary, 162–3
  in Italy, 158–9
  in post-1945 Europe, 167, 172–3, 209–17
  in Russia and Poland, 103–9, 155–8, 205–6, 214
  in the Soviet Union, 163–5
  modern form, 4, 86–7
  nationalism and, 93–4
  origins of term, 16
  religious form, 90–2
  rise of political form, 86–114
Anti-Nazi League, 191
Arrow Cross, 162
asylum seekers and refugees, 176, 182, 201–2, 217–18
Auschwitz, 42, 141, 149
Austria, 26, 49, 188
Austrian Freedom Party (FPO), 173, 198, 203–4.

Baker, Josephine, 136
Banister, Joseph, 110
Bardèche, Maurice, 193
Barkashov, Alexander, 207
Barrès, Maurice, 111, 159
Belgian Cinématographe des Colonies (1908), 80
Belgium
  colonial exhibitions, 77, 80
  Congo atrocities, 24, 25, 67
  eugenics, 47, 49
  immigration controls (1974), 188
  see also The Flemish Bloc, 198
Belloc, Hilaire, 110
Benoist, Alain de, 193
Berlin, 21, 67, 99
Bernanos, Georges, 159
Binding, Karl, 150
Birmingham Immigration Control Association (1960), 179
Bismarck, Prince Otto von, 38, 45, 51, 84, 100
Blacas, Jules, 160
blacks and racism,
  anti-black racism as a key modality, 2
  as servants in Europe, 71
  blacks in Europe before 1914, 58–85
  blacks in Europe (1914–39), 117–39
  black racism compared to anti-Semitism, 209–17
  deepening of racism after 1860, 63–6
  definition of term 'black', 3, 59
  early settlement in ports, 69–70
  exhibiting of, 73–8, 82–3, 133